WHAT'S THE MATTER WITH MATTER WITH CALIFORNIA?

CULTURAL RUMBLES FROM THE GOLDEN STATE AND WHY THE REST OF US SHOULD BE SHAKING

JACK CASHILL

THRESHOLD
EDITIONS

New York   London   Toronto   Sydney

Threshold Editions
A Division of Simon & Schuster, Inc.
1230 Avenue of the Americas
New York, NY 10020

First Threshold Editions hardcover edition October 2007

THRESHOLD EDITIONS and colophon are trademarks
of Simon & Schuster, Inc.

Designed by William P. Ruoto

Manufactured in the United States of America

10 9 8 7 6 5 4 3

For information about special discounts for bulk purchases, please contact Simon &
Schuster Special Sales at 1-800-456-6798 or business@simonandschuster.com.

Library of Congress Cataloging-in-Publication Data

Cashill, Jack.
   What's the matter with California? : cultural rumbles from the
golden state and why the rest of us should be shaking / Jack Cashill
      p.   cm.
   1. Social Problems—California. 2. California—Social conditions.
3. Pluralism (Social Sciences)—California. 4. Multiculturalism—California. I. Title.

HN79.C2C37 2007
306.097974—dc22   2007000840

ISBN-13: 978-1-4165-3102-9
ISBN-10:   1-4165-3102-5

**To Ray Lahr, a true Californian
and patriot**

★ Acknowledgments ★

Let's start with conception, and that honor goes to my agent, Alexander Hoyt, whose idea this book was, and an excellent idea it proved to be. To backtrack a little, let me thank Tom Lipscomb for introducing me to Alex and, moving forward, let me thank Mary Matalin and the good folks at Threshold and Simon & Schuster for approving the project.

Now let me pause for a moment to reread that paragraph. I am still wide-eyed enough to savor just how important it sounds.

Not living in the state, I am most indebted to the scores of Californians who helped me comprehend it, the great majority of whom I had never met before. Top honors in-state go to my San Francisco webmaster, Debra Blackstone, who assisted in any number of essential ways. It was she who cleverly managed to align *What's the Matter with California?* with my better-looking-than-I-deserve website, www.cashill.com.

Mucho thanks to the handful of people who have kept the Steven Nary story alive, including Edith Nary, Dr. Philip and Jeanette Dreisbach, Paul Averna, the late Artie Funair, and especially Peter Verzola, whose help on this project was indispensable.

In that any number of people ignored my entreaties or refused to talk to me, among them at least eight distinct radical Hispanic groups—e.g., the Watsonville Brown Berets: "We don't like what you write"—and nearly as many environmental ones, I am particularly grateful to those who shared their time, even suspecting that I would not necessarily share their opinions. These include Maywood city manager Ed Ahrens, Burning Man founder Larry Harvey, and Scientology president Heber Jentsch.

My great appreciation to those who trusted me to tell their

stories, among them Ben Chavis, Jorge Lopez, Tomas Osinski, Deborah and Michael Grumbine, Ray and Jackie Lahr, Terry Anderson, and Ben Shapiro.

My special thanks go to those good folks—not all of whom vote the way I do—who hosted events on my behalf and in the process introduced me to Californians of every conceivable age, ethnicity, faith, orientation, and gripe. These include Marcie Cecil in La Jolla, Melanie Grijalva and Diane Powers in the San Fernando Valley, Marilynn and Margot Goldberg in San Mateo County, Debra Blackstone in San Francisco, Janet-marie Persico and Tom Del Beccaro in the East Bay, Diane Crowley in Berkeley, Anne Forsyth in Ventura County, and Janice Benoit and Jill Yost also in the East Bay.

I was also the happy beneficiary of several eye-opening insider tours: producer Randy Olson's Hollywood, Peter Verzola's San Francisco, Terry Mulera's Oakland/Berkeley, and Dan Teigen's introductory tour of LA.

Several other smart people took the time to talk with me and share their insights: Melanie Morgan, Lance Williams, Cinnamon Stillwell, Lance Izumi, Xiaochin Claire Yan, Paul Bassis, Matt Toledo, Tad Lumkin, Harold and Steve Uhl, Victor Davis Hanson, Nathalie Brun, Bill Schoneberger, Bob Simmons, Dan Gifford, Ted Costa, Sonny Sarkissian. Gloria Hernandez, Mark Morrison, Roman Del Rosario, Karen England, Barbara Simpson, and special thanks here to Verna Weaver for sponsoring me at the Commonwealth Club and introducing me to any number of its members.

There are several other helpful individuals who will recognize their insights, but whose future is enhanced by remaining unnamed.

Top honors out-of-state go to my wife, Joan, for persuading me to purge the more ham-handed parts of the book and generally putting up with my stuff, and my editor and surprise homie, Kevin Smith, for his gracious assistance. Thanks too to

Joe Farah of *WorldNetDaily* and Joe Sweeney of *Ingram's* magazine for keeping my opinions in play and my name before the public.

A special tribute here goes to the faculty, staff, and students of Thomas Aquinas College, who went above and beyond the call of duty to help me understand what's not the matter with California. Not to slight anyone, but I would like to thank in particular Chris Weinkopf for introducing me to Santa Paula, President Tom Dillon and wife Terri for hosting me, and Anne Forsyth for arranging just about everything.

Finally, I must give my deepest thanks to the one person who put his soul on the line to bring this book to life, Steven Nary. Keep the faith, bro!

★ Contents ★

WHAT'S THE MATTER WITH CALIFORNIA?

PROLOGUE

The fault, dear Brutus, is not in our stars/But in ourselves, that we are underlings.
—Cassius, William Shakespeare's *Julius Caesar*

On Saturday evening, March 23, 1996, eighteen-year-old apprentice airman Steven Nary went looking for his regular carousing buddies on the USS *Carl Vinson,* then berthed at the Alameda Naval Air Station across the bay from San Francisco. Two of his fellow sailors were on vacation, however, and two were on leave, so Nary decided to go in alone, the first time he had done so. Bad move.

As usual, Nary took the Alameda bus to the BART and the BART into San Francisco. From the Montgomery Street Station, he walked up toward the Palladium, a co-ed dance club nestled amidst the porn shops and strip joints in the city's storied North Beach district. Still a little early, he stopped at a restaurant for some pizza and a pitcher of beer. He had only started drinking some months before. The Palladium catered to the under-twenty-one crowd, but it was a tough place to get a drink if you were underage.

After eating, Nary ran into a Navy buddy, Chaylon Hoffman, on the long line outside the Palladium. Hoffman, who was over twenty-one, suggested that the pair go to a nearby store and get some beer and this they did, a forty-ounce malt liquor for each. The two young sailors walked around talking and drinking, finished their forties, and bought two more. In their mindless wanderings, the pair ran into a bevy of girls outside a restaurant and started chatting them up. More than a little drunk, Nary dropped his half-finished bottle, which brought the proprietor out to chase them off. Pissed, in both senses of the word, Hoffman threw his bottle into the restaurant and took off running. Nary, a high-school basketball star from California's Riverside County, followed in hot pursuit.

In their dash to freedom, the two young men got separated. Nary headed back to the Palladium where he figured he would find Hoffman. Not seeing Hoffman inside, Nary came back out to look and then went back in again. He tried dancing but was still too unsteady so he sat down by himself and watched. After some time an older gentleman with two young girls joined him at the table. A few minutes later the two girls left, and the older man sidled over to Nary, now just drinking Cokes. As Nary would testify at his trial, the man asked him a whole series of questions about himself: who he was, where he came from, and what he did. That older man was a fifty-three-year-old Latino activist by the name of Juan Pifarre.

At the Palladium, Pifarre was more than twice as old as the average patron. He was old enough to be the father of Nary's mother. He also may have been the only guy there looking for other guys. If sex or companionship were what he wanted, Lord knows there were a hundred other clubs in San Francisco that promised a dramatically safer and easier score than this one. Pifarre obviously wanted something more.

The girls Pifarre sat down with had put Nary at ease. He suspected nothing. After Pifarre and Nary got to talking, Nary mentioned that he had to leave to catch the last BART train back to the ship. Pifarre offered him a ride. "He seemed like a nice person," Nary testified, "trusting person, and I'd get back to the base sooner." Nary accepted the offer. It would be the last ride the lanky teenager would take as a free man.

The Navy had taught Nary a good deal in the six months he had been in the service. It had even taught about some of the dangers he would face in the Bay Area, like violent crime and venereal disease and earthquakes. The Navy had taught him nothing, however, about the often cruel and indifferent forces that compose the state's cultural tectonics. No one knew enough to teach him.

The physical tectonics most people in California know a good deal about. As naturalist John McPhee explains in his stellar book *Assembling California,* the state pulled itself together relatively late in the geological game. McPhee describes California as a "collection and compaction of Oceanic islands." These islands did not merely drift in from the Pacific and lock into place like pieces in a jigsaw puzzle. Rather, they smashed up against and into the mainland, meshing and all but merging in some places but never quite losing their distinctive edges.

The "plates" that resulted from this "collisional assembling" are not terribly stable. They sit uneasily along a series of fault lines, each little shift sending shivers up and down the state. As to a major shift, that is something that everyone fears. "A big one will always be in the offing," says McPhee. He is speaking, of course, about geology.

In many ways the state's culture mimics its geology, including the omnipresent fear of a "big one." During the course of its brief human history, cultural island after island has rammed up and into the state. First the Indians came. Then the Spanish. The forty-niners followed. So did the Chinese, the Japanese, various waves of Mexicans, southern blacks, the American military, the Jews who invented Hollywood, the Armenians in the Central Valley, the Filipinos, the Okies and Arkies, the hippies, gays and lesbians and bis and transgendered, the Samoans, the Central Americans, the leather folk. When these plates sideswiped or collided, meshing here, mashing there, shock and occasional damage followed.

The spring 2006 immigrations rallies and boycotts registered about a 6.0 on the cultural Richter scale. The rolling blackouts of 2001 scored about a 6.5. The riots of 1992 that followed the innocent verdicts in the police Rodney King beating about a 7.0. Worse can come, and Californians sense it. They are just not sure which cultural plates—here and hereafter I freely improvise on the basic metaphor—will drift into each other and how great the shock will be.

If the state is to survive its future—and the nation is to survive the state's—it might pay to assess the forces that hold California together and those that pull it apart. For the reader's ease, I have categorized and color-coded the primary plates with an emphasis on current relevance. My apologies in advance if the color seems inappropriate to some. No insult is intended.

Plate	Description
Bronze	American Indian
Brown	Mexican, Central American
Yellow	Chinese, Japanese, Vietnamese, etc.
Black	African-American, Caribbean
Green	Environmentalist
Red	Right, conservative Judeo-Christian
Blue	Radical left, progressive, "creative"
Rainbow	Gay, lesbian, bisexual, transgendered
Beige	Middle class, homeowner
White	Pre-WW II American
Olive	Military

As should be obvious, it is possible for a Californian to locate him- or herself on more than one plate, depending on the issue. It is also possible to withdraw from a plate to which one might seem by nature affixed and seek a higher ground, a psychologically safer one, one removed from the aftershocks of societal jostling. California-based social theorist Shelby Steele refers to such an emotional sanctuary as a "zone of decency." Those who place themselves within enjoy a "conspicuous and social virtuousness." Those placed without are "decertified" from the good people club.

The reason that one might want to seek out such a zone is that some plates, when they cohere as a plate, are subject to more negative attention than others. What follows is an unscientific evaluation of each plate's negative attention grade, or NAG. The NAG represents the percentage of major media coverage that discredits the aspirations of a given plate. To get some relative sense of media affection, one need only contrast the coverage of the border "vigilantes" known as the "Minutemen" with that of the "undocumented immigrants" that they are monitoring. I would encourage a more rigorous testing of these numbers if anyone is so moved.

Plate	NAG Estimate
Red	70
Beige	65
White	60
Blue	30
Green	25
Yellow	20
Brown	15
Black	10
Bronze	5
Rainbow	2

I do not offer a NAG estimate for the "Olive" plate, as it varies from one part of the state to another. In San Diego, it is relatively low. In San Francisco, as Steven Nary would learn the hard way, it is all but off the charts.

No state has seen the seismic activity that California has.

How the state reacts to the shifts in its cultural environment may well foretell how America does. On the pages that follow I describe some of the larger forces at work, how they affect the state and nation, and why we all must pay attention *now*. There are a thousand predictive stories I could tell of individuals or groups caught in a seismic crunch and scores that I do. Steven Nary's is one of them.

THE BLUE PLATE
COMES UNGLUED

★ 1. Beverly Hills ★

Society cannot exist unless a controlling power upon will and appetite be placed somewhere, and the less of it there is within, the more there is without.
—Edmund Burke

I t was not until my third day on my very first trip to LA on a Sunday morning jog through Beverly Hills that I saw an undeniable sign—and more on this in a minute—that there really, truly was something the matter with California.

I had expected to find one sooner. Truth be told, I was predisposed to look for such signs, as I had never much liked the idea of Southern California and had no interest in going there, ever.

Fate, however, had intervened. A few months earlier, while waiting to pick up a large combo at my neighborhood pizza joint, my writer's pride prodded me to enter a radio-station-sponsored "Why I want to go to Los Angeles in twenty words or less" contest. With only about sixty seconds to kill before the kid with the nose ring—yes, even here in Kansas City—rang up the pizza, I wrote down the first thing that popped into my head: "Freeways, tacos, and smog, the without which not of my very existence."

The utter banality of my entry, however hastily conceived, made me doubt my career choice.

"Seventeen ninety-five," said the kid.

"Oh, the hell with it." I swallowed my pride and dropped the entry in a box. A month later I got a call at the ad agency where I then worked.

"Jack Cashill?" said the fellow on the other end rather matter-of-factly.

"Yes, this is he." Note the proper grammar.

"You've won a prize in the 'Why I want to go to LA contest.'"

"Oh, yeah," said I indifferently. "What prize is that?" I expected nothing more than a loaf of sourdough bread or tickets to some chronically undersold touring act like the Lippizaner Stallions.

But, lo and behold, my caller abruptly changed gears. "You've won the grand prize," he shouted in DJ hyperdrive, "a round trip ticket for two on Frontier Airlines to sunny Los Angeles and a free weekend stay at the luxurious Century Plaza Hotel and Tower."

"Can Frontier take me someplace else?" I asked ingenuously.

"C'mon, sport," said the DJ. "We're running this to tape. Let's try it over with a little more enthusiasm this time."

I got the message. I worked in advertising. I complied. "Wow, super, LA!" And my wife, Joan, and I were on our way to sunny Southern California. Obviously, the competition in the twenty-words-or-less contest had not been too keen.

Speaking of Joan, a few years ago I was waiting for her at an elevator bank on the top floor of a hotel for a radio station Christmas party. At the time I was doing a daily show for the station. The station's new program director, a recent California import, was standing there as well. Just in the way of making conversation, he said to me, "Are you waiting for your . . . for your . . . partner?"

"Wife," I answered. "Guys have wives in Kansas City, John. You can presume that without offending." Another sign that something was off-kilter in California.

Joan and I arrived at LAX on a Friday afternoon in February. A friend of ours from Kansas City met us at the airport in an old white Mercedes sedan. A gay actor manqué, Dan knew the sights the tour guides didn't and was prepared to show them—

including Polka Night at the Club Lingerie on Sunset Boulevard, an assemblage of the old, new, baroque, and blue unseen anywhere in the United States east of Vine.

There are, by the way, more actors manqué in greater LA than there are people in Omaha. To hear them tell it, though, they are not failed actors but aspiring screenwriters. Screenplays are, of course, the lottery tickets of the LA creative class. Everyone has one. Everyone waits for Steven to call or Quentin or Drew. Don't get in the way of that phone call.

Within minutes of arriving in their fair city, I realized that I had badly underestimated it. The sky had cleared after a few days of winter rain, and it was as fresh and fragrant and sharp as a sky could be. The fragrance came from the abundant plant life, much of it wildly exotic, that graced even the sidewalls of the freeways and the medians of ghetto streets.

This was not quite the smoggy, overcrowded wasteland that I had been led to imagine. Yeah, there were a lot of people here, but I had grown up in New Jersey, which has more than five times as many people per square mile as California. Essex County, Tony Soprano's point of origin and mine, is three times more densely populated than Los Angeles County. My hometown of Newark, even after losing half its population in the last fifty years, is more thickly peopled than LA. New York City, to which I commuted for high school, is nearly four times as dense as LA, and New York's figures include the relative wilderness of Staten Island.

Growing up, however, I did not know that I lived in a particularly crowded place. I never presumed that I was entitled to a seat on the subway, a diamond lane on the parkway, or a virgin stretch of beach to run around naked on. The people in California do, and that is, I would learn, part of what's the matter.

In Southern California, everyone does seem to be driving all the time. That much is true. I once did a call-in radio show to LA starting at 1:00 A.M. Pacific time, and the station was still running traffic reports. In Kansas City, those are over by 6:00 P.M. The last time I was in Los Angeles I got stuck in a downtown traffic jam at eleven o'clock—on a Sunday morning! Where were these people going, I wondered? In Los Angeles, it was not likely to have been church.

Nor is the massive traffic flow limited to LA. All freeways everywhere seem to be always busy and busy in every direction. The volume of traffic that staggers *into* both San Diego and San Francisco at the *end* of a workday befuddles the midwestern imagination.

Still, most of the time, the traffic does move. Off the freeways, in all the major cities, San Francisco and Los Angeles included, surface traffic, as they call it in LA, moves surprisingly well. And however grinding highway traffic can be, nothing in all of California compares to a semicomatose drive from Manhattan (drinking age eighteen back in the day) to Newark (drinking age twenty-one) on a sleeting night over the sagging, shoulderless Pulaski Skyway with a defroster on the fritz in a shock-free VW bug. You don't master that kind of driving. You survive it. Once you do, though, even the Santa Monica Freeway seems no scarier than a high school's Driver's Ed course.

Besides, by the time of my first visit, I had put enough distance between me and New York to like the idea that just about any citizen of the republic could hop into his or her own vehicle and drive from any point A to any point B at any time of the day or night without checking a schedule, finding exact change, or getting mugged at a bus stop.

LA had pioneered this kind of freedom. By 1920, an LA resident was four times more likely to own a car than an average American; eight times more likely than an average Chicagoan. By 1940, there was one car for every 1.4 adults in Los Angeles. In America writ large that figure was still one for every 4.8 adults. LA, in fact, had more cars per person in 1920 than the rest of America did in 1940 or than England does today. In 1923, entrepreneurs in San Luis Obispo obliged those Californians tired of necking in their cars by opening the nation's first establishment to designate itself a "motel."

As a consequence of the auto, Angelenos could live in single-family homes beyond the forced density and dirty politics of a streetcar line. By 1940, more than half did, a figure three times higher than in Chicago, the second city in the single-family rankings. If Joe Big Mac likes the idea of having his own car and home, urban planners don't. This is just part of the reason why they, like San Franciscans, New Yorkers, and most other totalitarians, hate LA, the city that columnist Westbrook Pegler called—and this nearly seventy years ago—"that big, sprawling, incoherent, shapeless, slobbering civic idiot in the family of American communities."

When running, you see even more than you do while driving. And so I did on that Sunday morning jog through the fabled Beverly Hills, not far from our Century City hotel. As I plodded up a Beverly hill on a winding street whose name eludes me, I began to notice something just a wee bit eerie and unexpected: ubiquitous gates and locks and walls and signs promising "armed response" and "armed patrols," and I knew then, Toto, that we were surely not in Kansas anymore.

It's not as if the people living here were movie stars. No, the stars all lived someplace cooler. These were the left-behinds, those with a major jones for the 90210 area code—accountants and orthodontists and owners of (multiple) Taco Bell franchises. Were a single *paparazzo* ever to stalk them, one imagines them hiring skywriters to spread the good news. Privacy was the last thing they wanted. If they did, the vegetation alone would have taken care of that. No, the inspiration behind their hermetic withdrawal was more ominous, and I sensed it. In the silent streets of Beverly Hills that morning I felt suddenly as alone and insignificant as a squirrel.

This enthusiasm for gates and fences might not have caught

my eye had it not been for a visit to KC by a French friend just a few months earlier. In the course of that visit, I took Michel on a drive through Mission Hills, the Kansas equivalent of Beverly Hills, about a mile from my house. Before the reader scoffs, be advised that if a Martian were to be plopped down in both burgs with no notion of property values, he would think Mission Hills the place where the real cream congeals. Its homes are easily the grander and gaudier of the two.

Mission Hills also happens to be the boyhood home of one Thomas Frank, the author of the unlikely bestseller *What's The Matter With Kansas?*, the book that more or less inspired this one. Frank apparently grew up in the South Central part of Mission Hills. As he tells it, a local juvenile delinquent pulled a knife on him when he was only ten—*Straight Outta Kansas*. Although the lad did not slice or dice the tender Frank, he frightened the common sense right out of him.

In his book the emotionally scarred Frank has projected the menace of these youthful mumblety-peggers onto their dads. He remembers their being routinely dispatched to the big house for fraud, forgery, tax evasion, and embezzlement. "Growing up here teaches the indelible lesson," writes Frank with an apparent straight face, "that wealth has some secret bond with crime—also with drug use, bullying, lying, adultery, and thundering, world-class megalomania."

Apparently, the locals did not know enough about the crime spree in their midst to be scared. To this day, even after Frank's shocking revelations, the palazzos in this ungated community sit as open to the world as the doublewides in a Kansas City, Kansas, trailer court, and this despite the fact that Mission Hills is much closer to the inner city of both Kansas Cities, Missouri and Kansas, than Beverly Hills is to any one such inner city.

If I had come to take this openness for granted, for Michel, it was a revelation. In his native France, every little handyman's special has its own menacing wall and *chien méchant*. An anticommunist leftist, as rare a breed in West LA as a born-again movie mogul, Michel rued the fact that the more proudly progressive a place was, the more likely it was to wall its citizens in. For Michel, the Berlin Wall, still standing at the time of his visit, represented the culmination of this paradoxical madness.

Walls do tell you something about a place. Ask a Kansan what's the matter with his unwalled state, and he'll likely respond, "Is there something the matter?" Ask a Californian, and he'll say, "How much time do you have?" As much as they love their state, and few want to leave, Californians sense that something is indeed amiss. They just don't know quite what.

To discover the "what" of all this, I decided to start by unraveling the paradox: Why is California so much more guarded—in every sense—than Kansas? The first thread leading from this paradox led me to where my hunches suggested it would, up the sinuous Benedict Canyon and off leftward to Cielo Drive. There, at the site of what once was 10050 Cielo, I found what I expected, the fiercest gate of all.

"Deep in the subconscious of every transplanted Californian," writes Hollywood producer Julia Phillips of the 1969 event that inspired the Cielo gate and many more, "lies a memory of that Labor Day weekend." A fifteen-thousand-dollar-a-week coke habit can cloud one's memory on specifics—her date's off by a month—but it did nothing to diminish Ms. Phillips's anxiety. That, she captures accurately.

At this point, I should offer one clarification. In the California spirit, I will shy from judgments like "good" or "evil" or even "just plain stupid." Instead, I will look at outcomes, namely how a given phenomenon affects the economy and the ecology of the state and the well-being of its citizens. Let me cite an example.

In his documentary-style novel of early eighties LA, *Less Than Zero,* Bret Easton Ellis describes a scene in which the affluent friends of our everyman protagonist, Clay, have abducted a twelve-year-old, drugged her, tied her to a bed, and repeatedly raped and sodomized her. True to the time and place, Clay has a hard time rendering judgment.

Says he, "It's . . . I don't think it's right."

Admittedly, this example is a bit extreme, but arguably no more extreme than those of the twenty-five hundred real Californians who are murdered each year and the thousands more who are drugged and date raped. Given the lack of a mutually agreed-upon morality, this book will focus on things material. In imagining the outcome of a case like the aforementioned—and at the heart of this book is a real case not unlike it—the reader would anticipate a few universally accepted negatives: the grave emotional wounds to the girl and her family, health care bills, extra police work, additional security at the junior highs, and the cost to the state of trials and incarceration.

The fence on the 7600 block of South San Pedro in Los Angeles exudes cost. It stands about eight feet high, maybe nine. Its steel pikes crowd against each other closely enough to screen out even an anorexic Crip, and just to be safe, a wicked spike curves out from the top of each.

The fence protects John C. Fremont High School from its South Central neighborhood. The fence was obviously something of an afterthought since this high school, like most throughout the state, sprawls Mission-style around a welcoming central courtyard. This style makes for a lot of fence. I would estimate a half-mile of it. Not surprisingly, the photos on the school's cheery website show no sign of the fence or the steel mesh that screens the face of the building.

Los Angeles spends a lot on fences and other security devices for its high schools. In the 2005–6 school year alone, the Los Angeles Unified School District (LAUSD) spent $73 million on such protections. The forty-four-year-old Nobel Middle School in Northridge made the news this past year when its parents and teachers rejected a school board proposal to fence in the school's twenty-acre campus. At Nobel, the students "don't feel like it's a prison," Principal Robert Coburn told the *Los Angeles Times.*

All other public-school students in LA do get to experience the prison feel, which, in many cases, provides useful conditioning for the career to come As it happens, Nobel is the only school of the 550 in the district not yet sealed off and shut in behind a security fence.

In part at least, one can trace the inspiration for the LAUSD fences to another event that took place in 1969, an unrelated one. To be sure, the Beverly Hills provocation was more dramatic and much better documented, but it was the South Central event that proved, in the long term, to be more consequential.

"In '69 the 'C' was born," goes the definitive origins story, a prison chant. That same folklore traces this seminal event, the birth of the "C"—the neighborhood association known as the "Crips"—to Fremont High School itself. The "C" would also produce Fremont's only Nobel Peace Prize nominee, Stanley Williams, nominated six years in a row in fact, but more on Mr. Williams and his colleagues later.

One more 1969 event, this one in New York City, on the steamy June night after Judy Garland's funeral, helps explain not so much the ominous fences of Coalinga, a Central Valley town halfway between LA and San Francisco, but the fact that twenty-nine-year-old Steven Nary grows old behind them.

These fences surround a facility with the absurdly congenial name of "Pleasant Valley," as in Pleasant Valley State Prison or PVSP for short. Fences have always surrounded prisons. This is not a sign that something is the matter with California. What is the matter is that there are more than five thousand inmates in a facility designed for half that number. What is even more the matter is that PVSP has had to take in these prisoners to accommodate an astonishing sevenfold increase in the state prison population—23,264 to 168,035—in just twenty-five years.

What goes beyond "the matter" to the truly tragic is that

among those numbers, PVSP BFB3-132L to be exact, is Steven Nary, once a proud apprentice airman in the U.S. Navy and before that the highest-scoring high-school basketball player in Riverside County. "Billy Budd," his handful of stalwart supporters call him, after the Herman Melville innocent hanged for a comparable offense. Had Nary done what he did anywhere other than San Francisco—or possibly Manhattan—he would not have spent the last eleven years of his life immured behind one wall or another. He likely would not have spent a day.

Scarcely a word has been written about Nary's case beyond San Francisco and few even there. That is not surprising. In no state have so many people of influence grown so thoroughly blind to the obvious. The fact is that California could solve its problems in a generation if only its creative classes could see what those problems are. This, they refuse to do.

In his dazzling book *City of Quartz*, for instance, Mike Davis shows an impressive mastery of the details of what he calls "Fortress LA." His description of "the most menacing library ever built," the Frank Gehry–designed Goldwyn Library in Hollywood, is alone worth a trip to your local bookstore.

For all his gifts of observation, however, Davis refuses to grasp the larger picture. As a case in point, where lesser mortals see the bellwether Watts Riot of 1965, he sees the "Watts Rebellion." Calling a riot a "rebellion." however, does not make it "an organized attempt to overthrow a government or other authority by use of violence." It was nothing of the kind. He knows that. No, it remains a riot, exactly as the dictionary defines "riot"—"a public disturbance during which a group of angry people becomes noisy and out of control, often damaging property and acting violently."

Davis represents something of a hip norm. By denying the obvious, observers like him, talented and otherwise, fail to get a handle on root causes. Depending on their skills and their biases, they fixate on the less true, the less relevant, the half-true, the irrelevant, and sometimes the downright false. So prevalent is this phenomenon that I have assigned it an acronym, ABETTO—as in, a blind eye to the obvious.

The late-century Reagan fixation nicely showcases the ABETTO factor. As to why LA has gone into semipermanent lockdown, Davis can do no better than cite, without a hint of irony, "the social polarizations of the Reagan-era." Julia Phillips takes precious time off from freebasing to campaign against Reagan because his election would mean that life "is about to get bleak." The notorious Crip author and gangbanger "Monster" Kody Scott teaches his love child to chant "Ronald Reagan pig" because his homies hold Reaganomics responsible for their "utter despair." And in the pair's stillborn 2003 CBS miniseries producers Craig Zadan and Neil Meron show the historically gay-friendly Gipper blowing off the AIDS crisis with a casual, "They that live in sin shall die in sin." Egad! I don't doubt that these and any number of observers know more about the minutiae of California life than I do, but as is evident above, they blind themselves to the big picture.

To be fair, that picture is not all bleak, not by a long shot. "It is so warm," an Austrian immigrant wrote a friend back home of his adopted Santa Monica. "In Graz I am always cold. Here is where I will stay. The sun shines." Nineteen sixty-nine just happens to be the first full year that Arnold Schwarzenegger spent in California. It was not just the weather that intrigued the twenty-one-year-old. It was the sweep of the place, the potential, the lively traditions of free speech and free enterprise. The girls weren't all that shabby either.

Alas, the metaphorical sun shines less brightly today than it did on a young Arnold nearly forty years ago. And it will shine less brightly every year hence—at least until its nabobs can bring themselves to call a cloud a cloud.

★ 2. Alta California ★

Now that the Americans are coming in all around us,
he is afraid and anxious all the time. He wants to get
a big fence built around our land to show where it is.
—Helen Hunt Jackson, *Ramona*, 1884

To understand why all the need for gates and locks, it helps to know at least a little of the state's history. The human part of that history also got off to something of a slow start with the state peopling itself as relatively late as it assembled itself. The heroic Sierras pushed up in the East by these monstrous geological collisions proved almost as daunting to our Indian friends as they did to the Donner Party some thousands of years later.

As to when the Bronze plate did drift in, no one is quite sure, perhaps only five thousand or six thousand or so years before the White, and these are pure SWAG (sophisticated, wild-assed guess) estimates. There is even less certainty about who got here first and how they got here. The various tribes seem to have arrived as randomly as an LA bus, with all the head banging one could expect from such a chaotic assembling.

Spanish explorer Pedro Font, who traversed much of California in 1775, was appalled by all the mindless violence. With only few exceptions, the Indians he saw were "in constant warfare between the different villages," as a consequence of which "they live in continual alarm, and go about like Cain, fugitive and wandering, possessed by fear and dread at every step."

"As with all of nature's children," confirms German Carl Meyer of the still unpacified Northern California Indians in 1851, "it is not law, but might, which is held to be right. Therefore, they fight in every way."

In fact, the California tribes were far less monolithic than the street gangs of LA and, on average, got along no better. Imagine the Spooktown Compton Crips jockeying for territory with the East Compton Piru Bloods, and neither being able to understand a single word the other says. Imagine this happening a lot. Indeed, before the first Spanish arrived, there were at least a hundred different tribes in the state, and 70 percent of their languages were as unintelligible to speakers of another as Mandarin was to Fremont High's Nobel nominee, the late Stanley "Tookie" Williams. Indeed, had Tookie spoken Mandarin, he might not have felt the urge in 1979 to cap Yen-I Yang, his wife, and his daughter and then diss them all as "Buddha-heads," but here I get ahead of myself.

By just about all accounts, too, the "disorderly and beast-like" California Indians, especially in Southern California, were some of the sorriest creatures on the planet. Pedro Font, like just about every other European visitor, was aghast at the "nakedness and misery" in which most of these early Californians lived. This wasn't just some sort of ignorant Eurocentric putdown either. Some of these guys, like British captain George Vancouver, had seen Indians on both continents and admired many of them, but not the Californians. "They are certainly a race," writes Vancouver, "of the most miserable beings, possessing the faculty of human reason, I ever saw."

There seemed to be some consensus about why the locals never bothered to develop a wheel or pots or even clothes. Life was just too dang easy. "The native in his primitive condition readily finds his chief needs, food and shelter, everywhere," observes Russian visitor Kiriil Khlebnikov, "there is consequently no reason for exerting his intellectual capacities in improving his state."

Two centuries later, Woody Allen would depict the Californians of his day as empty-headed and unproductive as the shellfish-happy Chumash Indians of yore and win an Oscar for his efforts, presumably for accuracy. "I don't want to live in a city," laments Allen's character of Los Angeles in *Annie Hall*, "where the only cultural advantage is that you can make a right turn on a red light."

From the beginning, it should be noted, the splendor of California impressed just about every Anglo-American visitor who lit upon its golden shores. Captain William Shaler raves about the "wild beauties" of the countryside and a view of mountains and forests "grand and sublime in the highest degree."

James Ohio Pattie, the first American to write an extended narrative, describes a place "remarkable for uniting the advantages of healthfulness, a good soil, a temperate climate, and yet one of exceeding mildness, a happy mixture of level and elevated ground, and vicinity to the sea."

Ten years later, in 1840, in his classic *Two Years Before the Mast*, young American sailor Richard Henry Dana exults about the "good harbors," the "fine forests," the "waters filled with fish," and a climate "than which there can be no better in the world."

Late-twentieth-century Californians, alas, would give these and other early Americans no credit for their environmental sensitivity. Disney composers Stephen Schwartz and Alan Menken presumed that when Europeans looked at America they did not see a "grand and sublime" landscape they could enjoy but rather "a dead thing" they could "claim." For the record, the pair won an Academy Award for this Europhobic children's favorite, "Colors of the Wind," written for the 1995 film *Pocahontas*.

"The Indian said, Kill only what you need," wrote another singer-songwriter of note in an equally self-hating ditty, "But the Whiteman likes to see things bleed." Although there would be no Oscar forthcoming for civil rights activist and environmentalist Charles Manson, he did manage to capture the spirit of the age.

The second major cultural island to jostle California's friendly shores hit surprisingly late in the real-life Risk game then being played by the European powers. It was not until 1769 that the Spanish chose to colonize *Alta California*, as they called it, literally "high California," a translation that would ring even truer in 1969.

This incursion would prove to be dramatically more benign than the Cortez-led incursion of Mexico more than two centuries earlier, and yet its impact was very nearly as powerful. Leading the charge with an incredibly light brigade was Father Junipero Serra. "The [Catholic] faith was a gift," says biographer Weber of Serra, "and he was determined to share it with others." This plate was fundamentally Red—traditional, Christian, and fully European. Father Serra and most of the early Franciscan missionaries had come directly from Spain.

The hugely popular 1884 novel *Ramona*, set in the years after California had become American and carefully researched by Helen Hunt Jackson, pivots on the unthinkable act of a Spanish woman hooking up with a well-educated Indian. "You marry an Indian. Never!" Señora Gonzaga Moreno tells her foster daughter, Ramona, despite the fact that Ramona herself is a half-Indian foundling. This DNA dissection would all be irrelevant today were it not for the claim by young Hispanic radicals that America somehow screwed the *Aztecs* out of California.

The Hispanic Californians of the pre–Gold Rush days were ripe for the screwing in any case. Although no one denies that Serra and most of his missionaries were men of extraordinary character, few secular observers applaud the results. Early European visitors to the missions often left dismayed. "One cannot help thinking," comments French captain Abel du Petit-Thouars in a typical review, "that perhaps the state of idiocy in which [the mission Indians] are found may be due to the cloistered life and to the slavery to which they have been bound since infancy."

"About Serra's worth as a man and a Christian there is indeed no controversy among those who know his career," notes American Josiah Royce in his precociously cynical 1886 history of the early days of his native state. Royce is far less sanguine about the project itself, which he calls "one of the most complete and fruitless of human failures."

The fact that with minimal help from the army or state, a group of poor and unarmed Spanish missionaries pacified the area from San Diego to San Francisco, converting some fifty-four thousand Indians along the way and building twenty-one missions, impressed some witnesses not at all. These children of the Enlightenment counted the "gift of faith" of no great worth and presumed that they could manage the cultural tectonics better than the Franciscans. History would prove them all wrong, but that would take time. In the interim, they set about bollixing things on their own, starting with a newly independent Mexico. In 1821, Mexico broke away from Spain. This ill-starred country shifted to a nominally Republican form of kleptocracy and introduced what would prove to be the enduring California sport of Christian-bashing.

Although there were only about three thousand white people in the state at the time and likely no more than a hundred thousand Indians and shrinking, the sudden shift from a fully Christian state to a boldly secular one caused a major shock to the Indians who depended on the missions and to the Spaniards who depended on the old order. "During the height of the despoiling and plundering of the Missions under the Secularization Act," Jackson writes of *Ramona*'s Señora Moreno, "she was for a few years almost beside herself." And well she might have been. "The old monastic order is destroyed and nothing seems yet to have replaced it, except anarchy," confirms Monsieur du Petit-Thouars, who visited in 1837.

Bostonian Richard Henry Dana had just turned nineteen in 1834 when he left for his "two years before the mast." During those years, he spent many months traveling throughout Alta

California gathering and curing bullock hides. He would prove to be as honest and accurate an observer as ever visited these blessed shores.

There was much that Dana liked. The countryside was beautiful and so were the women. The Californians of Spanish descent had good manners and nice voices, and danced well. The frijol was "the best bean in the world." The Hawaiians he worked with, and there were many in California at the time, were "the most interesting, intelligent, and kind-hearted people" he had ever known. Young and open-minded, Dana was not given to easy prejudice.

In those halcyon days before Hispanics had mutated into a minority group, Dana felt free to evaluate them as he saw fit. "The Californians," he would write, "are an idle, thriftless people, and can make nothing for themselves." That they actually had to buy wine from Boston appalled the young man. Even before California's beautiful people started squandering their fortunes on Napa vineyards, the country abounded in grapes.

"Among the Spaniards there is no working class," observes the budding sociologist. The postmission Indians had grown resigned to "being slaves and doing all the hard work." Dana bemoans a "caste" system determined solely by one's Spanish blood and a legal system that deprived Protestants of civil and property rights. "In fact," he writes in summing up his hosts, "they sometimes appeared to be a people on whom a curse had fallen, and stripped them of everything but their pride, their manners, and their voices."

Dana nicely anticipates California's future. He describes the Yankees, who had converted to Catholicism and married into the culture, as "having more industry, frugality, and enterprise than the natives" and notes that they had already begun to dominate trade and even civic life. "In the hands of an enterprising people," he enthused, "what a country this might be!"

Within a dozen years, Dana's dream would be realized.

California's exceptional state historian, Kevin Starr, nicely and fairly sums up those years after the rise of the secular republic: "The final decade of California's Mexican era was a confusion of revolution, counterrevolution, graft, spoliation and social disintegration as Northern and Southern factions struggled for power in a series of internecine clashes." Otherwise, everything was great. Curiously, the *Nortenos* and *Surenos* still fight over California, but now as prison gangs.

The ever-progressive Harvard instructor Royce, who published his book *California: A Study of American Character* just forty years after the conquest, writes of the Californian of this final era, "In politics, as in morals and material wealth, he was unprogressive." And Royce, by the way, sympathized with the Hispanic plight.

This little history helps put the *"reconquista"* dreams of today's radical Latino movement in some perspective. According to one of the movement's founding documents, *El Plan Espiritual de Aztlán*, only "the brutal 'gringo' invasion of our territories" has separated the "northern land of Aztlan," aka California, from the Mexican motherland. Rightfully, it "belongs to those who plant the seeds, water the fields, and gather the crops and not to the foreign Europeans."

Is there a nice way in Spanish to say "clueless"? In 1846, one set of largely European descendants, namely Americans, removed another set of largely European descendants, namely the Mexicans, from control of what would soon come to be the state of California. The Mexican Republic had governed California for only twenty-five misbegotten years. Hispanics had been there only seventy-five. At the time, there were fewer people of Hispanic descent living in all of California—twelve thousand max—than there are Eskimos living in California today. By all accounts, they considered the planting of seeds, the watering of fields, and the gathering of crops beneath their dignity. "California in a nutshell," said Sir George Simpson in

1841. "Nature doing everything and man doing nothing." That would change.

California would endure no greater cultural shock than the first great White-Brown sideswipe. The American makeover began with the brief and relatively painless Bear Flag War of 1846—an adventure largely improvised on the spot by American settlers—and exploded with the discovery of gold in 1848. Anthropologist James Rawls calls it, rightly, "the great discontinuity in the state's history."

Two early books written about this transition tell us as much about the California of today as the California of old. Just thirty when he wrote his history of California, Josiah Royce did something almost unprecedented in American letters. He ruthlessly demythologized the origins story of his native land, namely the Bear Flag War, and rendered it as a comic opera with tragic repercussions.

More provocatively still, Royce cut the mythic legs right out from under the war's most heroic figure, Captain John C. Frémont. This he does with mischievous glee, crediting "the gallant Captain Frémont" with little more than introducing "civilized warfare," the clearest sign of which was that "somebody always gets badly hurt."

Although the Anglo-American gift for self-criticism has much to recommend itself, Royce pushed it to the edge. In so doing, he helped shape the whole concept of the zone of decency a century before it became de rigueur. When he writes of his fellow Californians, "We exhibited a novel degree of carelessness and overhastiness, an extravagant trust in luck, a previously unknown blindness to our social duties, and an indifference to the rights of foreigners of which we cannot be proud," he doesn't really mean "we." He means "they." Had Royce been there at the beginning, he would have known and done better.

Helen Hunt Jackson was to fiction what Royce was to history, a pioneer of the decency zone. In *Ramona*, a tragic romance set in the time of transition, and an enormously popular book nationwide, she rebels against her New England roots by embracing the then-exotic Catholicism of old California and by making her fellow Protestant Americans the boogeymen.

The book, like so much California conversation then and now, is really about real estate. The story Jackson tells is of how the Americans in California imposed the rule of law on a region that had never really known it before. This imposition was not always pretty. As described in the book, the Moreno family and its many peons had once inhabited a Connecticut-sized estate that included forty miles of ocean front and the entire San Fernando Valley. Its boundaries, however, were "not very well defined." Sadly for the Morenos, the Land Act of 1851 defined their property for them, whittling it down to about the size of Sherman Oaks. Although Jackson would like the reader to think otherwise, this was not exactly tragic.

Meanwhile the Indians in *Ramona* get whittled down to just about nothing. "These Americans will destroy us all," the heroic Indian Alessandro tells the deeply pious half-breed Ramona. "I do not know but they will presently begin to shoot us and poison us, to get us all out of the country, as they do the rabbits and the gophers." As the plot works itself out, Alessandro and Ramona run off to find a priest to marry them—those were the days—only to be undone by snarling Americans at every turn.

Today in nonjudgmental California, charging other Americans with genocide is no more exceptional than charging them with littering on the beach or tailgating on the freeway. This is especially so in the state's education system. Even the normally sober state historian Kevin Starr would say of the Indian that he "was exterminated at the wish and the expense of the legislature." And yet the oft-repeated "exterminated" makes no more sense as a way of describing the fate of the California Indian than "rebellion" does to describe the fate of Watts.

Yes, many Indians were killed, some gratuitously, but both

before and after the conquest, Californians tried a thousand different solutions to accommodate them. This wasn't genocide. Hell, there are six times as many Indians in California now as there were then, and most of them own casinos. This was government as usual.

More so than any other group in the tectonic history of the state, the Indian got caught in the grinding of the plates. The Americans were sure that they could do better by the Indian than the Mexicans had, so as early as 1846 the San Francisco naval commander John B. Montgomery declared that the "Indian population must not be regarded in the light of slaves." In 1849, the forty-eight delegates who met to declare the state's first constitution—eight of them Hispanic—unanimously voted to outlaw slavery for anyone, no small accomplishment in these volatile days before the Civil War. Still, they had no idea what to do with the Indians and never really would.

Despite the good intentions of the coastal Californians, the hinterlands were bad news, and the Indians were hardly blameless. In San Francisco, Colonel William Thompson published *Reminiscences of a Pioneer,* an account of his journey west. Along the way, he details several friendly encounters with various tribes and some not friendly at all. Writing in 1912, Thompson is clearly bothered by "mock sentimentalists" like Jackson, who "have walled their eyes to heaven in holy horror at the 'barbarities' practiced by white men." Had they witnessed the "scenes of diabolical atrocity" that he had, Thompson is confident that they too would have slipped off the veneer of civilization "as a snake sheds his skin."

Jackson would hear none of it. Like a Sumo wrestler, she had shoved Thompson out of her pristine little decency zone. In fact, she may have been the first to introduce to California what I call ZSM, or zero-sum multiculturalism, whose credo—"I'm OK, you're not"—marks it as the evil twin of a more benign California product, transactional analysis.

Jackson fully identifies with the beleaguered Indians of the novel, who are morally superior to the mestizos, who are morally superior to the Mexicans, who are in turn morally superior to the Americans. The Americans, particularly the men, are as brutish as the bad guys in a Spaghetti Western. A *Ramona* reader can only wonder how they managed to turn California from the semibarbarity of the Gold Rush into the orderly allure of the Golden State in an historic eye-blink.

Here, Royce gives credit where it is due. He acknowledges the "marvelous political talent of our race and nation." More important still, he argues, is the "courage, the moral elasticity, the teachableness, of the people." To be sure, Californians had made "grievous errors," but what distinguishes them from other peoples is that they went on to correct those errors, "good-humored and self-confident as ever."

It is precisely this self-confidence that enabled Helen Hunt Jackson to become a star. No matter what she thought of Americans, Americans loved *Ramona*. They are the ones who got the book reprinted three hundred times and spawned the movies, plays, and festivals to follow. The *Ramona* phenomenon helped revive the mission tradition, fuse the jostling plates, and give California a distinctive spiritual and multiracial identity that endured for a century—at least until the Helen Hunt Jacksons of the twentieth century started mucking with it.

★ 3. Lakewood ★

In L.A., nobody touches you. We're always behind this metal and glass. I think we miss that touch so much that we crash into each other just so we can feel something.
—Detective Graham Waters, *Crash*

It is occasionally said that the opposite of California is New York. I use the word "opposite" guardedly here, remembering the enlightened NYC grade-school teacher who taught her charges that the opposite of an apple was an orange and the opposite of a frog a tadpole. Still, from Hollywood's perspective at least, New York and California are the two contrasting poles between which the rest of America pivots. This is New York's perspective too.

This dichotomy, however, is contrived. New York is no more the opposite of California than the Soviet Union is the opposite of Nazi Germany. If the former tends toward the brooding, the intense, and the international and the latter toward the parochial, the pagan, and the homoerotic, they are both nonetheless socialist states with a mighty totalitarian urge. (To be clear, I speak, here, of the Soviet Union and Nazi Germany respectively.)

No, if California has an opposite, that opposite is Texas. One cannot imagine a Josiah Royce or a Helen Hunt Jackson debunking the Alamo and Sam Houston and surviving until dawn the next day. It would take another century for such moral preening to become commonplace, and even today it is risky west of the Pecos.

Much of the difference lies in the respective history of the two states. Texans will tell you that they have, as Royce might have phrased it, a more "manly" story to tell. They had to deal with the astonishingly vicious Comanche, not the groovy Chumash of Santa Barbara. They had to beat back Santa Ana and his five-thousand-strong army, not the sundry Zorro wannabes of José Castro, whose eponymous neighborhood now flies the Rainbow Flag. They remember the Alamo. Californians remember the sixties, and that only dimly. They fought valiantly for their scrubby chunk of real estate and are proud of that fight. Californians, by contrast, are proud largely of the real estate. If Californians defend themselves with gates, Texans defend themselves with guns. But hey, we all know about Texans. They like to boast.

Californians tend to be more modest than they ought to be or used to be—at least about their state. For that first American Century, no place in the world had ever managed so much tectonic activity with so little raw control from above. The rule of law made it all work, imperfectly to be sure, but work. So did a common language and a congenial Christian tradition, largely shared.

To know how future governor "Pat" Brown got his name is to understand the one most powerful unifying influence during those years, the force that kept the plates in check. In the way of background, one of Brown's grandfathers had immigrated from Germany, and the other from Ireland. In 1917, when Brown was in the seventh grade in a San Francisco public school, Irish rebels were conspiring with Germany against America's allies in World War I. Without hesitation, young Edmund Gerald Brown entered the fray on the American side. So passionate was his "Give me liberty or give me death" war bond speech that his fellow seventh graders dubbed him "Patrick Henry Brown" or "Pat" for short.

The state identity played almost as great a role in helping these disparate people cohere as the national identity. Sixth-generation Californian Joan Didion, arguably the best writer to write about her native state, has preserved her eighth-grade graduation speech on the subject of "Our California Heritage."

Those who came to California, she told the attentive audience, "were not the self-satisfied, happy and content people, but the adventurous, the restless, and the daring." San Francisco's population multiplied almost twenty times by 1906, she boasted, and the city was rebuilt almost as quickly as it burned down. "We had an irrigation problem," she continued, "so we built the greatest dams the world has known. Now both desert and valley are producing food in enormous quantities."

"We must live up to our heritage," young Didion concluded triumphantly, "go on to better and greater things for California." This was June 1948. California was in a triumphant mood. From the end of World War II and on for the next twenty-five years some twelve hundred people a day came to California, the great majority of them ambitious, American, and middle class.

Native Californians, like Joan Didion's family, called them "the new people" and weren't entirely thrilled to see them arrive. "Native Californian," by the way, is a phrase that one hears often. In no other state, with the possible exception of Texas, is "native" status more dearly treasured, and multigenerational status even more so.

I have never heard the phrase "native Missourian" or "third-generation Kansas." Upon moving to either of these nicely humble states, one is considered as worthy as Harry Truman's grandkids. In fact, from Thomas Frank's perspective a guy like myself doesn't even have to live or work in Kansas to be honored as a Kansan. To my astonishment, he did a five-page profile on me in *What's the Matter with Kansas?* though I have not spent two consecutive nights in the Sunflower State and don't work there either.

Still, despite a certain native resistance, it has never taken a transplant long to feel at home in the accent-free clime of the Golden State. Besides, the postwar new people had little choice but to feel at home. Like those who preceded them, they had left almost everything—and everyone—behind. At the time, pundits called it "the last great migration." It wasn't, but it seemed like it and sounded good.

Whole new towns sprang up, seemingly overnight, to accommodate the new people and their baby boom children. The most ambitious such town was Lakewood. Built on a scrubby wasteland south of LA and east of Long Beach, the town housed sixty-seven thousand people before it was ten years old. In fact, its developers sold seventy-four hundred houses in the first ten months. As Lakewood administrator D. J. Waldie notes in his wonderful memoir, *Holy Land,* "Buyers needed only a steady job, and the promise they would keep up the payments."

The average age of the wives in that first early 1950s wave of Lakewood homebuyers was twenty-six, the husbands thirty-two. In 1953, when *Harper's* magazine asked the young homemakers of Lakewood what they missed most in moving there, they usually replied, "My mother."

A century earlier, a well-meaning legislative committee, in contemplating the fate of California's Indians, regretted that "there is no longer a wilderness west of us that can be assigned them." And so it was with this great wave of new people. There was no place farther west they could go. Having left some lesser place for this golden land, usually with much fanfare and fond farewells, they could go back only in failure. They may have been strangers here, lonelier than they would ever dare admit, but they were strangers in paradise. And who would ever quit paradise, especially after those too many, too proud postcards home.

Expectations were lofty then and would remain so into the 1960s, when California, under Democratic governor Pat Brown, built schools, universities, highways galore, and what Brown would call "the greatest California waterworks of all." In 1962, the state, now 17 million people strong, reached something of a high-water mark when it passed New York State in population, its go-go, can-do ethos still intact.

The national magazines celebrated the milestone on their front covers. *Newsweek*'s cover line may have best summarized the world's take on California: "No. 1 state: Booming, Beautiful California." Implicit in all the coverage was California's role in reshaping America's future. "Most important of all," wrote George Leonard in *Look* magazine, "California presents the promise and challenge contained at the very heart of the original American dream: here probably more than at any time, the shackles of the past are broken."

In 1962, forward-thinking people throughout the state were in no more mood for shackles than they were for rainy days. The more forward among them saw shackles everywhere, even in traditional notions like state, nation, family, and faith. So these thinkers started to hammer away, unaware that they had nothing to replace them with but walls, fences, gates, and prisons.

★ 4. North Beach ★

Just call me Lucifer/cause I'm in need of some restraint.
—Mick Jagger, "Sympathy for the Devil"

In her autobiography, Susan Atkins shows a picture of her family from 1958. Every baby boomer that grew up in California has one like it. Nine-year-old Susan slouches beside the family sedan next to older brother Mike. Younger brother Steve smiles through the back window. Mom stands coolly in her shades next to Mike. Dad, tall and bespectacled, leans proudly against the car next to Mom, his hand on the roof. The Atkinses are dressed as if going to church—even the boys wear jackets and ties—but if so, this sunny day was likely Easter or maybe even Christmas, since they rarely went otherwise.

What so many of these postwar California photos lack, Susan's included, is the presence of others. Neither in her photos nor in her narrative is there any reference to cousins, aunts, uncles, grandparents, or even good family friends. As her family moved from Millbrae to San Jose to Cambrian Park, all on the peninsula south of San Francisco, the only outsider the reader gets to know is "the divorcée" with three children who lives next door to the Atkinses and occasionally takes Susan to the Cambrian Park Baptist Church.

Susan Atkins's little nuclear family began to collapse shortly after the photo was taken. Cancer grabbed hold of her mom and killed her soon thereafter. The bottle meanwhile did in her dad. A functioning alcoholic when his wife was well, he turned fully dysfunctional when she wasn't. Just fifteen, Susan found herself alone, adrift, an emotional orphan with no larger familial or community support in her time zone.

Within five years of her mother's death, Susan Atkins went on to achieve a level of fame few in Cambrian Park would have expected of her. She did so by composing one of the era's most memorable slogans. It was one word long. That word was "Pig." She splashed it on the front door of the house on Cielo Drive. What really grabbed local attention was the medium she used to make her statement, unorthodox even by California standards: the blood of fully pregnant actress Sharon Tate.

The concept "Susan Atkins" has considerably more explanatory potential than "Charles Manson," which is an answer to no particularly useful question. The architect of the 1969 massacre on Cielo, the Ohio-born Manson could have popped up anywhere. "Dickensian" does not do justice to his early life. "Feral" is closer to the mark.

Manson came into the world in 1934 as "no name Maddox," the unwanted son of an unmarried sixteen-year-old. As a child, he bounced from relative to relative to reform school while his indifferent mom focused her career ambitions on petty crime and prostitution. At seventeen, the diminutive Manson moved to California looking to fit in, but the only place he did so was in prison. When prison authorities booted him in 1967, he didn't want to leave.

The California of 1967, however, differed considerably from the one he left behind in 1960. Many of the "shackles" that *Look* magazine had fretted about in 1962 had already been corroded or broken. "This is a whole different time," Atkins's first real boyfriend had whispered seductively to the suddenly upended child. "Things have changed." With her mother dead, and her father drunk, the unsteady Atkins succumbed to the lad and experienced a good deal of that change in the form of promiscuity, drugs, and miscellaneous "moral chaos"—her term.

The same year that Manson left the pen, the eighteen-year-old Atkins washed up on the shores of San Francisco's North Beach. At the time, of course, there were no literal shores. North

Beach had not been a beach since anyone could remember, having long ago been filled in and paved over. Once largely Italian, and home to the DiMaggio brothers, the neighborhood had proved hospitable to the emerging Beats in the 1950s and to the booming sex trade of the 1960s.

That trade traces its emergence from the shadows to the date of June 16, 1964, when a former prune-picker from Napa Valley, Carol Doda by name, agreed to wear, on stage at the Condor Club, a topless swimsuit recently designed by Palo Alto's own Rudi Gernreich.

Hoping to topple the topless towers of Ms. Doda, Big Al's and the Off Broadway Club fired back with bigger, if not better, topless dancers of their own. Topping them all was the naturally freakish Yvonne d'Angers of Off Broadway. Undaunted, Doda responded to the challenge the way Barry Bonds would to Mark McGwire's. She invoked science to overcome nature and explored the promising new field of silicone injection. Hard to believe, but just forty years ago there was still a "public decency" to be outraged in San Francisco, and it prodded the police to raid the topless clubs. Close the clubs they could, at least until the courts intervened, but they could not unwhet the public's deeply whetted appetite. This genie had fully escaped the bottle, and all the sheriff's men could not put her back in.

Thirty years later, in 1995, by the time the Billy Budd of our story, Steven Nary, first ventured into San Francisco from the nearby Alameda Naval Base, North Beach sex had morphed from the optical to the fully interactive. The scene scrambled the brain of the virginal eighteen-year-old from the literal desert and those of his buddies as well.

"There wasn't a place in that area that would ask our age," says a wiser Nary today from behind the walls of Pleasant Valley State Prison. He speaks here of the strip clubs, bars, peep shows, massage parlors, clubs, and hotels that included what Nary calls "in-house prostitutes." He had never seen anything like it before San Francisco, "except of course through media exposure."

Given the nature of the beast, every time he and shipmates went to North Beach, they would try "to outdo the previous nightly adventure." Nary first sampled physical sex with an in-house prostitute that a buddy paid for. Although he was hardly the first sailor to be deflowered thusly, he remembers feeling bad for the girl for several weeks afterward, as she was an obvious crack addict not much older than he.

Still, by his own admission, Nary was "hooked." When he did meet a girl whom he truly connected with, he couldn't commit because he'd "much rather have had that nightly experience." He had sexual encounters with street prostitutes, massage parlor girls, strippers, and so-called girl friends that he met at the dance clubs. All of these women he now sees as "enslaved" in the sex industry by fear, manipulation, addiction, and a media-driven mania to satisfy one's needs. At the time, though, he wasn't doing much thinking at all.

Susan Atkins played her own minor role in the devolution of North Beach. In their quest to meet the growing appetites of their patrons, club owners had been feeding them one more thrill after another, including amateur topless nights. In early 1967, Atkins entered one such contest and took top honors. This turned the head of the eighteen-year-old who had not had a kind word said to her since her mother died. Her victory led to a full-time job as a stripper even though she was underage. No big deal. Club owners in San Francisco—"a black flower of sin," Royce called it a century earlier—have never fussed too much with propriety. Nor did this one. He just gave Atkins an alias and sent her out for a walk whenever the police showed up.

That same year, Atkins's boss saw another opportunity to push the envelope, and he seized it. He teamed up with an emerging local legend, Anton Szandor LaVey, he of the shaved head and lascivious air. Pooling resources, as it were, the new partners collaborated on a live, X-rated "witches' sabbath." When the boss asked Atkins to audition for the vampire role, she hesitated. A newcomer to the city, she did not know exactly what a witches' sabbath was. "It's a big thing around here," her boss assured her, and besides, LaVey was a "full-fledged honcho in that stuff."

In Topeka, one becomes a "honcho" in commercial real estate or midget car racing. Only in San Francisco can one become a "honcho" in Satanism. LaVey had founded the Church of Satan a year earlier, in April 1966, the culmination of an increasingly unorthodox career, one that intersected Atkins's at a particularly vulnerable point in her life. Although he conceded that she made a "fine vampire," he would later write her off as "just another Haight Street burnout." He had, however, made more of an impression on her than she on him. As LaVey's sympathetic biographer Blanche Barton acknowledges, "Atkins indicts LaVey as the catalyst for her downfall."

Born Howard Stanton Levey in Chicago in 1930—identity shifts are as common in California as seismic ones—LaVey moved as a boy to San Francisco and grew up weird from the get-go. Although biographical materials on LaVey are notoriously unreliable, he seems to have learned from his uncle's gangster cronies one key conceit: "Everything is a racket, including the church." The way he learned it, only "the fool continues to go straight for God and country." Not surprisingly, at the very height of the red scare, LaVey flirted openly with communism as well as Satanism.

If LaVey ever succeeded in evoking Satan, there is not much evidence of it. In fact, he may never have really tried. He used Satan more as a visual symbol of the happily lascivious id that he hoped to see unleashed on the land. "Man is the only god," he concluded early on, and he seems to have persuaded much of San Francisco society of the same.

Beyond the shock of an occasional freak show, the Satanic

platelet has never really spiked the cultural Richter, not even in the Bay Area. Satanism has had much more of an impact when it has prodded the larger Blue Plate up and against the Red. From the beginning, LaVey made no bones about the nature of the enemy. In fact, he designed the rococo rituals of his Satanic Church as blasphemous parodies of Christianity in general and Catholicism in particular. "You have to take Satan within yourself to smash that Christian orientation," he would tell his followers.

More analytical than LaVey, and more influential in the dark arts, is one Marvel Whiteside Parsons, also known as John Parson, also known as Jack Parsons—under any name one of the more twisted life forms to have blossomed in the California sun. Parsons was born at LA's Good Samaritan Hospital in 1914, just about the time that future mentor Aleister Crowley was staging his notorious "Paris Workings." Within a year of his birth, Parsons's mother divorced his wayward father. Not one to shy from self-analysis, Parsons would later write of this rupture in the third person, "Your father separated from your mother in order that you might grow up with a hatred of authority and a spirit of revolution necessary to my work." This is a critical understanding. Writ large, as we shall see, antidad fallout has surely fueled the thrust of late-century California culture.

Speaking of fuel and thrust, Parsons would himself emerge as one of the most influential rocket scientists—yes, literally—that our country has produced. Something of a hands-on autodidact, Parsons helped perfect jet-assisted takeoff and found the famed Jet Propulsion Lab in Pasadena. "Without his contribution to both solid and liquid fuels," writes biographer John Carter, "the American space program would not be where it is today." As testament to his influence, the International Astronomical Union named a moon crater after him, on the dark side, to be sure.

It was the dark side that inspired Parsons and toward which

he turned his passions. In 1935, Crowley, the self-declared "wick-edest man in the world," opened the first American franchise of his operation, Ordo Templi Orientis, appropriately enough in franchise-friendly LA. There, Parsons discovered Crowley, the spiritual papa that he had long been seeking. "Dear Father," his letters to Crowley would inevitably begin.

Those who think these dark arts inconsequential should consider the career of Pulitzer Prize–winning *New York Times* correspondent Walter Duranty. In 1913, the young Duranty fell in with Crowley in Paris and became something of a deacon in those "workings," a series of black masses. The mantra of this unholy affair, *sanguis et semen* (blood and semen), nicely captures its over-the-top, homoerotic edge, one that flourished under Parsons's care in the even more fertile fields of Southern California.

Duranty would not say much about these workings, only that having gone through them, "He no longer believed in any-thing." His career proved that. As the *Times*'s main man in Mos-cow, he pursued his newfound fondness for kinky sex. His hosts kept him well entertained, almost assuredly to blackmail him. They seem to have succeeded. Duranty was largely responsible for the suppression of all news about Stalin's terror-famine, one that would ultimately cost some 7 million Ukrainians and Rus-sians their lives. His callousness rivaled Stalin's own, no mean feat.

"Russians may be hungry and short of clothes and com-fort," he wrote in the *New York Times* in 1932. "But you can't make an omelet without breaking eggs." As a tip of the hat to the Crowley commandment—"Do as thou wilt"—Duranty had given his Soviet memoirs the altogether appropriate title *I Write As I Please.*

Jayson Blair, the *Times*'s spectacularly disgraced cub report-er of a few years back, found Duranty's gilt-framed photo in the *Times*'s hallowed hall of Pulitzer winners on the eleventh floor.

All that distinguished Duranty from his fellow honorees was an asterisk beneath his picture and a disclaimer: "Other writers in the *Times* and elsewhere have discredited this coverage."

Even Blair had the good sense to be appalled by Duranty. No one in the history of journalism had shown the deadly potential of the ABETTO factor—a blind eye to the obvious—as Duranty had. Indeed, the ABETTO factor binds New York and California as it blinds them. The media mavens on either coast choose not to see much of anything but their reflections in each other.

Try as he might, Parsons had no more luck invoking Satan than LaVey would. Where he had more success was in ginning up a philosophy that rationalized his hatred of authority and his affection for oddball sex. This he disseminated through a pamphlet on "the rights of man" that he called *Liber OZ*. Among its more provocative and prophetic declarations are the following:

> There is no god but man.
> Do what thou wilt shall be the whole of the Law.
> Every man and every woman is a star.
> Man has the right to love as he will:
> to speak what he will:
> to write what he will:
> to draw, paint, carve, etch, mould, build as he will:
> to dress as he will.
> Man has the right to kill those who would thwart these rights.

Given his security clearance, Parsons had to be more discreet than Crowley. To help protect that clearance and these newly declared rights, Parsons joined an outfit tailor-made for a man of his bold disposition, the American Civil Liberties Union.

Although his literary career never got much beyond pamphleteering and an untitled antiwar, anticapitalist manuscript, Parsons helped shape the culture through his protégées. One,

Robert Heinlein, went on to become arguably the most influential of American science fiction writers. As fate would have it, Heinlein was raised in Kansas City and moved to Los Angeles after his discharge from the Navy. There he fell under the sway of Parsons, a fact that his wife would dispute, but only after burning his letters. Heinlein's popular 1961 novel, *Stranger in a Strange Land*, helped open the door to the sexual revolution and the 1960s counterculture. "Some still say," writes futurist Robert Anton Wilson, "Jack Parsons' magick/libertarian ideas permeate every page of it." Wilson, in fact, believes that through his proxies Parsons all but spawned the "magick trinity Sex and Drugs and Rock 'n' Roll."

There is little to doubt about Parsons's relations with the second of his protégées, the Nebraska-born Lafayette Hubbard, known to Parsons as "Ron." In fact, so deeply did the gregarious, red-haired Hubbard get involved with the movie-star-handsome Parsons and his sexually charged rituals that he eventually ran off with Parsons's sexually charged wife, Betty. Later, Hubbard's people would claim that he had merely infiltrated Parsons's "black magic rites" as an agent of the U.S. Navy and "rescued a girl they were using." But then again this was in 1969, when the institution of Hubbard's design had taken root, and he had a reputation to protect.

L. Ron Hubbard and the Church of Scientology will resurface later, but allow me to add a unifying note from a Joan Didion essay on the 1960s called *The White Album*. As she is cleaning out a beach house that, to her, embodied that turbulent decade just past, she comes across a couple of emblematic items, "a piece of Scientology literature beneath a drawer lining," and "a copy of *Stranger in a Strange Land* stuck deep on a closet shelf." For Didion, the two gents responsible for this literature sum up the strangeness of that very strange time.

Parsons's influence outlived the 1960s. Among other trendy works, Ellis's *Less Than Zero* is neck-deep in the Parsonsian ethos.

When challenged on the rightness of drugging and raping a twelve-year-old, for instance, one character responds, "What's right? If you want something, you have the right to take it. If you want to do something, you have the right to do it."

Parsons tests one's commitment to the nonjudgmental. At one point, for instance, he was very nearly busted for having a pregnant woman jump nude nine times through a fire ring in a backyard ceremony, "not," as Seinfeld might say, "that there's anything wrong with that."

High too in the dubious category was the nature of Parsons's exit from this mortal coil. While mixing explosives on the ground floor of his carriage house, the then-thirty-seven-year-old, hands-on to the end, literally blew his arm off and died soon thereafter from the wounds. His loving mother swallowed a lethal shovelful of sleeping pills when she learned of his fate.

Just as well. Among the charred ruins of the Parsonses' abode were found home movies of Parsons and his mom having sex not only with each other but also with his mom's rather large dog. If California rocker Jim Morrison projected his Oedipal complex into song—"Father/Yes son?/I want to kill you/Mother, I want to fuhhhh you"—California rocketeer Parsons projected his on the living-room wall, not that there's anything wrong with that either.

"Christian piety and Capitalist predation co-existed as equally sacred idols," writes futurist Wilson about the America of Parsons's day. Parsons's goal, and LaVey's as well, was to shatter both, an iconoclastic mission of the highest order and one that continues to attract young missionaries by the thousands.

★ 5. El Monte ★

I was still looking for a panacea, for some kind of
relief from all of that life, from all that damage.
　　—Tatum O'Neal, *A Paper Life*

God is everywhere and everyone is God," Charles Manson would tell Susan Atkins soon after meeting her. Atkins was ready for a little God in her life. "I felt he might be
Christ," she remembers thinking. Like so many others in that
time and place, Atkins felt radically unmoored. This was a sensa-
tion that Manson masterfully reinforced. "All your roots are cut,"
he would tell his charges, sounding much like a *Look* editorialist.
"You are freed from your families and all their old hang-ups. You
are cut loose into the now."

To cushion these lost souls from the shock of "the now,"
Manson created his idea of a family with himself at the head.
"Charlie had instantly seemed more a father to me," says At-
kins, "than my own father." On the night of August 8, 1969,
Manson directed four of his children—Atkins, Linda Kasabian,
Patricia Krenwinkel, and Tex Watson—to kill the inhabitants of
the house on Cielo.

How Manson had come to choose this house deserves a
sidebar. Some time in 1968, Dennis Wilson was driving down
the Pacific Coast Highway when he spotted two female hitchhikers, picked them up, and took them home. In the way of
background, Dennis was the grandson of Buddy Wilson, who
had moved out to LA from Hutchinson, Kansas, in the 1920s to
work on a massive water project. Buddy never quite found his
footing. A "no-good alcoholic," he beat his wife and alienated
his son, Murry. Murry adapted no better. He abused his wife
before divorcing her and alienated his sons, Dennis most of all.

According to his biographer, "Dennis's only ambition was to be as different from his father as possible." To accomplish this, he left home as soon he could support himself, which he was able to do quite young and quite well. By the age of twenty-three he had been married, divorced, and addicted but still managed to have his own home in Malibu. There he let the hitchhikers and their friends nestle in, Charles Manson prominent among them.

It was a shame about Dennis. Just a few years earlier, he and his brothers Brian and Carl, their cousin Mike, and friend Al had burst out of LA County's South Bay as triumphant and together as the state they embodied. Like California perhaps, the Beach Boys peaked in the early 1960s and found almost nothing more certain in their later lives than disorder.

Manson was not the cause of that, just another symptom. Although Dennis would always remain elusive about their relationship, he likely saw in Manson the father that Atkins did. In any case, Dennis arranged for Manson to audition for record producer Terry Melcher, Doris Day's son by her first marriage. Melcher, who then lived at 10500 Cielo Drive with Candice Bergen, turned Manson down, and Manson never forgave him.

Dennis Wilson did not need Manson to kill him. His was a slow, steady suicide that merely climaxed with an alcohol-assisted drowning in Marina Del Ray. "I'm lonesome. I'm lonesome all the time," Wilson was quoted as saying on the day he died. Not yet forty, he left behind a wife, Shawn, his fourth, who just happened to be the illegitimate daughter of his cousin, Mike Love, as well as assorted children.

Whether Manson intended to kill Melcher or merely scare him by killing the new tenants is uncertain, but to the victims it scarcely mattered. "I'm the devil," Tex Watson told them, "and I'm here to do the devil's business." That, not one of the five adults killed on Cielo Drive doubted.

On the next night, August 9, Charlie took a group of his

acolytes out for another ride into the wilds of West Los Angeles. At one point, he stopped in front of a church and went in, promising to "kill a priest and hang him upside down on the cross." Finding no one there, he continued until he came to a house on Waverly Drive in Hollywood and there dispatched Krenwinkel, Watson, and Leslie Van Houten to murder the inhabitants. It was no more than this whim that sent Rosemary and Leno LaBianca to their graves.

Manson was a freak, but Atkins, Krenwinkel, Kasabian, Van Houten, and the twenty or so other young women under Manson's sway were not. To see them now is to see one's own sisters and wives and mothers: attractive, middle-aged, middle-class women, well spoken and well spoken of, even if at least four of them are still in prison. Under slightly different circumstances, they all might have prospered.

They obviously have not, and the question is why. In her biography of Leslie Van Houten, Karlene Faith offers an essential clue as mere detail. As Faith tells us of the Van Houtens, "They were a clean-cut, loving family in a comfortable middle-class house with a pool, in a Southern California suburb." Van Houten's father, an automobile auctioneer, and her stay-at-home mom were "devoted to their four children."

Not that loving, not that devoted. As the reader learns, "Major change was in the offing." The Van Houtens divorced in 1963, when Leslie was thirteen. By sixteen, Van Houten had experienced acid, sex, pregnancy, and abortion, and by nineteen, first-degree murder—"major change" in just about anybody's book.

A cyber trip to the "Manson Girl Info Center" fills in the blanks on the other two would-be killers. Born in 1949, Linda Kasabian witnessed her parents' divorce, her mother's remarriage, and her stepfather's contempt. Mad at the world, she dropped out of high school, married at sixteen, divorced that guy, married again, turned "hippie," dropped acid, visited communes, and drifted into Manson's orbit after giving birth to daughter Tonya in Los Angeles in 1968.

Patricia Krenwinkel was born to an insurance salesman father and a homemaker mother, making her second go at marriage. The child from that first marriage never adapted. By the time Krenwinkel hit her teens, that half-sister was already a junkie, and she hooked her younger sister on diet pills. While still in high school, Krenwinkel watched helplessly as her mom divorced once more, this time from her own dad. After a semester of college, Krenwinkel dropped out, moved into a Manhattan Beach apartment with her now-heroin-addicted half-sister, and was more than ready for a new family when Manson came knocking.

There is an obvious thread here. The reader sees it. If I were to go twenty-five deep on the Manson girls the thread would grow as thick as bridge cable, but Van Houten biographer Faith would still insist on not seeing it. "Manson's followers had certain things in common with each other," she writes. "They were idealists and social rebels and spiritual seekers in the 1960s." In this regard, they were like "millions of other young people who shared their values and visions."

That's it! Faith, like most of the era's chroniclers, chooses to remember the children of the sixties, even the butchers and murderesses, as seekers of peace and justice. After all, America was groaning under the weight of "every traditional value, every hypocritical practice, every war and injustice." The yoking of "traditional value" and "injustice" makes perfect sense to Faith and has become a commonplace trope in her circle. She applauds Van Houten and her peers for "bursting out of cultural constraints" and "constructing a vibrant counterculture to their liking."

James Ellroy did not share those values and visions. The brilliant noir writer, author of *Black Dahlia* and *L.A. Confidential,* among other works, had a different take on what he calls "the Tate-LaBianca snuffs." With the possible exception of Tatum O'Neal, Ellroy was living what may have been the most desperate, drug-addled young life ever recorded as memoir. In his well-titled *My Dark Places*, Ellroy recounts that life in chilling detail beginning with the divorce that precipitated it. "I took it hard," he remembers. "I threw tantrums for weeks running." He was six years old at the time.

The state was noisy with tantrums. "The 50s divorce boom was peaking," Ellroy recounts. So he and his mother moved from Los Angeles to the unlovely East LA satellite burg of El Monte, "The City of Divorced Women." There his mom set out to find new love in all the wrong places with all the wrong people, one of whom murdered her when Ellroy was ten. Dispatched back to his increasingly dissolute father, the young Ellroy roamed the streets of Los Angeles like a wolf boy.

In August 1969, Ellroy was multitasking as a burglar, voyeur, and drug addict when the Manson murders took place. "I saw more private patrol cars out trawling," he recalls. "I saw security-service signs on front doors. I stopped B&E'ing cold turkey. I never did it again." In time, Ellroy found his way to Alcoholics Anonymous and eventually, as fate would have it, to Thomas Frank's Mission Hills, Kansas, where he lived for a number of years. O'Neal, herself a product of a brutal divorce, also found her way to a life-changing experience through AA.

Although the same age as the Manson girls, and just as druggy, the self-aware Ellroy never could quite see himself as part of "a vibrant counterculture." Rather, he saw himself as a child of divorce, which, he says only half-jokingly, "stigmatized little kids and fucked them up for life."

As it happens, during the same year that Manson was preparing his flock for Helter Skelter, state assemblyman Jim Hayes of Long Beach was going through a nasty divorce. To make life easier for people like himself he introduced a bill, which would result in the nation's most progressive no-fault divorce law. Not that Californians needed much help getting divorced. Josiah Royce argued that California divorces were "far too numerous and easy," and that was in the 1850s.

On September 4, 1969, just four weeks after the Tate-LaBianca murders, Governor Reagan—Reagan again!—signed the bill into law, an endorsement that he would later regret. "He wanted to do something to make the divorce process less acrimonious, less contentious, and less expensive," son Michael Reagan writes of his once-divorced dad in his book *Twice Adopted*. He also made divorce a whole lot more available.

Marin County divorce authority Dr. Judith Wallerstein calls the bill "an upheaval akin to a cataclysmic earthquake." "People were jubilant," adds Wallerstein. They rejoiced in the same shortsighted way the people in England did when Chamberlain brought back "peace in our time." Only in California, they celebrated by getting divorced.

In 1970, the first full year of the no-fault law, the state registered a record 112,942 divorces, a 38 percent increase from just the year before. To put that number in perspective consider that, in 1960, there had been only 105, 352 *marriages* in California. Population growth—27 percent for the decade—accounts for some of the discrepancy, but the marriage/divorce ratio, no matter what the qualifiers, signaled a massive disruption in family life.

In 1970, California's divorce rate was 60 percent higher than that of the nation as a whole, and it continued to trend upward throughout the decade. By 1980, California had registered a new record 138,361 divorces. In other words, 276,722 Californians got divorced in 1980 alone. That was more than twice as many as in 1966, and in 1966, the California divorce rate was already 50 percent higher than the national norm. In fact, the divorce rate increased four times faster than the population did in the years 1966–80.

Only Oklahoma had no-fault divorce before California,

and no one paid attention to Oklahoma. People did pay attention to California. A national lawyers group, the self-designated Uniform Law Commission, quickly composed a model no-fault law based on California's, and by 1985, just about every state in the union had adopted it in one form or another, with predictable results. By 1980, the nation's divorce rate was higher than California's was in 1969.

In 1980, embarrassed by the divorce plague in their midst, California lawmakers implemented a quick fix of world-class caliber: They would no longer keep or publish statistics! Imagine the anxiety lawmakers could have spared their constituents if they had tackled AIDS with the same ingenuity.

These divorce reforms went unchallenged, argues Wallerstein in her breakthrough book *The Unexpected Legacy of Divorce*, because of "an almost conspiratorial silence" about its unhappy effect on kids. Wallerstein began rethinking her own relatively tolerant take on divorce after a chance encounter with a child she had counseled long ago. Twenty-five years after her parents' divorce, the young woman was still struggling with its consequences. This meeting inspired Wallerstein to undertake a long-range, close-up study of the kids with whom she had worked twenty-five years earlier, the deepest such study ever undertaken. The results, as Wallerstein admits, "hit a raw nerve" in America. Many in positions of influence simply did not want to know what she had learned.

Among her discoveries is that most children never really recover. "Divorce is a life-transforming experience," Wallerstein writes. "After divorce, childhood is different. Adulthood—with the decision to marry or not and have children or not—is different." She refrains from judging that difference as good or bad, but her subjects don't. Not one of the roughly one hundred interviewees wanted their own children to go through what they had.

In general, adolescence begins early and lasts late for these kids. The girls are more likely to seek out sex, the boys drugs and alcohol. They marry later if at all, get divorced more, trust less, and have fewer children. Even as adults, they nurse a "continuing anger at parents," more often at the dads, whom the kids regard as "selfish and faithless." As Jack Parsons deftly put it, that anger can work itself out as "a hatred of authority and a spirit of revolution." Indeed, were it not for divorce, there might not have been a "sixties." We might remember California in that decade largely for the Beach Boys, the skateboard, and Silicon Valley.

When not ignoring divorce completely, the media have done their best to trivialize it. In July 1999, the PBS children's show *Sesame Street* offered a perky little vignette on the subject. In it, Kermit the Frog, here an inquiring reporter, asks a cute little bird where she lives. As she tells Kermit merrily, she lives part of the time in one tree where she frolics in her mother's nest and the rest of her time in a separate tree where she frolics with her dad. "They both love me," she chirps.

Had James Ellroy written this scene—*Sesame Street Confidential?*—the tone might have been a little different. He remembers his own nest-hopping as a "bifurcated life divvied up between two people locked in an intractable mutual hatred."

Ellroy's hard stare is too much for Hollywood as well. "Oh, my dear Katie," counsels Aunt Euphegenia Doubtfire on her kiddie TV show. "You know, some parents get along much better when they don't live together. They don't fight all the time and they can become better people. Much better mommies and daddies for you."

Such is the sappy and largely false advice Robin Williams's drag character, Mrs. Doubtfire, offers at the end of the movie comedy of the same name. What sets the movie apart, though, is not that it takes a wrongheaded stand on divorce—"You'll have a family in your heart for ever"—but that it takes any stand at all. *Mrs. Doubtfire* is one of the handful of halfway serious cinematic looks at the effects of divorce on children, even if its message is no deeper, or different really, than *Sesame Street*'s.

While *Sesame Street* and *Mrs. Doubtfire* both at least try to address the emotional fallout of divorce, neither addresses the ecological one. If Mom has a nest, and Dad has a nest, California needs a whole lot more nests than it otherwise would, not to mention more resources to heat, cool, light, and water those nests and more gas to ferry the baby birds between them.

There is a secondary factor at play here. One shared trait Wallerstein finds among her subjects is a relentless "fear of loss, fear of change, and fear that disaster will strike, especially when things are going well." This may help explain "Helter Skelter." Susan Atkins and the others interpreted this innocuous phrase from a Beatles' song to mean that "things were going out of control in the world, and the end was coming."

Today, children whose parents divorced in the sixties, seventies, and eighties have enormous influence in California's political and civic life. One has to question how their anxieties have skewed the state's thinking not just on social issues but on issues like growth and the environment. There are many well-placed Californians capable of confusing a new strip mall or subdivision with the end of the world as we know it.

In the course of my research, I asked hundreds of Californians what's the matter with their state. Because they can afford to, the affluent offer a wide range of responses, none of them, however, "divorce" or "family breakdown." Not surprisingly, working-class Californians pretty much stick to one: the extraordinarily high cost of housing. If fear of the future contributes to that cost, so too does bifurcated nesting. It's just that hardly anyone will talk about either.

★ 6. Pleasantville ★

I actually smoke freebase in the hospital right up
until the abortion.
    —Julia Phillips, *You'll Never Eat Lunch in This
    Town Again*

More than one-fourth of California's people live in
Los Angeles County. For better or worse, what these
people think matters. For very nearly a century they have had
more influence on world culture than any comparable group
of people since imperial Rome. This influence began with the
movies, then bled into television, then into music, then music
videos, and even into video games. Locals sense their power.
One screenwriter with whom I spoke referred to himself casually as a "Roman citizen" in just the sense I mean above, namely,
someone who shapes the world, satisfies his own whims, and
leaves the potholes to the plebeians.

"Back where you come from you have the freedom to do
this," he confided, holding his hands about half a foot apart.
"Here," he said stretching his hands about three feet apart, "we
have the freedom to do this."

As much as we might like to deny it, Hollywood still has
a grip on us. Back in Kansas City, no story that I tell about my
California travels grabs more attention than the one in which
Brad Pitt sits at a table next to me at Shutter's in Santa Monica.
All else pales. That much said, Hollywood is not what it once
was. It has gone wrong in a thousand different ways, only one
of which will time and continuity permit me to pursue, namely
the one leading from the Cielo gates, that is the Hollywood take
on family.

In a mercenary way, at least, family matters a great deal in

Hollywood, perhaps more than ever. There is no other rational explanation for the career of Tori Spelling, even if she didn't show up at the old man's funeral. Nepotism rules here more so than in any other competitive endeavor. How many winners of the U.S. Open or the Nobel Prize in Literature or the Tchaikovsky Competition have spawned a winning heir or even one who made the final cut? None. None. None. By contrast, Ryan O'Neal's ten-year-old daughter, Tatum, took home an Oscar on her very first try, and she is just one of scores, nay hundreds, of the Hollywood offspring to prosper.

The problem, however, goes much deeper than the triumph of the half-talented and the homely. Hollywood has become a closed loop of bad vibes and worse information, especially on the issue of family. "I didn't want to be this crazy mother," Tatum O'Neal says of her own mom, "which I sort of ended up later on being." Many in this industry simply have never seen a happy, functioning family, let alone a community of such families. "We are a little bit out of touch in Hollywood every once in a while," boasted Rosemary's handsome nephew, George, at the 2006 Oscars. "I think it's probably a good thing." No, George, it is not. Ignorance never is, not when you have the power to teach the world.

To test my assumptions about Hollywood and the family, I wrote down the names of the twenty most prominent children of the entertainment industry I could think of and traced their family status during childhood through the Internet Movie Database (IMDb). There is nothing scientific about this survey. If the reader thinks some personality should be on this list and is not, it is likely because I forgot.

Drew Barrymore	Parents divorced
Jeff Bridges	Parents together
Jamie Lee Curtis	Parents divorced

Laura Dern	Parents divorced
Michael Douglas	Parents divorced
Robert Downey, Jr	Parents divorced
Carrie Fisher	Parents divorced
Bridget Fonda	Parents divorced
Jane Fonda	Parents divorced
Melanie Griffith	Parents divorced
Kate Hudson	Parents divorced
Timothy Hutton	Parents divorced
Angelina Jolie	Parents divorced
Jennifer Jason Leigh	Parents divorced
Gwyneth Paltrow	Parents together
Sean Penn	Father previously married
Campbell Scott	Parents divorced
Charlie Sheen	Parents together
Kiefer Sutherland	Parents divorced
Patrick Wayne	Parents divorced

In every one of the "divorced" cases cited, the parents did so when their children were still minors. Many children watched their parents divorce more than once. Curiously, those that have become bigger names than their parents—Jeff Bridges, Charlie Sheen, Sean Penn (actress Eileen Ryan and director Leo Penn), and Gwyneth Paltrow (actress Blythe Danner and director Bruce Paltrow)—are the ones that grew up in two-parent homes. Divorce is not the key to emotional depth or star appeal.

Plus, as the cases of Sheen and Penn make clear, a two-parent household is no guarantee of sanity in a universe where family disorder has reached critical mass. "The family grows best in a garden with its kind," Josiah Royce observed correctly more than a century ago. "Where family life does not involve healthy friendship with other families, it is apt to be injured by unhealthy if well-meaning friendships with wanderers."

Yet despite their limited perspective, these wanderers and friends are the very same people who have been tasked to show the rest of the world how American family life and culture work. This makes no sense. It is like having Jack Parsons teach a class on handling explosives—or on handling one's mother, for that matter. No wonder everyone hates us.

To be fair to our myopic media pals, they do at least sense that something is the matter. They are just not sure what it is. This anxiety reveals itself in those few serious cinematic attempts to explain contemporary family life in California, beginning with the archetypal California movie, 1955's *Rebel Without a Cause*, a movie whose cluelessness is built into the very title.

"Man existing alone seems an episode of little consequence," a scary old astronomer at LA's Griffith Observatory tells the gnarly young rebels at the film's beginning, and it is left to them to find whatever consequence can be had. In this still-innocent era—*Rebel* premiered the same year as Disneyland—writer/director Nicholas Ray felt free to pose the idea of family as an alternative to that aloneness. The idea is one thing, however. The reality is another, and in mid-fifties California, at least for the three main characters, family just wasn't happening. All are estranged from their folks. The parents of Sal Mineo's poor rich kid, Plato, skipped town and left him with the maid. By the time of Ellis's *Less Than Zero* everyone seemed to be skipping town and leaving the kid with the maid, but in 1955 that still seemed pretty shocking.

Desperately adrift, Plato tries to find safe harbor with James Dean's stuttering Jim and Natalie Wood's equally unsteady Judy. "If only you could have been my dad," Plato tells Jim before being gunned down by the overeager LA cops. "He tried to make us his family," sighs Jim afterward. In real life, there would not be much family for any of the three actors.

When sixteen-year-old Natalie Wood first read the script for *Rebel*, she heard a voice buzzing in her head saying, "You are

Judy." In many ways, hers was the perfectly synthetic California life. Born Natalia Nikolaevna Zakhraenko to Russian parents in San Francisco, young Natalia had metamorphosed into the All-American girl-next-door Natalie Wood by the age of five. After just one small film role, Natalie's overly ambitious, once-divorced mother uprooted her, her half-sister, and her alcoholic father—"a shadow figure in his own household"—to Los Angeles in the hope that Natalie would become a star. That she did, experiencing just about every culture shock California had to offer along the way. These included an affair with the forty-three-year-old Ray when she was still sixteen-year-old "jailbait," a brutal rape at the same age by a major Hollywood star twenty years her senior, and a marriage to movie star Robert Wagner undone, according to Wood at least, when she caught him in bed with another man.

Wood would go on to divorce Wagner and remarry him. She shouldn't have. On Thanksgiving weekend 1981, the forty-three-year-old actress, Wagner, and their friend, actor Christopher Walken, sailed to Catalina Island, a surprisingly untouched and unpeopled slice of California twenty-six miles across the sea from Long Beach. After a disturbed, deeply alcoholic evening, the hydrophobic Wood apparently tried to escape their yacht and ended up drowning, her cries for help either unheard by Wagner or, more likely, unheeded. That Wagner walked away from this tragedy legally unscathed is a testament to the enduring clout of Hollywood.

As it happens, Wood outlived her *Rebel* costars. James Dean met his untimely end on what is now Route 46 near Cholame when a Cal Poly student with the unfortunate name of Donald Turnupseed crossed blindly into Dean's lane and ran head-on into his Porsche 500 Spyder. "My fun days are over," Dean reportedly said to the EMTs who carted him off. His prerelease death helped make *Rebel* a huge hit. In 1976, the thirty-seven-year-old Sal Mineo was in rehearsal for his role as a gay burglar in the LA production of the play *P.S. Your Cat Is Dead* when a not-so-gay burglar stabbed him fatally in a West Hollywood alley. Nick Adams, another *Rebel* costar, died of a drug overdose in his Beverly Hills home in 1968 at the age of thirty-six. Volumes have been written about the alleged gayness or biness of all three of these actors, some of which may even be true.

At the time of *Rebel's* release in 1955, Hollywood still saw the family as worth saving, worth reconstructing. On television especially, the nuclear family dominated that decade and into the next, as evidenced by chirpy classics like *Leave It to Beaver*, *Father Knows Best*, and *Ozzie and Harriet*, each with a stable father figure.

In those shows without two parents, typically it was the mom who went missing—chastely to her grave, of course—and it was the dad who soldiered on even as he mothered his children. *Andy Griffith, My Three Sons,* and *The Courtship of Eddie's Father* all mined this theme, as did Westerns like *The Rifleman* and *Bonanza*. The movies meanwhile served up the apotheosis of widower pophood in Atticus Finch, the hero of 1962's *To Kill a Mockingbird*.

Yet even in these families, at least the ones set in contemporary California, no one had cousins or aunts or even grandmothers. No one went to christenings or first communions or even to church. No one prayed on fifties TV, not Beaver, not Bud, not David and Ricky. If they still saluted the flag, they had lost touch with the rituals of extended family and faith. They were as deracinated as the young families of Lakewood. As two-parent families came under siege in California life, Hollywood's fictional families would lose touch with their fathers as well. Today, practically the only nuclear families left standing on TV are the Sopranos and the Simpsons.

In film, especially in serious films about California, the feud between the emotionally fragile child and a faithless father has become something of an angry staple. Robert Altman in *Short Cuts* (1993), Irwin Winkler in *Life As a House* (2001), Erik Skjoldbjaerg in *Prozac Nation* (2001), and Paul Thomas Anderson in *Magnolia* (1999) serve up some of the least attractive screen dads since Jack "Here's Johnny" Torrance in *The Shining*.

In the equally angry 1993 Joel Schumacher film, *Falling Down*, the Michael Douglas character, William Foster, wanders across the baroque badlands of Los Angeles on a deranged odyssey to reclaim his estranged wife and daughter. "I'm coming home," he tells them repeatedly and pathetically.

For Michael Douglas, this film has an element of the personal. His father, Kirk Douglas, quit the nest when Michael was six. Michael saw his dad and his new half-brothers only on holidays. In turn, Michael left his wife Diandra and son Cameron. According to the IMDb, Diandra "was sick of [Michael's] womanizing, absenteeism, and not being 'a proper father to Cameron'" In *Falling Down,* Douglas's character is shown to have been no more proper a father than Douglas himself, his memory of a happy home proving pure illusion. As with Plato, the police shoot Foster down, too, standard deus ex machina in Hollywood.

By century's end, the film community had so lost touch with the workings of a normal, happy family that it began to treat such a family as myth, a hoax even, and in no movie more insidiously than 1998's seemingly benign *Pleasantville*. Gary Ross, an occasional speechwriter for Michael Dukakis and Bill Clinton, wrote and directed this sly little bit of cinematic subversion. The LA-born son of a blacklisted screenwriter—or so he alleges, commie roots being boastworthy in Hollywood—Ross has an agenda. Unlike the other auteurs, his is political, not personal. He does not try to illuminate the family but to undermine it.

The movie opens in a contemporary California high school with an apocalyptic bent. In one class, a counselor tells the students that the job market is collapsing. In another, a health teacher cautions them that HIV is running wild. In a third, a science teacher warns them that the globe is on high broil. "Okay. Who can tell me what famine is?" he asks.

If anything, life at home is scarier still. "No—you have custody the first weekend of every month and this is the first weekend," the mom shouts on the phone. Her two high-school-age children meanwhile suffer visibly through this messy divorce and their mother's ensuing affair with a man nine years her junior. Jennifer is a mindless slut; her brother, David, a feckless nerd who seeks refuge from his chaotic life in an old *Leave It to Beaver*–like sitcom called *Pleasantville*.

Through some mildly entertaining gimmickry, David and Jennifer find themselves teleported into a living, breathing, black-and-white Pleasantville. Here, they emerge as Bud and Mary Sue Parker, model children of the equally perfect George and Betty Parker. A serious student of the show, David has the inside skinny not only on the quirks of the characters, but also on the culture of the town. He attempts to instruct his wayward sister in both.

Jennifer will have none of it. From minute one, she can sense Pleasantville's psychic shackles and proceeds to pare them off as quickly as she can. Sex, Jennifer understands, cuts through everything. When she liberates the town's virginal jocks from their restraints, they mutate from black and white to color. They, in turn, spread the charms of sex to their friends. These newly deflowered lads and lasses blossom in full color as well. So do the flowers around them in this anti-Eden. Soon enough, Jennifer enlists David in her polychromatic rebellion—I would say "rainbow," but Hollywood had yet to discover gay sex—and the revolution is on. Jack Parsons or Anton LaVey could not have scripted it better themselves.

The quietly restless Betty Parker discovers her own color by—blush—masturbating in the bathtub. She becomes fully radiant when she betrays the dull but decent George and beds down with the aptly named "Mr. Johnson," the soda shop manager. Mr. Johnson taps his inner palette not just through adulterous sex but also through truly awful abstract art.

The forces of change soon shake, rattle, and roll the once-complacent burg. The kids at the soda shop switch from sweet fifties pop to raunchy R&B. David introduces his new friends to literature—as if! They now read presumably subversive classics like *Catcher in the Rye* and *Huckleberry Finn*.

In writing about Gold Rush San Francisco, Royce had described "the true sin of the community" as a general sense of "irreligious liberty." As Royce saw it, San Franciscans "considered every man's vices, however offensive and aggressive they might be (short of crime), as a private concern between his own soul and Satan." As Ross sees it a century or so later, that same "irreligious liberty" is the salvation of the community.

This plot line might have been amusing enough were our heroes merely rebelling against *Pleasantville*, the show. But by blurring the line between the fictional Pleasantville and the real Mid-America, Director Ross grinds his edgy Blue provocations right up in the face of the Red.

It is only a matter of time before the town fathers, black and white to the man, fascist to the core, attempt to suppress "the coloreds" and reinstate their own "values," a word that drips acid when spoken. This frantic little effort climaxes in a court trial whose set smugly, if preposterously, mimics that of *To Kill a Mockingbird*. But it's too late. The sixties are spreading through Pleasantville like the Blob, and folks are too buzzed to get the fire extinguishers from the high school to freeze it in its tracks.

Ross targeted the young and hit home. "The film addresses the limits of conservatism, the hypocracy [sic] of hiding your head, the fascism of fear," writes one typical reviewer on *Ain't It Cool News*. "It brings up the other C word, not communism, but Change. The most violent act we have."

Before they contract AIDS, catch fire freebasing, or start up

Pleasantville's own Trench Coat Mafia, David and Jennifer are miraculously teleported back to the present. To his tiny credit, Ross acknowledges the chaos of the world these kids inhabit. Nothing has changed in their absence. The mom, distraught over a botched weekend with her Cub Scout of a beau, tearfully tells David, "It's not supposed to be like this."

Before his Pleasantville experience, David would have agreed. But like the epic hero-trippers of yore, David has returned home a savvier if more cynical dude. He has learned that morals are a scam, marriage a fraud, innocence an illusion, and "family values" a euphemism for bigotry. The wise man, he knows now, avoids moral judgment at all costs or at least pretends to. With his newfound wisdom he reaches out to his weeping mom and reassures her with a bit of teen sophistry so tellingly empty it could have been this book's title—"It's not supposed to be anything."

If the adults of California insist on blinding themselves to the obvious, the children are all eyes. It would take a thirteen-year-old, Nikki Reed, to write the screenplay for the truest and scariest cinematic portrait of a family in meltdown, 2003's *Thirteen*.

In the way of background, Reed's California parents divorced when she was two. As Judith Wallerstein might have predicted, Reed's problems exploded when she hit adolescence. Her father's girlfriend, production designer Catherine Hardwicke, suggested that Reed keep a diary to cope. She wrote a screenplay instead. Impressed, Hardwicke helped her shape it and went on to direct the film, her directorial debut.

Shot in semidocumentary style, and set at and around the very real Portola Middle School in the San Fernando Valley, *Thirteen* ingenuously captures the mayhem that the culture of divorce has wrought on California life. The film's protagonist, the shrewdly named Tracy Freeland, begins her seventh-grade career at Portola as a studious innocent. From day one, she finds herself awed and intimidated by the school "hot" girls already well along in their self-liberation. Envious of their status on campus, Tracy begins to mimic them.

Following the lead of one Evie Zamora—a rare biblical allusion these days—Tracy proceeds to dispense with one cultural restraint after another: modesty first, then temperance, then chastity. Living in the sexually overcharged LA environment, the girls and their friends spread the spirit of "irreligious liberty" throughout the junior high. They steal clothes, drink, do drugs, tramp around, self-mutilate, and sample gay sex, all the things that David and Jennifer might have gotten to do if *Pleasantville* had had a sequel.

Left by her parents with a drugged and indifferent relative, the shackle-free Evie leads the way. Tracy has all the restraint that a divorced and distracted mom can impose. Those distractions include a full-time business, a house, two children, an unhelpful ex, and a sometimes live-in boyfriend struggling with his own coke habit. In a reversal of roles much like the one seen in *Pleasantville* and not at all uncommon in divorced families, Tracy asks her mom, "Why are you doing this to yourself?" The mom, who looks, as Evie points out, "like the hot big sister," has no good answer.

The yuppie dad has no answers at all. When called in to help by the older brother, he chafes, "Can someone please tell me what is the problem—in a nutshell?" Only in a world where life and love are so routinely commodified could a problem possibly come in a "nutshell." This one, however, is not so easily cracked. As much as the dad would like to help, he cannot let his little bird frolic in his nest even for a weekend. "I am trying to kick ass at this new job," he tells Tracy. "I am trying to get you and your mom more money."

The movie, painfully realistic and believable, has no answers either. It offers hope at film's end that the mother's desperate love for her daughter will save her from a dissolute culture, but it offers no guarantee for Tracy and not a prayer for Evie—nicely played by Nikki Reed herself. In the wrong time and place, Evie becomes Susan Atkins.

In general, the critics liked the film, but not a one that I read talks about the role of divorce in Tracy's fevered embrace of the vulgar. A typical review cites as the "themes" of the movie "insecurity, confusion, wanting to be liked and accepted." Yeah, okay, Mack, but why?

What the movie shows smartly and un-self-consciously is how broken homes undermine the common culture and how that culture, in turn, undermines the home. In this regard, it is the exact opposite of the absurd *Pleasantville*, which the same critics liked even more. In Hollywood, life really is not supposed to be about much of anything.

★ 7. South Central ★

The truth is you're the weak. And I'm the tyranny of
evil men. But I'm tryin'. I'm tryin' real hard to be a
shepherd.
    —Jules, *Pulp Fiction*

In the relentlessly naturalistic *Thirteen*, Tracy and Evie
hook up almost exclusively with minority boys, mostly
black. They do so for no particular reason other than that the
black kids in their orbit have even fewer checks and balances in
their lives than they do.

The unbloodied thirteen-year-olds in Tracy's circle have
turned an unsweet sixteen when they show up on the mean
streets of Inglewood in the LA-based *Grand Canyon*. Mack, the
film's lawyer protagonist played by Kevin Kline, encounters the
lads one night after a Lakers game when they drive by his stalled
Lexus and come back to harass him. "You know, this is a nice
car, mister," says one of them in a scene that sends chills down
the collective California yuppie spine, if yuppies do indeed have
spines. "I could use me a car with a phone in it."

Were the makers of *Thirteen* and *Grand Canyon* merely
dabbling in stereotype, California would be a happier place. But
unfortunately, they are not. These lost boys represent the rolling,
pulsating edge of what in the year of *Grand Canyon*'s release,
1991, was California's most volatile cultural plate. A year later
their real-life models would spark the single greatest shock to
the state since the Manson murders of 1969 and send even their
sympathizers scrambling for ornamental iron and the locks to
secure it.

Yet just fifteen years later California seems almost unaware
that these kids and their culture still exist. Astonishingly, not one

of the hundreds of nonblack Californians with whom I spoke, north and south, mentioned race relations or anything like it as a first response to the "what's the matter" question. As I came to discover, it's not that they look more kindly on their black brethren. It's just that now they don't really look at all.

Stanley "Tookie" Williams bore some responsibility for California's averted gaze, but not nearly as much as he liked to claim. Williams lied about a lot of things, not the least of which was his innocence. He also took credit for having founded the notorious confederacy of street gangs known as the Crips. He did not. That dubious honor belongs to one Raymond Washington, the fourth of five boys from a broken home, an occasional student at Fremont High, and an industrial-strength bully.

In 1969, the same year as the Manson murders and the new divorce bill, the ambitious sixteen-year-old quit a local gang called the Avenues and cannibalized the brand to start his own offshoot, the Baby Avenues. According to Tookie, Crips was a drunken corruption of Avenue Cribs, a derivative of Baby Avenues. Another tale, more widely circulated, has the Baby Avenues beating a group of Asian merchants with walking sticks and robbing them. When one merchant told the press that the walking sticks made the thieves look like "cripples," the gang gleefully exploited the publicity and ran with the new identity.

The true story is much more prosaic. One of Washington's brothers badly sprained his ankle, and someone wrote "Crip" on his Chuck Taylor Converses to commemorate this minor crippling. Brother Raymond liked the name and adopted it. From that humble origin grew the most gratuitously lethal American tribe since the Comanche.

No one ever beat the brutal Washington in a fight, and he fought all the time. In that relatively innocent era, before gangs armed themselves like Hezbollah, Washington would confront the leader of a rival organization, beat the black out of him if he resisted, and absorb the awed subordinates. In 1971, eying a potentially rival fiefdom west of the Harbor Freeway, this street-corner Caesar persuaded its leader to join the Crips, and Tookie Williams did just that, now as the manager of his own franchise, the Westside Crips.

So relentless were the Crips and so violent that unaffiliated gangs like the Piru in Compton and the Brims near USC formed their own confederacy as an act of self-preservation. They called this new assemblage the Bloods, complete with its own brand identifiers, including a dizzying array of hand signals, legends, idioms, clothing styles, codes of silence, and color coding—red to the Crips' storied blue. The battle for South LA was joined. More Americans have died in it than died in both Gulf Wars combined.

In 1953, the year both Washington and Williams were born, the state of California recorded 276 homicides, or about two per hundred thousand residents. At the time, Los Angeles's black population had more apparent reason to be angry than today. Most lived materially poorer lives in steamy little homes in rigidly restricted neighborhoods. They were expected to pay market rent, their own doctor bills, and actually *buy* lunches for their kids. Should they apply for a job or their kids apply for college, those applications more likely settled to the bottom of the pile than to the top.

In 1979, fifteen years into LBJ's Great Society, nearly three thousand Californians were murdered, ten times more than in the year of the boys' birth and a stunning six times more per capita. And this was *before* the crack epidemic gave urban apologists something to blame murder on other than murderers. Raymond Washington was one of the three thousand. As luck would have it, the LA media had more on their plate that day than the shotgun slaying on South San Pedro of an uncelebrated man just shy of his twenty-sixth birthday. August 9, after all, was the tenth anniversary of the Manson slayings.

Tookie Williams contributed four homicides of his own to

the 1979 tally. In February of that year, he pumped two shot-gun shells into the back of twenty-six-year-old 7-Eleven clerk Albert Owens as he lay facedown in a storage room. Owens, a father of two and an Army veteran, made the mistake that day of coming to work Caucasian, as Williams "was killing all white people." In March 1979, Williams broke into the office of the Brookhaven Motel and blasted seventy-six-year-old Yen-I Yang, his wife, sixty-three-year-old Tsai-Shai Yang, and their forty-three-year-old daughter Yee-Chen Lin, killing all three "Bud-dhaheads." He then looted the cash register and vamoosed. With more than a few Bloods already notched on his belt, the equal-opportunity Williams had pulled off a multicultural trifecta. Not the most circumspect of thugs, he was soon arrested and off the streets for good even before Washington was.

The question that has to be asked, of course, is what hap-pened between 1953 and 1979 and why has that murderous surge not reversed itself? Despite the removal of all legal barriers to equality, a massive transfer of funds to the poor, and the vir-tual force feeding of opportunity, why has it become more cin-ematically honest to show a young black male as a convict than as a collegian? And why is this not true of all ethnic groups?

The statistics freeze the blood. Since the founding of the Crips in 1969 roughly one hundred thousand Californians have been murdered, some unhealthy portion by California gangs. There are four times as many black males in California prisons today as in California colleges. Roughly one out of every three young black males has a current place in the California criminal justice system—in jail or prison, on probation or parole, or un-der pretrial release. An African-American in California is nearly four times more likely to be in prison than an Hispanic and nearly seven times more likely than a white.

To read even the mainstream media, however, one would think that the reason so many blacks are imprisoned is Califor-nia's three-strikes law or the bias in drug prosecution or racially unbalanced juries or racial stereotyping by police or injustice in sentencing or some exotic combination of the above. In Tookie's case, the ACLU attorneys argued that only a "racially-coded closing argument that compared Williams in trial to a Bengal tiger in the zoo" put the Tookster on death row—and they weren't intending to be funny.

The argument for some vestigial bias against nonwhites would make more sense were it not for the fact that a black Californian male is a mind-boggling twenty times more likely to be incarcerated than a yellow one. Even if the ACLU could spring half the blacks from the state's prisons, they would still house proportionately ten times more black males than males of Asian descent. Besides, there is no longer a "majority" population in California to serve as oppressor. Non-Hispanic whites make up less than 45 percent of the state population, a percentage that drops by the day.

Sad but true, the reason California incarcerates so many African-Americans is that they commit so much crime. This much is obvious if unspoken. Given the reluctance by many in the black community to report crime or to finger perps—an understandable instinct—blacks may get busted less often for comparable crimes than other minorities, whites included. The gangbanger autobiographies certainly reinforce that impression. These guys are "working" every day.

Yet, a half-block in any direction from the epicenter of the 1992 Rodney King riots, Florence and Normandie, one finds rows of pleasant bungalows with generally trim lawns. In San Francisco's Hunter's Point, the vegetation is lush and the views of the East Bay are extraordinary. This isn't Bed-Stuy or Harlem or Chicago's South Side. This is twenty-first-century California, sunny, open, free of restraint, at least semiprosperous, and potentially mobile in every which way.

So why the mayhem?

Hollywood, when it bothers to try, cannot muster even

a dumb rationale. "This ain't the way it's supposed to be," laments Danny Glover's everyman character, Simon, the black tow truck driver, as he negotiates Mack's way out of the carjacking in *Grand Canyon*. "Everything is supposed to be different than the way it is." Unfortunately, neither Simon nor the writer/director, Lawrence Kasdan, has any more sense of how anything in postshackle California is supposed to be than the mom in *Pleasantville*.

Neither do the other characters in *Grand Canyon*. "What's going on in the world?" asks Mack in despair. "The world doesn't make any sense to me anymore," agrees Mack's wife, Claire. And while the characters sit at the literal edge of the Grand Canyon trying to conjure up some sense, carloads of wayward young boys continue to roam the streets of Los Angeles locked and loaded for Armageddon.

The young black directors who have tried to answer the question—why the mayhem?—have done so with considerably more insight, most notably John Singleton in his 1991 feature, *Boyz N the Hood*. Just twenty-three years old at the time of the film's release, Singleton tells a South Central coming of age story not unlike his own. As the film's protagonist, Tre Styles, approaches adolescence, his divorced mother ships him to his father's house knowing full well the pressure the streets can bring to bear on a fatherless boy.

"You may think I'm being hard on you right now, but I'm not," the father explains to Tre. "I'm trying to teach you how to be responsible. Your friends across the street, they don't have anybody to show them. You gonna see how they end up too."

These friends, a pair of half-brothers living with their strung-out single mom, fulfill the father's prophecies. The one is murdered, and his brother turns murderer in revenge. In an impressive act of will, Tre opts out of the revenge party. As the movie makes clear, the moral reinforcement from his father has given him the strength to do so.

At film's end, the surviving brother tells Tre about watching TV the day after his brother's murder and scanning the news in vain for some mention. "I started thinking, man," he continues. "Either they don't know, don't show, or don't care about what's going on in the 'hood." For a variety of reasons, the "they" care less even today.

In 1993, twin brothers Albert and Allen Hughes cowrote and directed the film *Menace II Society*. They were just twenty-one at the time. Although rougher-edged than *Boyz*, *Menace* imposes something of a biblical allegory on the mindless chaos of contemporary California.

In the way of prologue, we see the young protagonist, Caine Lawton, growing up in a Watts household awash in drugs and violence. In one scene he and his junky mom watch his dope-dealing dad needlessly shoot a man. The dad is himself shot and killed when Caine is ten, and Caine is dispatched to his grandparents' home in the projects.

In their portrayal of the grandparents, the Hughes brothers signal their recognition of a stronger and more orderly African-American past. Critical to that order is the grandparents' traditional Christianity. As best they can, they infuse Caine with love enough to keep him whole and values enough to keep him focused at least until high-school graduation, a rare distinction among the young men in his lost world. "The Lord's Grace is with you, boy," says his grandpapa.

The Lord has his work cut out for him in contemporary LA. Once out on the streets, Caine proves as resistant to grace and as keen on violence as his namesake. "We supposed to be brothers!" pleads one black victim of Caine's swelling greed, but Caine is clearly not this or any other brother's keeper. He robs this one, beats another, and kills another still. All of his victims are black just as all the victims and victimizers in *Boyz* are black. Unable to help, and unwilling to condone, his grandparents are finally moved to cast Caine out.

As Caine suspects, the violence he has unleashed comes back to haunt him and ultimately to kill him. "I had done too much to turn back, and I had done too much to go on," he regrets as he lies dying. "And now it's too late."

A less artful film from this same period, Steve Anderson's *South Central*, focuses even more intently on the role of the father. Based on Donald Bakeer's book, *Crips, South Central* tells the story of O. G.—original gangster—Bobby Johnson. After ten years in prison, Johnson returns to the streets of South Central LA a wiser man. He has one mission in mind—to save his young son from the gangbanging life that he himself had led.

In the movie's climactic scene, Bobby faces off against the new gang leader, who has all but stolen his son's heart and mind. "Ray-Ray," implores Bobby, "that boy you're holding is my son. My son. I told a man in prison that I would save my son's life, even if it took my life." When Ray-Ray resists, Bobby hits home with a plea so universal in its appeal that Ray-Ray relents, "All I want is to give him something that you or I never had—a father."

Unlike their white counterparts, these young black writers and directors know that life is supposed to be about something. They know that the key to that something is the love of a woman and the transmission of values from father to son. And although there is some peripheral rhetoric in all three movies about white this and that, they know too that the essential problem is theirs to solve.

One hears almost identical themes in the gangbanger autobiographies, the most interesting of which is the eponymous *Monster,* the nom de guerre of Kody Scott, now known as Sanyika Shakur.

"My mom's house is a moderate three-bedroom mid-sixties dwelling with two huge picture windows on either side of the front door," writes Scott knowingly. "We had a nice front lawn and a huge rubber tree out in the yard that gave us great shade in the summer." This is not exactly the asphalt jungle.

In addition to providing shade, the rubber tree "camouflaged military launches at night." The "launches" he talks about have nothing to do with play and everything to do with a very real, if incredibly stupid, civil war. Although Scott will occasionally carry on about living in "an oppressed nation, colonized by capitalist-imperialists," he is not inclined to self-pity. In his comfortably godless world, Scott enjoyed being Monster Kody, "playing God, having the power of life and death in my hands."

Scott rode to his first hit on a bicycle. He was not yet old enough to drive. It was the fall of 1980, the most absurdly violent year yet in gang history. Statewide, homicides would jump 16 percent over the record year of 1979. By this time, the fighting was no longer between blacks and whites or blacks and Hispanics or even Crips and Bloods but among the various Crip "sets." That year alone Scott's Eight Trays Crips had shot eight of the Rollin' Sixties Crips, and they in turn had shot five of the Eight Trays.

Scott has a keener sense of what prods a kid to gangsterism than does the entire Sociology Department of UCLA. For him, the descent began with his parents' divorce when he was about five. "And there has not been a man in your lives since," his mother tells him later. "I wonder if that's how I lost you and [your brother] to the streets."

Even before the divorce, his father treated Scott like the bad seed. Later, he found out why: His mother had an affair with a pro football player during a period when she and her husband were estranged. And so the monster was forged, with nature from a three-time Pro Bowler and nurture from a two-timed loser, a lethal combination. "Absentee fatherhood was despicable," Scott reflects on both his dads. "I can't imagine having children and not being able to raise them, to live with them."

By the time Scott hit the streets, such lost boys had reached critical mass in South Central. "You guys have turned from my darling little ones into savage little animals," his mom laments. It was almost inevitable. With no extended family, no faith, no father, and no effort at school to endear him to nation—he refers to white people as "Americans" and himself as a "New Afrikan"—Scott invested all of his self-described "patriotism" in the Eight Trays.

"My homeboys became my family," he recalls at one point, "the older ones were father figures." They were more than family. "The set functioned as a religion," he adds. "If you died on the trigger you surely were smiled upon by the Crip God."

At age sixteen Scott was shot in the back during an armed robbery gone awry. When the doctor examined Scott, he noticed an earlier bullet still lodged in his abdominal cavity. Yes, of course, he had been shot before. Who hadn't? By this time, the police had Scott's number. They wanted him and a pal for a robbery. "We had done so many robberies," Scott remembers, "that I was at a loss to figure out which one we were wanted for." No, these weren't innocents unjustly hassled because they were black. They were gangsters and proud of it.

Finally apprehended, Scott was sent away at sixteen to Bad Boy's Island or some such place, the first of many of the tightly walled environments that he would come to know as home. There he would struggle in vain to find a new identity through Che, Mao, the New Afrikan Liberation Movement, and other self-defeating nonsense best restricted to college campuses.

Tookie Williams was one of Monster's early father figures. Like Scott, Williams was uprooted from his familial home in the Old South, Louisiana to be precise, and shipped to LA. Williams remembers the world he left behind as bathed in an Edenic glow. He tells of a wonderfully kind, Christian grandmother "whose religious influence was evident in each of her sixteen children" and of a "huge, muscular, loving, pensive [grandfather] who worked tirelessly on the railroad" to support those children.

Although he claims a precocious distaste for a white Jesus, Williams has warm memories of a vibrant, musically inspired black church. His grandmother's food was "heavenly" too, particularly the sweet potato pie, the cornbread, and the gumbo.

In this powerful "family equation," there was, however, one "weak link," a critical one, Williams's father. He had abandoned the family before Williams's first birthday. So in 1959, Williams's sixth year on the planet, he and his mom boarded the Greyhound for "the so-called City of Angels," where his beleaguered mother hoped "to achieve prosperity."

The Williamses settled in South Los Angeles west of the Harbor Freeway. Tookie describes the neighborhood in purposeful paradox as "a colony of poverty behind a facade of manicured lawns and clean streets of Cadilacs, Fords and Chevys." Like Scott, he is a little defensive about this relatively charmed little hood. Throughout his autobiography, *Blue Rage, Black Redemption*, he works hard to make the case that despite the nice home, the private bedroom, the trim lawns, the sharp cars, the plentiful food, the cool clothes, the subsidized juco education, the good job, and his maternally enforced proper English, he really is poor and thus righteously angry.

After twenty-five years on death row, much of it in solitary, Williams still cannot think his way out of this cell. He can find no better explanation for his thuggery than white racism, which he believes thwarted him at every turn. In an unattractive bit of self-pity, he sees himself as a "beneficiary of more than 500 years of slavery." Actually, two hundred years is more accurate on the American end, but Williams falls short on more than math and history. He fails to connect his own dots when he gripes, "I was left only scattered remnants of a broken culture."

That "scattered remnants" guff would make more sense if he had not so lovingly described his grandparents' world—their love, their faith, their family bonds, even their food, all of it African-influenced. This they accomplished amidst real poverty in a time and place where "racism" meant a lynching, not a suspicious look from a Korean merchant. It didn't take two hundred or even five hundred years to break this culture. It took one or two generations. "The Crips became my family," says Williams. Fine, Took, but whose fault is that? As Williams's lament makes clear, the ABETTO factor cuts across all classes in California and is one very good reason why so many of its citizens are behind bars.

Although their families tend to be stronger, and thus their crime stats lower, Hispanics are not immune to the lures of California life. In his well-observed book, *Barrio Gangs, Street Life and Identity in Southern California*, sociologist Diego Vigil profiles in some depth four gang members that he sees as "representative examples" of the larger population. He does not emphasize their family backgrounds, but the pattern smacks the observer upside his head.

Wizard, a member of El Hoyo Maravilla, moved with his family six times around the LA area before he was eight. For most of that time, his father was "in and out of jail and seldom around the household." His parents finally divorced, and Wizard spent even more time in the streets, "fearful of being rejected" by other young males and desperately seeking affirmation. This he found by acting like a real *vato loco*—crazy guy—fighting, stealing, and sticking people up until finally imprisoned for armed robbery.

Also from LA, Geronimo belonged to a gang called Varrio Nueva Estrada. His parents divorced when he was two, and he "never saw his father again until he was twelve." Looking for approval outside the home, Geronimo began to emulate the *cholo* style and behavior of the older kids. At fourteen, he was charged with robbery and kidnapping. Vigil caught up with him in a state youth penal institution.

Born in Riverside, Freddie had "mostly pleasant memories" until the age of ten. Then his parents divorced, and "the experience left Freddie and his siblings confused and disoriented." By fifteen, he was a full-fledged gang member, drinking, doing drugs, and cutting people up. A stabbing got him sent to boys' camp, and the love of his child's mother helped turn his life around.

Henry, from Chino, saw his world collapse at age three when his father died. Although his mother never remarried, she bore another man's son out of wedlock. With a more stable family background than many of his peers, Henry quit the gang as they moved from petty thievery into violence. When Vigil talked to him, Henry was a mechanic's helper.

Although Vigil did not profile Jaime Castillo, his case differs only marginally from the others. Castillo's father, a *ranchero* musician, abandoned the family when Jaime was a boy. His mother survived on welfare as the family kicked about the various low-rent suburbs of East LA. Expelled from school, Jaime found refuge from the chaos of the streets largely through music. In time, he hooked up with a band in LA whose leader "became more of a loving father to me than any man I've ever known." When the band moved to Texas, Jaime followed and there found "the one true, stable family I've ever had."

On April 19, 1993, seventy-four members of Jaime's adopted family died following a federal assault on their makeshift community. Among the dead was Jaime's surrogate father, David Koresh. If it seems unusual for a Latino to have found safe harbor among the presumed rednecks at Waco, a look at the roster suggests otherwise. In fact, more than half of those killed that dark April day were racial minorities, twenty-seven of them black, six Hispanic, and six of Asian descent.

Although usually eggshell-sensitive to the concerns of racial minorities, the American media turned a strategically blind eye to their very presence at Waco. As intended, scarcely a black person in America knows the hell visited on his brethren in those early uncertain months of the Clinton era. As to Castillo, he was sentenced to forty years in prison on charges that made no sense to anyone but the judge who sentenced him. It would take seven years and the Supreme Court before the sentence was abridged.

The gang, says Vigil, is a "spontaneous street social unit that fills a void left by families under stress." This much seems transparent. Knowing the dynamics, you would think that all the social workers and educators in the state would do all they could to shore up the two-parent family and the props that support it, like church and extended family. To think thusly is to misunderstand Blue California.

Lest it step on any ideological toes, the City of Los Angeles mostly just spends money and spreads it around, now some $82 million a year on twenty-three antigang programs. It doesn't much help. "We frankly haven't gotten gang violence under control at all," bemoaned Councilwoman Janice Hahn this past year.

Earl Paysinger knows that all too well. The veteran deputy chief would tell the *Los Angeles Times* that in the thirty years since 1976 the "killing fields" of his South Bureau bailiwick had experienced seven thousand murders and a hundred thousand shootings, roughly ten shootings a night in his area alone. A resident of this neighborhood is nearly forty times more likely to be murdered than the average American.

To control the madness, the City Council commissions studies, which predictably argue for more money. Those who do the studies, however, often give the impression of having been born within the last week or two. "Researchers mapped out neighborhoods where gang violence is greatest," reported the *Times* about a recent study, "and found a correlation in many cases with high school dropout rates and poverty."

Like legions of researchers before them, these analysts admonished the City Council to better address "root causes" and then zeroed in on things as painfully secondary and superficial as dropout rates. Not surprisingly, no one in the *Times* article mentions family or father or faith or any other tradition that discourages the individual from doing what he or she wilt. That, to be sure, might be construed as judgmental.

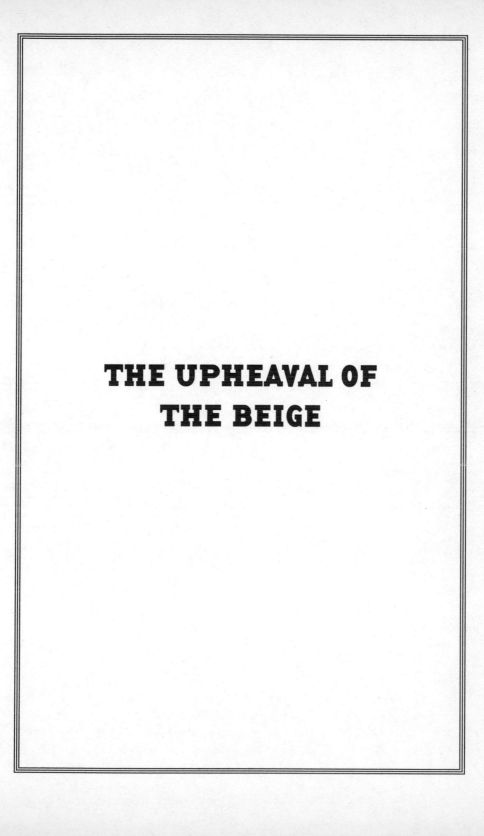

THE UPHEAVAL OF
THE BEIGE

★ 8. Sacramento ★

I have nothing but contempt for those who say that
no new taxes are necessary.
  —Pat Brown, governor, 1959-67

A few years back, while writing a feature on what I called
the "murder industry," I tracked a shooting from the
moment the call came in to its denouement at the tail end of the
legal-investigative complex. I learned a lot. I watched as the call
taker switched the intake information to the police dispatcher,
who in turn directed patrol officers to the scene. I tagged along
to the site with the homicide detective on duty, saw the EMTs
cart away the victim—he was not yet dead—and observed the
crime scene investigators gather up the evidence.

From the crime scene, the detective and I drove to the hospital where the nurses and doctors were scrambling to save the
victim's life. "Has our boy got a future?" asked the cop. "Yeah,"
said the hardboiled ER doc, "as an organ donor." Subsequently,
I visited with the other interdependent subsets in this industry:
the medical examiner, the crime lab technicians, the prosecutors,
the public defenders. Although the mood among the cops and
other pros throughout the chain was matter-of-fact, even lighthearted—hey, it was just some dude shooting another dude—all
parties focused on doing their job right. As I learned, no function in government is handled more thoroughly or more effi-
ciently than the mopping up of a murder. No statistics are more
accurately kept.

Although it is hard to measure, I could see that even a
seemingly inconsequential case like this one costs a whole lot of
money. The salaries and overhead were just the beginning. This
one stupid act—even the shooter didn't know why he did it—

robbed four young men of their most productive years. Three of them would waste away in the pen and the fourth in a long-term care facility, all for a long time, all at public expense.

No bias inflates murder statistics. These are hard numbers. Softer are the numbers for the beatings, break-ins, and muggings that LA's young "working" gangsters chalked up in the scores of thousands. Many of these went unrecorded, but none went unfelt. They all cost.

So did the children that Monster and Tookie sired and left behind. Curiously, state and federal officials were encouraging young men like them, criminal or not, to abandon their kids. They did not do so wittingly, but they did so just the same. Nineteen sixty was the year that the Aid to Dependent Children Program became the Aid *to Families* with Dependent Children, or, more realistically, Aid to *Moms* with Dependent Children. A working dad at home did not fit the state definition of *Family*. In 1964 the Feds sweetened the pot for forsaken moms with food stamps and in 1965 with Medicaid. Shortly afterward, public housing switched from fixed rents to rents based on ability to pay, a change that made the working dad all the more an albatross.

The reforms of the 1960s targeted black families and hit them hardest. In 1950, five out of every six black children were born to married parents. By 1990 that number had plummeted to a woeful two out of six nationwide. If it were not for federal welfare reform that number would likely have continued to slide. California's generous welfare payments assured that the state would at least match the national norms in pathology. By 1990 only Alaska offered a more ample benefits package. After the federal welfare reform act was passed in 1996, California stubbornly hung on as one of the few states in the country to provide lifetime welfare benefits.

Although the percentage of black children born out of wedlock is higher than the Hispanic, unmarried Hispanic women tend to have more children than black women. Worse, as their marriage rates continue to drop their fertility rates continue to rise. In Southern California, social workers "are in despair over the epidemic of single parenting," writes Heather McDonald in *City Journal.* "Not only has illegitimacy become perfectly acceptable, they say, but so has the resort to welfare and social services to cope with it."

The impact of this breakdown on the state budget is not hard to track. The state earmarked 17 percent of its projected 1959–60 general fund budget dollars for social welfare and health. By 1977–78 that figure had more than doubled. Percentagewise at least, the state's once-proud education system bore the brunt of the change, dropping from 62 percent of all general fund budget dollars in 1959–60 to 42 percent in 1977–78. More and more too that system had to shift its emphasis from teaching students to restraining them.

Despite the drop in percentage, no one actually cut education spending. The state and local governments simply collected more revenue to pay for the increased social costs. Estimated state revenues soared from $1.2 billion in 1959–60 to $12.4 billion by 1977–78. Inflation and population growth accounted for some of that differential, but not all. Controlling for both, the State of California was still collecting three times more real tax dollars per capita in 1978 than it had been in 1960, an oddball symmetry in that the state's aspiring felons were committing three times more violent crime per capita in 1978 than in 1960.

To understand how the growth in tax revenue could be so dramatic, the reader needs to grasp one more variable: the growth in the California economy. Between 1960 and 1978, even when controlled for inflation, the Gross State Product (GSP) doubled. During the same period the population increased only 42 percent. In other words, the California economy was going great guns, more than just literally. Jobs were plentiful and diverse. Despite all the gripes about bedmaking and burger-flipping, between 1958 and 1977 the state added more than five hundred thousand jobs in manufacturing alone, a growth of some 44 percent in employment and 258 percent in payroll.

This all leads to a conundrum that the state's Blue punditry has never quite been able to wrap its mind around: How could a gangbuster economy spawn a gangbanging culture? Opportunity all but exposed itself to even the most timid of minorities. Crack had yet to check in at Hotel California, and Reagan was still in exile.

True, few employers showed much enthusiasm for investing in the inner city, but there was a reason why: unfathered men in unstable family situations of their own, black or white or brown, make for a less than productive workforce. High absentee rates, excessive worker comp payouts, staggering drug and alcohol abuse, and lots of lawsuits from the slighted or fired, often on "civil-rights" charges, could send Mahatma Gandhi & Sons fleeing to the suburbs.

To preserve the stand-by excuses of racism and poverty in the face of all contrary evidence, Blue theorists had to give those excuses an extreme makeover, and this they did quite skillfully. Now dressed up as "institutional racism" and "structural poverty," these phenomena promised eternal victimization for the poor and eternal employment for the do-gooders. There was no way to solve either. This was Sisyphean government at its purest.

The only snag was that the do-gooders had to squeeze Sisyphus's salary out of the taxpayers. In most states this would be a simple matter of leaning on the legislators, most of whom are beholden to special interests, California's no exception. In 1910, however, citizens had risen up against the California legislature, then under contract to the Southern Pacific Railroad, elected a progressive new governor, and forced a redrafting of the constitution. The new constitution put three innovative mechanisms at citizen disposal—recall, referendum, and initiative—and from that moment on neither governor nor legislature was safe from the wrath of its citizens.

Among the most righteously wrathful of those citizens was a Southern California septuagenarian by the name of Howard Jarvis. The retired appliance manufacturer had lived a Forrest Gump of a life. He had shoveled ore in a silver mine, boxed professionally, played semipro baseball, and published a Utah newspaper. In the middle of the Depression, he up and quit Utah for California, where he made his way into manufacturing and Republican politics.

Never shy, Jarvis managed to pop up Gumplike at critical junctures of history. "Finally Churchill said to me," begins one typical Jarvis reminiscence, presumably true. "I advised Nixon not to debate Kennedy," begins a second. In still another cinematic moment, the appliance manufacturer finds himself at the bar of a Colorado Springs country club just as President Eisenhower walks by on the way to the golf course. In the retelling, Ike does a double take, walks back, and asks, "Aren't you the fellow who didn't want Earl Warren on the court?" When Jarvis admits that he was, the president offers an aside of no slight historical import, "You were right."

Starting in 1962, Jarvis launched a more verifiable sortie into the history books. His crusade began humbly enough in the living room of a neighbor's home in Los Angeles. There he and about twenty other homeowners got together to strategize about the spiraling assessed valuations in Southern California and the property taxes that came with them. Little did anyone in that parlor know that they had just created California's first Beige plate of consequence—largely but not exclusively white—since 1910. Under Jarvis's direction, it would continue to grow and shift and grind up against the establishment, resulting ultimately in a political tremor of historic proportions.

By 1970, Jarvis had emerged as the leading tax activist in the state or, as the *Los Angeles Times* uncharitably phrased it, "the chief spokesman for a large group of disgruntled California property owners." What disgruntled these taxpayers was that they were being taxed out of their homes, often their only asset of significance. As Peter Schrag concedes in his unflattering look at the Jarvis movement and its aftermath, *Paradise Lost*, real estate values in Southern California had managed to "double and then double again in a period of four or five years." As a result, "thousands of people, particularly on fixed incomes, were genuinely fearful they would lose their homes." This was not mere paranoia. Between 1974 and 1978 home prices statewide increased from an average of thirty-four thousand dollars to eighty-five thousand dollars, and in many cases, local property taxes kept pace.

The localities, not the state, collected and spent the property taxes. But in that it was politically easier to reassess a property than pass a tax increase, there was a good deal of burden shifting going on. Jarvis and his Beige cohorts objected. They believed that property owners should pay only for services related to property, such as garbage and sewers, and not be made "the goat for schools, food stamps, welfare, libraries, and all the rest."

This reasoning did not endear Jarvis to the powers that be. At the time, state legislators feared the taxpayers less than they did the recipients of those taxes. These included not only the various welfare rights groups but also, and especially, state and local government employees. In a generation, the presence of such employees among their fellow Californians had fully doubled, swelling from one in thirty workers in 1950 to one in fifteen by 1978.

These employees had also gained the right to unionize, and the unions had gained the right to extract dues for political campaigns. Not surprisingly, the unions representing these 1.5 million workers had become the most potent force in California politics. Some 117 of 120 legislators took their money, and they weren't about to pass any kind of legislation that might stand between a union member and his paycheck. As Governor

Arnold Schwarzenegger discovered in 2005, when he proposed to limit union political power, these unions have become, if anything, more fiercely protective of their prerogatives. They are so protective, in fact, that they may well lead California into a fiscal crisis of third world proportions when those baby boom pensions come due.

Any meathead could propose an initiative—and some have—but for a genuine grassroots movement to get an initiative on the ballot and past the voters took a near miracle. Of the 148 initiatives proposed between 1960 and 1978, only 26 had made the ballot, and only 7 of those passed into law. To qualify for the ballot, Jarvis and his partner on this drive, Paul Gann, first had to gather five hundred thousand valid signatures. Today, most such petition drives recruit their "volunteers" from day labor centers and the like. This one depended fully on the real unpaid McCoy. By the end of 1977, just to be on the safe side, those volunteers had gathered 1.5 million signatures, and Proposition 13 was officially on the ballot.

Titled "the People's Initiative to Limit Property Taxation," Prop 13 restricted the real estate tax on a residential property to 1 percent of its assessed value, with a maximum increase in that value of only 2 percent a year. If the property resold, however, it could be assessed anew. Prop 13 also required a two-thirds majority in both legislative houses for any future increases in state tax rates, including income tax rates.

The then (and Zen) governor, Jerry Brown, rolled out the heavy artillery. He predicted that Prop 13 would cost no fewer than 450,000 state and local government employees their jobs. The panicked labor unions rushed headlong into the ensuing breach. As Schrag acknowledges, they had lots of company, "almost the entire establishment." This included the League of Women Voters, Common Cause, the chambers of commerce, the major industry groups, city and county officials, the Democratic Party, the California PTA, and all the big newspapers except the

LA Herald Examiner. The Republican Party stayed neutral, and the State Farm Bureau manned the defenses, the only organization of size to back Prop 13.

The media treated Jarvis and Gann only a wee bit more charitably than they had the recently retired Zodiac Killer. The *Monterey Peninsula Herald* accused the pair, whose only property was their own homes, of being "slick Southern California real estate operators" running a con on the "outrageously deluded" voters of California. "Proposition 13 is the difference between putting a mechanic to work on an engine that's out of tune," opined the *San Diego Union* inelegantly, "and giving a chimpanzee a hammer to beat on it until it falls apart."

The *Los Angeles Times* hammered even harder and less adroitly than the aforementioned chimp. "Los Angeles County would eliminate all of the Fire Department's paramedic units, and would close half of the 129 fire-stations," began one Chicken-Littlish editorial that ended its catalogue of catastrophes with the "even darker" prospect for LA schools of eighteen thousand furloughed teachers and half-day classes.

Not before or since has the California establishment flown the ABETTO flag more conspicuously than it did in the run up to D-Day, June 6, 1978. And never before had fewer citizens saluted. Howard Jarvis and friends smashed through the opposition like the Allies through France, scoring an in-your-face 65 percent of the vote sweetened by a 69 percent turnout. In the aftermath of defeat, Berlin could not have been much gloomier than Sacramento. Still, the state would eventually have its way. Blocked on property tax, lawmakers would eventually find new strategies to separate Californians from their paychecks. Indeed, only twenty thousand public workers were laid off in the year that followed passage.

As these workers discovered, finding a job in the private sector was not all that hard. Just as Jarvis had predicted, the tax cut "stimulated the state's economy by giving the consumers more money to spend." In the ten years after Prop 13 became law, incomes in California grew 50 percent and jobs 100 percent faster than in the nation writ large. The explosive growth in the economy surprised even Prop 13 supporters.

As so often happens, or at least used to, political tremors in California sent shock waves through the nation. In the next five years, nearly half of the states managed to place restraints on the taxing power of their legislators. As history records, no Californian benefited more from this tax-cutting wave than Ronald Reagan, who rode it right up Pennsylvania Avenue.

The naysayers could find comfort only in the belief that revenge is best served cold. For more than a decade a booming state economy kept their I-told-you-so's on ice. In the early 1990s, however, their patience finally paid its petty dividend. Post–Cold War defense cutbacks and a massive 1991 tax increase—the largest ever by an American state—helped push California into a recession even deeper than the national one.

"The Tax Revolt That Ruined California"—so read the headline of a 1994 *Money* magazine cover story by Richard Reeves that placed the blame for the recession squarely on Jarvis's now fifteen-year-old initiative. The *New Republic* blamed Jarvis for the state's losing the O. J. Simpson trial, given the "inadequate tax base" for its cops and prosecutors. National Public Radio, ignoring the impact of a score of silly reforms, blamed Jarvis for the precipitous decline in California test scores. And, in book form, the *Sacramento Bee*'s Peter Schrag blamed Jarvis for stirring up the "hyper-democracy" that caused his *Paradise* to be *Lost*.

Apparently, late-century progressives had lost the enthusiasm for democracy that had so moved their early-century namesakes. No matter. The Beige plate remains ready to rumble anew. Twenty years after the initiative passed, a large majority of surveyed voters said they would vote for Prop 13 again.

★ 9. Malibu ★

> I drive down Wilshire and then onto Santa Monica
> and then I drive onto Sunset and take Beverly Glen to
> Mulholland, and then Mulholland to Sepulveda and
> then Sepulveda to Ventura and then into Tarzana and
> then Woodland Hills. I stop at a Sambo's.
> —Bret Easton Ellis, *Less Than Zero*

On a crystalline Saturday afternoon in mid-October 2005, I took the 405 north from Newport Beach in Orange County thirty or so miles to the 10. I then took the 10 west into Santa Monica and turned right on the Pacific Coast Highway. I took the PCH north about three miles or so and headed up Coastline Drive on the right to the front door of my friend Ray's house. Like Ellis above—or Joe Friday on *Dragnet*—I feel the urge to tell you exactly how I got from place to place, in large part because so many of the streets sound famous. Just about everyone who writes about Los Angeles does the same thing.

Please note too that all highways in the Los Angeles area are special, so special that they are preceded by "the," even the numbered highways. As evidence, consider this submission to an *LA Times* "worst highway" bulletin board:

> The worst place is the cross-over that occurs at the 605 and the 10. Traffic must cross within only a couple hundred feet. It's a disaster waiting to happen. I've had co-workers choose to drive surface streets from the 210 to the 10 instead of taking the risk at 605/10.

I get the impression that if a highway passes through Los Angeles, it gets to keep its "the" designation even when it leaves town. Consider the following from the same board:

*The scariest road to me is 395 from near Ridgecrest south to the I-15.
I will stay overnight at Bishop to avoid traveling it in the evening.
People going to/from Mammoth or other recreation sites overload the
road on the weekends.*

Since "the I-15" exits greater Los Angeles on its way to Las
Vegas, it retains the *the* designation even to the point where it
intersects with a remote highway that never was a *the*.

In any case, I had given a talk that morning at the Balboa
Bay Club in Newport Beach and stayed there the night before.
I had never before stayed at a place quite so swell. (Yes, someone
else was paying.) Ray's house, the most nicely situated anyone
had ever let me into, sits on a bluff overlooking Santa Monica
Bay. Like many in his generation, Ray just happened to take root
in the right place at the right time. This retired airline captain
bought his Malibu home forty years ago for seventy thousand
dollars and has watched it increase in value thirty times since.
Thanks to Proposition 13, he can still afford to live there.

This October day I began to understand why the green-
eyed monster flourishes so in California. Here, the affluent can
afford not only bigger and better homes, but also boats, views,
access to the water, ski lodges, and even better weather. Ray does
not have air-conditioning. He does not need it. The average August high on his Malibu deck is 70 degrees. The average August
high around a backyard barbecue pit in Riverside, on the eastern
edge of the same metro, is 95 degrees, a stunning 25-degree difference. And it's not as if Malibusters suffer in the winter. Their
average January high is 64. Those who can afford to find 64 too
bracing flee to their second homes in places like Palm Springs
about one hundred miles east of LA and dependably warmer
and sunnier in the winter.

In the San Francisco area, the extremes are nearly as great.
In the city itself, the average July high is a room temperature,
72 degrees. In Lafayette, less than fifteen miles east of the Bay

Bridge, the July high registers 15 degrees higher than in San Francisco, a toasty 87.

The swank San Diego beach community of La Jolla posts an average high of 76 degrees in July. The inland San Diego suburb of Rancho Santa Fe clocks in at 89 for its July average high. In 1997, Marshall Applewhite and thirty-nine of his fellow Rancho Santa Fe residents beat the heat by taking a last lethal ride on the spaceship hiding behind the Hale Bopp comet where it was presumably a good deal cooler.

In California, the truly wealthy are capable of living much grander lives than the middle class. This is not true everywhere. In Kansas City, spared the distraction of oceans and mountains, the rich live only slightly better than their inferiors. Their homes are no warmer in the winter, no cooler in the summer. Their cars are no bigger. Their views are no better. Their weekends are no more fun. They live no closer to their work. By all appearances, they eat considerably less, especially the women. And their weather is, if anything, worse. The average July high in Mission Hills is 90. In the blue-collar suburbs of Independence and Raytown in Missouri, it is only 87. The "hills" in Mission Hills provide only as much relief from the heat as you'd expect from an added sevety-five feet or so of landfill, which is none.

As a result, envy stirs the emotions much less in Kansas than it does in California. A "growing disparity in income" means little to a blue-collar worker who has everything he thinks he needs, including a minivan for the family, a 4 x 4 for himself, HBO, and a ranch house with central air. As to food, twenty minutes' work pushing earth or running parcels can buy him a fully plucked, packaged, and cooked chicken. He lives better than his parents, and he knows it.

In California, where timing counts more than toil, the parents live better than the kids. Those forming new families anywhere in the state today have picked the wrong place at the wrong time, dramatically so. Barring a collapse in the state housing market—and that would pose even more serious problems—young families face a series of bad choices. The housing opportunity index that follows will give the reader some sense of the problem. The number to the right of the city's name indicates what percent of the homes in a given area a person of median income could reasonably afford to buy in 2006. The median income is less in some areas than others. So, for instance, even though homes tend to cost more in San Francisco than in LA, LA's opportunity index is still lower.

San Francisco/ San Mateo	7.8
Los Angeles/ Long Beach	1.9
Santa Barbara	3.2
Modesto	3.9
San Diego	5.2
Bakersfield	16.5

Let's say that the Rios family made fifty-six thousand dollars and change last year, the LA median. Jason Rios teaches junior high and wife Maria does telephone work from her home as she tends to the two little ones, Brad and Angelina. With the birth of Angelina they need more space than their apartment in Encino affords. They begin to look and look hard because less than 2 percent of the homes for sale fall within their price range. Then too they are not even sure they want to live where some of those homes are located, like the "charming fixer-upper" in the not so charming Compton.

Jason has begun to listen to his brother, Frank, who moved to Kansas City a dozen years ago and wants Jason to join him. For years, Jason would say, "Oh, I'd miss the mountains and oceans too much." But all he can see down this road is a mountain of bills and an ocean of debt. Plus, let's face it, he hadn't been to the beach but about twice in the last year or so—Maria complains that a tan makes her look like a field hand—and he doesn't know where a real mountain is or what he would do with it when he got there. As with most suburban American parents, the closest the Rioses get to the "great outdoors" is the sidelines of the neighborhood soccer fields.

When Frank emailed Jason the 2006 housing opportunity index for some typical flyover cities, Jason could not believe what he was seeing.

Kansas City (2003)	87.9
Dallas	61.8
Indianapolis	90.1
Jacksonville	54.8
Columbus	71.8
Tulsa	77.7

As Frank explained, Jason could afford seven out of every eight homes that go on the market in greater Kansas City, real homes with four bedrooms, a big yard, and an attached garage. "And the soccer fields look exactly the same."

"Hmmm," said Jason. "Hmmmm!" Still, California is California, and the Rioses bit the bullet and bought a $460,000 bungalow in Riverside, an hour, on a good day, from his LA job. In California one hears often about heroic commutes. I know of one black family from Hunter's Point in San Francisco that moved two hours east to Stockton to buy a house they could afford. To beat the traffic, the father would leave for his job in San Francisco at 3:00 AM, arrive about 5:00 AM, and sleep in his car until work started a few hours later. The whole family would then come back on Sunday for church. The flight to the Central Valley represents something of a trend, one that has real conse-

quences for rush hour traffic. Stockton resident Sean Snaith got
an insight into the phenomenon during a recent bout of insom-
nia. "It wasn't unusual," reports Snaith, "to see people lining up
at 4 in the morning at the gates of the community where I was
living to begin their commute to the Bay area."

I asked one San Francisco cop how he and his fellow officers could afford to live in San Francisco. "They can't," he told
me. Like many of his fellow officers, perhaps most, he lives on
the far side of the seven-mile-long Bay Bridge. When I asked
how the officers living in the East Bay would respond to an
emergency like an earthquake, he answered, "They couldn't."

There is a precariousness to living in California that one
does not find elsewhere. People are keenly aware of what they
now have and what they might have. So much of what they do
have is tied up in their property that they tend to orient their
lives around real estate: the price of it, the location of it, the taxes
on it, the means of paying for it, the threats to it. A physical disaster can wipe out everything that they have. So can a lost job.
These people are as sensitive to changes in the political environment as they are to changes in the physical one. Anything—or
anyone—that threatens the security of that property can mobi-
lize property owners.

Like most Malibu residents, my friend Ray worries more
about physical disasters—earthquakes, fires, mudslides—than fiscal ones. For all its environmental sensitivity, no burg in America
is more precariously imposed on its landscape than Malibu, and
Ray's cliffside house is as precarious as the next. Still, except
when the foundation starts groaning, he doesn't think much
about it. He greeted me at the door when I arrived. Just back
from his morning tennis, he looked tan and fit as always. "Did
you know I graduated from USC?" he asked. I didn't, but I read
the hint in his question. "Well why don't we hang around and
watch the game then?" I said.

Admittedly, the century was not quite six years old, but the media were hyping the Notre Dame–USC game as the "game of the century," and those who saw it will agree that it actually lived up to the hype. I didn't tell Ray that growing up in an Irish Catholic neighborhood in a state whose *most* competitive football team was Princeton, we all followed Notre Dame as if we had gone there. Although much of that sentiment was purged during my graduate-school years at Purdue, I still could never bring myself to root for Southern Cal. Hell, everyone but Southern Cal grads hates USC, the slanderously labeled "University of Spoiled Children." O.J. didn't help much either.

Not overly political, Ray represents the sunny side of the Beige plate. As a pilot he learned to adjust to changing conditions. True to form, when I asked Ray what was the matter with California, he answered, "Nothing particular that I can think of." Of the hundred plus times I asked this question, his was the only such answer. The barrage of ads during the game for or against the various propositions in play for the November 2005 special elections did not much faze Ray either. Like almost every non-union member on the Beige plate, Ray was backing the propositions that the governor was. He had confidence in Arnold.

Slow to rile, the Ray Lahrs of California know when something is amiss. Two years before my visit, the state's great Beige plate showed that it still had the seismic juice to shake things up. As with Proposition 13, however, the chattering classes refused to believe that what did happen could happen. In fact, when Ted Costa and Shawn Steel walked their 275 petitions over to Governor Gray Davis's office on February 4, 2003, to launch the recall effort of that governor, no one paid them any mind. Steel, the maverick Republican Party chairman, had invited his fellow Republicans to a press conference to announce the recall. Only one showed up. Most of the rest shared the sentiments of the two Democrats who came carrying "Shawn Steel Is Nuts" signs.

Costa had even less standing than Steel. The protégé of Prop

13 coleader Paul Gann, Costa had inherited his People's Advo-cate office in a building behind a downtown Sacramento Krispy Kreme that should have been urban renewed a half-century ago. Still working on his college degree at sixty-something, Costa paid himself thirty-eight thousand dollars a year and drove a twenty-year-old Ford compact. The *Los Angeles Times* did not bother reporting the pair's effort for five days. The mainstream media would continue to ignore the recall effort even when it was polling in positive territory, just as they ignore Costa to-day when he talks about public service pensions, the next likely provocation of the Beige plate.

For his part, Gray Davis had all but invited the recall. A longtime party loyalist, the colorless governor wore the name "Gray" as if it were a description. Davis had inherited his job much the way Costa had inherited his, by being there and show-ing up. First elected governor in November 1998, he presided over a booming economy and a budget surplus, but the good times came to a quick end with the NASDAQ crash of 2000, the electricity crisis of 2000–2001, the recession of 2001–2, and the aftershocks of September 11. Davis responded with all the dash and creativity of a Herbert Hoover. He continued to play special-interest politics, especially with the public service unions, and to spend other people's money as if it were, well, other people's money. In November 2002, Davis barely survived a re-election against unsteady opposition. Shortly after the elec-tion he revealed that—oops!—the budget surplus had morphed into a possible $30 billion shortfall. "He had deliberately mis-characterized the problem," said Melanie Morgan of KSFO radio in San Francisco. "There was tremendous anger and re-sentment." The Beige plate had begun to rumble.

In 2003, that plate had a voice it did not have in the 1978 Prop 13 upheaval—talk radio. "The first time Shawn Steel men-tioned the word 'recall' on our show," Morgan told me, "My cohost and I lit up like pinball machines."

Hosts like Morgan, Eric Hogue of KTKZ in Sacramento, John and Ken on KFI in LA, and Roger Hedgecock on KOGO in San Diego not only hyped the recall effort on air, but also helped gather signatures—nine hundred thousand were needed. Better still, they made the whole process kind of fun. Morgan, a Kansas City native, would do live broadcasts from Costcos and BART stations and invite listeners to come down and sign petitions. Others did much the same. To gather nine hundred thousand signatures, however, required some major infusions of cash, and the bulk of that came from wealthy San Diego area congressman Darrell Issa, who would choose not to run himself.

Issa did not run in 2003 in part because a new and improved people's champ was waiting in the wings to replace Davis, a Hiram Johnson on steroids, as it were, Arnold Schwarzenegger. The itch was clearly there. The body builder turned movie star had gotten his first sweet taste of California democracy the year before when he led a successful drive to pass Prop 49, a benign before-and-after school-care initiative. The timing, however, was tricky in 2003. Schwarzenegger's latest movie, *Terminator III*, would not open until July. He had an obligation to promote it and a stake in doing it right.

If there was a defining moment in the recall campaign, it came in June when Schwarzenegger, not yet a declared candidate, gave the keynote speech on the twenty-fifth–anniversary celebration of Proposition 13. After memorializing Howard Jarvis as the "Tax Terminator," Schwarzenegger held his head quizzically and claimed to have forgotten the name of the current governor. The audience chuckled nervously, not quite sure if the political novice was joking. He was. With the next line, Conan the Republican secured his future. "But I know you will help me recall him." When the laughter subsided, everyone knew that the Beige plate was his for the asking. On July 2, the day *Terminator III* opened, the signature gatherers were waiting outside the theaters. In his excellent book on the recall election, *The*

People's Machine, Joe Mathews traces the birth of "blockbuster democracy" to that synergistic day.

A month later, his intentions still unknown even to himself, Schwarzenegger appeared on *The Tonight Show* with Jay Leno. Leno prodded Arnold about the recall, and Arnold fended him off with a few jokes. Then he turned serious. "When I moved to California in 1968, California was a fantastic place. It was the greatest state of the greatest nation in the world." Schwarzenegger was saying what most Californians used to say routinely. "Now it is totally the opposite," he continued. "The atmosphere is disastrous." The one man most responsible for that disaster was none other than Gray Davis. "He's failing [the people] terribly," said Arnold, "and this is why I am going to run for governor of the state." The eruption of the audience drowned out whatever else Schwarzenegger said at sentence's end. Blockbuster democracy would not be denied.

During the 2005 Notre Dame–USC game at Ray Lahr's house, just about every thirty-second TV spot attacked the "Governator." As Ray explained, the public service unions were spending upward of $100 million to show the public how Schwarzenegger was silencing them. At halftime, weary of the commercials, I insisted we go out on the deck. The day and the view were too spectacular not to. Never mind an ocean, there is not so much as one natural lake in either Kansas or Missouri. After about twenty minutes, though, I really questioned whether the view was worth the $2 million difference in value between Ray's house and mine, especially since the game was more seductive than the view, and I do have a TV, three actually. Plus, I don't have to worry about my house tumbling onto the Pacific Coast Highway.

With about one minute left in the game, Southern Cal down four and driving desperately, the phone rang. Ray answered it. "Mom," he said with a touch of filial exasperation, "the game's on! I'll call you when it's over."

When Ray returned to the couch, I could not help but ask, "Ray, how old can your mother possibly be?" I did not know Ray's exact age, but I do know that he was a Navy pilot in World War II and that war ended more than sixty years ago. Do the math.

"Oh, she's just 101," said Ray casually.

"Don't you think," I said, laughing, "that maybe you better take that call?"

"No, she'll be all right till the game's over."

I thought for a second. "Ray, sixty years after you graduate from USC, she still doesn't know you well enough not to call you during a Notre Dame game?"

"You know moms." He smiled.

After Southern Cal scored its winning touchdown on the game's last play, Ray explained that his mom lives just down the road in Santa Monica with his son. Lest the reader think that everyone in California is at loose ends, Ray's three children and their children all live in California, and Ray still nests happily with his lovely bride of nearly sixty years, Jackie. I walked behind them when we went out to dinner that night, and they were holding hands.

The unions prevailed in 2005, and the pundits got to work writing Arnold's political obituary. But you don't get to be Mr. Olympia six times by rolling over and playing dead. A year after my visit, Ray and Jackie and people like them defied conventional wisdom once again and re-elected Arnold by a landslide in an otherwise awful year for Republicans. Although Arnold himself will not likely be the answer to the state's problems—that is beyond the power of any one individual—his success testifies to the state's orneriness and originality. California will not yield easily to stereotype.

THE FALL OF THE
SKY BLUES

★ 10. Big Sur ★

A loss of belief is what separates us from the much-handled things we grew up with.
—D. J. Waldie, *Holy Land*

In 1911, the residents of a remote mining town found a lone Indian scrounging for food and perhaps companionship as well. He called himself "Ishi," and he was the last of the Yahi. He had been living alone since his one other remaining relative died several years earlier. When found, the likable young Indian had no more sense of civilization than Tarzan or the Encino Man, but that civilization embraced him like a lost child.

Although not radically inclined—Mike Davis chides him for being "Whiggish"—California's state historian Kevin Starr goes native for Ishi. "Peace, dignity, a harmonious relationship to mature, appropriate technology, culture and identity, all of it joyously rooted in place," he gushes, "bringing such a message, Ishi became a Founder, an enduring representative of an inner and better California landscape." That was a heck of a lot of message for one disoriented little Indian to bear.

Ever since the Franciscans were kicked out, Californians have been desperate for a message. In a critique of late-twentieth-century California, *Nation* magazine accurately described the state as a land "plagued by spiritual starvation." Starr traces that starvation to its source in the "uprootedness" of Californians and their "detachment from Midwestern anchorages in solid religion." As is obvious in his own treatment of Ishi, Starr may have a little spiritual hankering himself.

Like Hazel Motes, the embittered protagonist of Flannery O'Connor's prescient 1952 novel *Wise Blood*, one Californian after another has set out to address this hankering by creating "a

Church Without Christ," a church without God, for that matter, a church where, in O'Connor's words, "there was no Fall because there was nothing to fall from and no redemption because there was no Fall and no Judgment because there wasn't the first two." The phrase "Sky Blue" seems to fit here. It captures the ethereal essence of the spiritual progressive and distinguishes him or her from his or her more political kin.

The problem that the Sky Blues pose for contemporary California is not so much what they believe in, but rather the belief that they have denied others. "There is only one truth," Motes insists in precocious postmodern patois, "and that is there is no truth." To make their own improvisations work, the Sky Blues have had to convince their followers that the Judeo-Christian beliefs that they have held to be true were, in fact, not true at all. All of this re-educating has had consequences.

The story might profitably begin at Big Sur. A half-century after Ishi's discovery, a pair of almost equally disoriented Californians, Mike Murphy and Richard Price, began to re-create that "inner and better landscape." They chose as a site for their experiment a Murphy family property on this glorious stretch of central California coastline. When the two young men had met in San Francisco in 1960, they had each just stepped off an emotional rickshaw ride. Murphy had quit his premed studies at Stanford to embark on a spiritual odyssey. His wanderings had taken him to an ashram in India and to the edge of an emotional Hades before dumping him back in the city by the bay.

Price's road was bumpier still. He had bounced in and out of college and done a tour in the Air Force before landing at the Soto Zen temple in San Francisco. There he married his wife, Bonnie, in a Japanese-language ceremony that was in every which way incomprehensible to his Jewish parents. In part at least, he did so to shock, having already dismissed organized religion as an elaborate ruse used mainly to control behavior.

As Price began to sense, however, his own behavior needed some serious control from somewhere. He found that control in spades at Connecticut's generously named "Institute of Living." There, for several grim months, he was on the receiving end of the shock—the electric shock, that is, and the equally unpleasant insulin shock as well. For the three robotic years after his release, his Zen marriage annulled, Price passed his days mindlessly *chez les parents* until one day he hit the road for California, never to look back.

The partners hoped to create at Big Sur a center for the exploration of new ideas, one that pulled East and West together. They named their creation after an Indian tribe that had once lived in the neighborhood. In that the tribe went belly-up, the first tribe in California to become extinct, "Esalen" seemed an unlikely brand inspiration. Yet despite the bad juju, Esalen prospered. Before the decade of the 1960s, the partners' first in the business, was out, Murphy and Price had turned Big Sur, in Starr's words, into the "American Tibet."

Sky Blue pilgrims came to Esalen to discover just about every spiritual nuance imaginable, except, of course, God. God was way too demanding to be part of the weekend package. Besides, the up-and-coming shamans at Esalen—Abraham Maslow, Fritz Perls, Will Schutz—had no need for God. They had moved on to newer and cooler things, most notably their fabulous selves.

Humanism ruled at Big Sur. As a philosophy, it had begun to cohere in the early part of the twentieth century and staked its claim to seriousness with the Humanist Manifesto of 1933. Signed by thirty-four intellectual worthies, the manifesto boldly declared "the religious forms and ideas of our fathers no longer adequate." That much said, it declared "the quest for the good life" to still be the "central task for mankind."

Rarely does a philosophy so nicely fit a place as secular humanism fit California. The pursuit of "the good life" was at the seductive heart of the California experience. This, after all, was the state that had pioneered surfing, suntanning, smoking dope, and sleeping—or whatever—at motels. Now, it had a governing philosophy, one that as a bonus encouraged its adherents to slough off the restraints of religious tradition. Not surprisingly, George Leonard, the *Look* magazine editor who had praised the state for breaking "the shackles of the past," wrote brochure copy for Esalen.

In 1939, inspired by the manifesto, a restless crew of slightly confused Quakers decided to form a "nontheistic society" based on the humanist vision of a marriage between science and ethics, "one that would put into action a new kind of naturalistic religion." Nothing if not practical, these highly innovative folks incorporated under the state laws of California as a religious organization. This charter empowered the newly christened Humanist Society—*Serving Humanism since 1939*—to train and ordain its own ministry with the same rights and privileges as priests, ministers, and rabbis. The same tax status, too. This was among the first of the godless religions incorporated in California, but it would not be the last.

From the beginning, secular humanism has had a powerful, if a tad puzzling, hold on Christianity. God and godlessness would seem to make for odd bedfellows. Still, it was a highly respected Unitarian minister, Edwin H. Wilson, who had actually guided the drafting of the *Humanist Manifesto*. In this whole endeavor, he would have lots of equally curious Christian company. "Esalen was remarkably cozy with churches," observes Esalen chronicler Walter Truett Anderson.

Although several different individuals—just about all of them Californians—would claim credit for creating humanistic psychology, a quick read of the manifesto suggests that it had already been created. "Religious Humanism considers the complete realization of human personality to be the end of man's life," reads the manifesto's eighth point, "and seeks its development and fulfillment in the here and now." The psychologists who followed didn't create. They tweaked. This eighth point would form the core truth of humanistic psychology, a movement of great influence, most of it dubious, much of it downright destructive.

Arguably the most influential of these psychologists was a fallen-away fundamentalist named Carl Rogers. Already well known—he was wont to marvel at the "astonishing impact" of his work—Rogers settled in at the Western Behavioral Sciences Institute in La Jolla within a year of Esalen's launch.

With Freudianism more or less discarded as yesterday's news, Rogers found himself locked in a grouchy dialectic with the behaviorists. They insisted that the environment largely, if not solely, shaped human behavior. Rogers took a cheerier and more American route. He argued that the individual could be the "architect" of his own being—"self-realization," Rogers called it. To self-realize, though, that person had to be willing to change, to reject "the conformity of institutions and the dogma of authority." Given these two positions, one dark and one bright, but both rigidly materialistic, America's swelling army of pop psychologists opted largely for the bright one.

Up the coast at Esalen, Abraham Maslow was likewise finessing the *Humanist Manifesto* just enough to avoid a plagiarism rap. "The Good Person can equally be called the self-evolving person," preached Maslow, giving man credit not just for his identity, but for his very existence. Where Rogers and Maslow differed was in Maslow's appreciation of man's capacity for evil. This Mister Rogers approached the world as blithely as his kiddie-show namesake. Ironically, this is what made him so dangerous.

If Rogers was talking about "self-realization," Maslow was preaching "self-actualization," and it was Maslow's phrase that stuck. A clever wordsmith, Maslow introduced the concept of the "peak experience" into the lexicon as well. Like Rogers, he and his acolytes were "hearing" people, being "open" to their feelings, "getting the sense" of what they were saying, encouraging them to live "in the moment," and generally rewiring the world of human interaction.

At Esalen too the semifamous Fritz Perls was making his own contribution to the *zeitgeist*. "I do my thing, and you do your thing," began his "Gestalt Prayer" in language that would morph from hip to trite in a seeming nanosecond. By aiming even his prayers at his fellow man, Perls was flaunting his indifference to the supernatural. His creation, Gestalt Therapy, stuck firmly to the here-and-now. It offered individuals the hope of recovering their own feelings and reintegrating as fully alive human beings if only they got with the program.

Looking for a generic name for that program, which would come to include encounter groups, Rolfing, psychedelics, and a grab bag of other nostrums, Murphy and Price borrowed a phrase, "the human potentiality," from Aldous Huxley, who had lectured at Esalen shortly before his death in 1963. In due time, this lumping of humanistic cures would mutate into the "Human Potential Movement," and true to form, Carl Rogers would claim to be its founder.

As a historical aside, Huxley had previously written a book on his experiments with mescaline, *The Doors of Perception*, which impressed not only the folks at Esalen but also a young singer/songwriter in Los Angeles. In the way of homage, Jim Morrison named his inchoate rock group The Doors. He too was going to "break on through to the other side." Whether he succeeded remains unclear, but his mortal remains were mysteriously left behind in a Paris bathtub when Morrison was just twenty-seven.

On the eastern front, Swami Paramahansa Yogananda had considerably better claim to the concept of self-realization than either Rogers or Maslow. This Indian transplant started the Self-Realization Fellowship in 1920 and in 1935 incorporated it as the Self-Realization Fellowship church in, of course, California.

Although this particular swami had no direct effect on Esalen, other Asian Indians did, none more so than Bhagwan Shree Rajneesh. In 1978, Esalen cofounder Price changed his handle to "Geet Govind" and made a much-publicized pilgrimage to see Rajneesh in India. The trip, however, proved to be a "bummer"—another West Coast neologism—and good old Geet skedaddled home as a chastened "Richard Price."

Apparently, the Bhagwan's encounter groups proved a bit too rough for Price's tastes, resulting as they routinely did in abrasions, bruises, and broken bones. At Esalen, such encounters culminated in group hugs or getting naked or maybe even sex in the hot tub with someone else's spouse. Only occasionally did they lead to divorce or suicide—well, maybe more than occasionally. Truth be told, Esalen had to abandon its residential program for "the overwhelming reason," writes Anderson, that "too many of the people in it ended up committing suicide."

Michael Murphy may have kept his name—no Murphy would dare give that up—but he sampled Weltanschauungs as freely as other Californians sampled wine. Unlike Price, he favored domestic varieties like est and Scientology. Still, after all the sampling, he never really felt grounded anywhere other than on a golf course. In 1972, in fact, he published his first novel, an unusual tale of golfer/shaman Shivas Irons called *Golf in the Kingdom*.

At the end of the 1970s, the end of an era really, no one was terribly surprised when Murphy turned management of Esalen over to a British woman whose thing was "channeling" eight-million-year-old space aliens from the star Sirius—not, of course, that there's anything wrong with that.

★ 11. Marin County ★

> You don't have to believe nothing you don't
> understand and approve of. If you don't understand
> it, it ain't true, and that's all there is to it.
> —Onnie Jay Holy, Flannery O'Connor's *Wise*
> *Blood*, 1952

I f the synthesis between East and West didn't quite take, the one between West and Midwest did considerably better. The man who made it happen changed his name too, but he did so to cover his tracks after abandoning a wife and four children back east.

Before fleeing to St. Louis, Philadelphian Jack Rosenberg went by the name Jack Frost, a better name for a used car salesman than, say, a Zen master. When Jack decided to lam out of town for St. Louis, he changed names again, emerging with the impressively Teutonic "Werner Hans Erhard," and it stuck. The pregnant woman who accompanied him, June Bryde, changed her name too, to Ellen, but who can blame her?

Erhard was no ordinary salesman. In St. Louis, he switched from used cars to encyclopedias and poured himself into the latest sales and motivational techniques. In 1962, the year of Esalen's birth, the good-looking twenty-seven-year-old fatefully relocated to San Francisco. There he began to read Maslow and Perls and L. Ron Hubbard—didn't everyone?—and to fuse their Sky Blue psychologies with the more orthodox motivational philosophies on the market.

Like Richard Price before him, Erhard discovered Zen in San Francisco, and Zen proved to be the critical, final ingredient in the philosophical bouillabaisse that he was concocting. In March 1971, Erhard experienced an epiphany of sorts while driving down Highway 101 in Marin County. It dawned on him that he was "all right" and had always been "all right" and that things were the way they were because that's the way they were.

I guess you had to be there. Whatever the inspiration, by October 1971 Erhard was ready to launch his own brand in the human potential movement, which he called "est"—with a small "e." He pulled the name from a science fiction novel, but he made it stand for Erhard Seminars Training and/or Latin for "It is."

To get the dope on what that "it" was, I spoke to Rebecca, a San Franciscan who had been instructed by Erhard himself and who later lived in the world of est with one of his chief lieutenants. As she explained, the est training typically lasted for sixty hours over a two-weekend period. The sessions were famous for their ardor. More than a few critics, in fact, have called Erhard a fascist. The stories of trainees being scolded or denied bathroom privileges are legion, and in the softer suburbs of San Francisco, that level of deprivation conjures up holocaust imagery. The name "Werner Erhard" didn't much help either.

Rebecca, however, remembers her experience as "mostly positive." She describes Erhard himself as an "excellent, tough, and honest communicator" with "outstanding seminar-leading skills." Just twenty when she took the course, Rebecca found Erhard's appeal to personal responsibility a welcome reprieve from the new "discourse of victimization" then being force fed to young women. To see oneself as a victim, Erhard argued, was to deny oneself the chance at "transformation."

Like the folks at Esalen, Erhard instructed his "seminarians" that there was no larger meaning to the world other than the meaning they imposed on it. "Tell the truth and your word becomes law," he told Rebecca. To reach this point, however, the trainees had to abandon the "rackets" that had previously constrained their behavior.

"Don't give me your goddamn belief system," a trainer would typically shout at some deluded soul in the audience. "Get rid of all that shit." Like so many of the humanistic therapies, est wallowed in coarse language. Indeed, in many of the worlds then evolving in California—humanistic, pornographic, gay—all euphemisms for making love were yielding to the least euphemistic of all, the F bomb. This was the naughty side of liberation.

In this newly constructed universe, Erhard began to see himself as the principal lawgiver. He had transcended the conventions of society and its codes as well. The fact that he was making goo-gobs of money only heightened his Olympian sense of self. He was "the Source," he informed his employees, and he expected them to treat him as "akin to God." When asked on one occasion, "Are you the messiah?" Erhard, in spontaneous biblical cadence, gave the one response more vain than a simple yes. "No," he answered. "I am who sent him."

In Erhard's twenty-year career, a million people would pay to hear the Source or his hand-picked clones. Among the eager participants were many of America's brightest and shiniest, and they in turn eagerly amplified his message to their minions. "Indeed," says biographer Steven Pressman, "he stirred up Hollywood the way no other self-help master had ever done before, and the town has never been the same."

Although for most of the million paying customers est would inflict no more than two weekends' worth of damage, an unhealthy percentage hung on as volunteers or paid staff. "You have no rights," Erhard would tell them, and he meant it. He would work them like vassals and choose sexual partners from among the faithful as blithely as did the late and unlamented brothers Hussein. "We were a bunch of zombies," agreed a top aide.

Erhard would probably still be riding herd over his zombies had he not made one enduring enemy, a man last heard from when he ran off with Jack Parsons's wife, the inimitable L. Ron Hubbard. Although his Church of Scientology has made itself at home in Hollywood, as seems somehow fitting, Hubbard was too outsized for any one state to claim. He belonged to the world, if not to the galaxy. In 1950, not yet forty years of age, he published the book that transformed him from hack sci-fi writer to big-league guru, *Dianetics: The Modern Science of Mental Health*.

In February 1954, some questing Angelenos incorporated the Church of Scientology of California, a franchise of the mothership that Hubbard had himself incorporated in New Jersey a few months earlier. Hubbard had been encouraging his franchise holders to convert their operations into independent churches for the same reasons other pseudoreligions did. "Writing for a penny a word is ridiculous," Hubbard had said at a science fiction meeting in Newark a few years earlier. "If a man really wants to make a million dollars, the best way would be to start his own religion." It was not just money that turned Hubbard religious. It was the freedom. Religious status frees an organization from a good deal of government oversight, and Hubbard needed all the freeing he could get.

"In Scientology no one is asked to accept anything as belief or on faith," reads the official literature. "That which is true for you is what you have observed to be true." There it is in a nutshell. Scientology has flourished in Southern California because it does not trouble anyone's conscience. It provides a sense of belonging, feeds an inflated sense of self, and yet makes almost no moral demands. "It is despicable and utterly beneath contempt," writes Hubbard, "to tell a man he must repent, that he is evil." In LA, no one repents. They recover.

America's most successful recovery program, Alcoholics Anonymous, is unabashedly theistic in its orientation. "We found that as soon as we were able to lay aside prejudice and express even a willingness to believe in a power greater than ourselves," notes AA's *Big Book,* "we commenced to get results, even though it was impossible for any of us to fully define or comprehend that Power, which is God." Scientologists, however, have no particular use for God. That does not stop them, however, from imposing their nontheistic beliefs on nonbelievers. For example, a wonderful, only-in-Hollywood spat broke out in 2005 when actor Tom Cruise publicly chastised actress Brooke Shields for becoming dependent on the antidepressant Paxil, following the birth of her daughter Rowan. What troubled Cruise, the world's most famous Scientologist, was that Shields had resorted to the wrong nostrum. Forget faith or prayer or sheer virtue. "You can use vitamins to help a woman through those things," opined Cruise helpfully. Shields was not amused. Said she in angry rebuttal, "His comments are dangerous. He should stick to saving the world from aliens." To be sure, there is lots of truly weird sci-fi cosmology involved with Scientology—all that Prince Xenu stuff for starters—but on the plus side, there may not be a Scientologist in all of Southern California able to recite it chapter and verse.

The almost inevitable conflict that erupted between Hubbard and Erhard was no more a religious war than the one between Pepsi and Coke. They were battling, said one private eye hired by the Scientologists, over "potential customers," and Hubbard was losing. What made it all the more galling for Hubbard was his conviction that Erhard had ripped off many of his techniques, which was true enough. Hubbard responded with a series of dirty tricks and dirt-digging exercises, an endeavor that survived his (presumed) death in 1986.

With the help of several private dicks, the Scientologists planted little nuggets on Erhard for the media to find, and find they did. In 1991 CBS's *60 Minutes* convinced Erhard's daughter Deborah to share some dirt about her dad, and the conversation barely cleared the censor. "He beats his wife and he beats his children and he rapes a daughter, and then he goes and tells people how to have marvelous relationships," a former governess summed up the case to CBS's Ed Bradley. "I'm sorry. That's what I have against Werner Erhard." Even before the show had aired, Erhard sold the company to his employees and hightailed it to Costa Rica.

As to Hubbard, he is likely off somewhere in the Galactic Federation having an infinitely good long laugh.

★ 12. Hollywood ★

"I'm doing everything for myself," she told her group. "I'm going to have an abortion." Everyone clapped.
—Carol Lynn Mithers, *Therapy Gone Mad*

D r. Joe Hart was no quack autodidact in the Erhard model. Like so many of his colleagues at the time, he was a thoughtful, well-credentialed quack. He had studied under Carl Rogers at the University of Wisconsin and then finished his Ph.D. in psychology at Stanford in 1965.

Dr. William Coulson, one of Rogers's most serious critics, describes Rogers nonetheless as a "terrific human being." Just about everyone who knew Rogers says the same. Where Rogers blundered was in thinking that protégés like Hart would be as responsible as he and his deeply Christian parents were. He was wrong. In 1987, after two years of legal ordeal, California's Board of Medical Quality Assurance revoked Hart's license and disciplined a dozen members of his staff, and with good reason.

Back in 1965, however, Hart was a rising star in the profession. After Stanford, he took a job at the new University of California campus at Irvine in Orange County, or UCI. There he proved to be a masterful teacher, attracting a circle of worshipping admirers, none more consequential than the charming and cocky Richard "Riggs" Corriere.

This being the late 1960s, Hart and Corriere longed for an experience more visceral than clinical psych. So they started sampling the witches' brew at Arthur Janov's Primal Institute in Beverly Hills. An LA native, Janov put patients through an intense three-week session during which they would regress to infancy and "feel the pain" an infant feels. After enough "primaling," they no longer felt the need to please Mommy and Daddy but could go on to please themselves, their only guideline now for future behavior.

The Beatles' John Lennon and his lovely bride, Yoko Ono, deserve credit—responsibility at least—for putting the Primal Center on the map. "We primal almost daily," Lennon would enthuse in a *Rolling Stone* interview. "I think Janov's therapy is great." The lyrics of Lennon's breakaway 1970 album, *John Lennon/Plastic Ono Band*, are a veritable tribute to Janov and primaling with their endless blather about one's mummy being dead and Jesus being obsolete and John and Yoko being the center of their own spectacularly self-absorbed universe.

To a person, the Sky Blue shamans proved much more adept at purging old belief systems than at putting new ones in place. Janov was no exception. After a brief infatuation with the man, Hart and Corriere pulled back his curtain, and even they could see nothing behind it but a "cruel hoax." More wide-eyed than a Ph.D. in anything ought to be, Hart was shocked to see "that most [patients] had been faking their primals."

Disillusioned with Janov, Hart, Corriere, and a few others launched their own center in 1971. These budding therapists now preached that neurosis derived not from the traumas of infancy but from years of parental "disordering." To remedy this, they would create a full-blown "therapeutic community," one in which hundreds of patients could live and play and pay for therapy together.

No fools, the founders chose to go hunting where the ducks were, and there was no wetter psychological wetland than Hollywood. In time, the staff and patients all but took over the Gardner Street neighborhood around the center. Here, as a community, they engaged daily in what the partners called "feeling therapy." As one veteran recounted, "In this world, all that mattered was having and expressing feelings."

As with virtually all of the humanistic strategies, the therapists got to those feelings by peeling off traditional restraints like so much dead skin. "Your whole mythology of who you are and who you should be was completely blown away," said Corriere to the community in summarizing that strategy.

The techniques, often improvised, targeted a patient's cultural sensitivities. With one female patient, for instance, Corriere played the role of a priest. The patient knelt before him as if in confession and screamed out, "I refuse to give in to what you taught me," the "you" meaning the Catholic Church. For Corriere, "Catholic" was shorthand for "repressed." Nevertheless, he and his colleagues were commissioned to design programs for Catholic priests. One strains to imagine their content. To be fair, the therapists showed a commendable ecumenism in their abuse, mocking their patients, when appropriate, as "Jew boys" or "fat bitches" or "fags." They were competing with Erhard, after all, who once famously blamed a Jewish woman for creating the major "racket" in her own life—that minor historical hang-up commonly known as the Holocaust.

About halfway into the center's roughly ten-year experiment, the founders rolled out "a completely new model" of therapy. Now, astonishingly, feelings were beside the point at the Feeling Therapy Center. Instead, patients were to pursue good looks and worldly success in the expectation that good feelings would catch up. To prod the patients down the road to success, the center launched or incubated any number of businesses, all of them run relentlessly, even ruthlessly, to achieve results. "Forget the old ways," the therapists told their charges. "This is what works." Writes Carolyn Mithers in her book *Therapy Gone Mad*, "Center values were beginning to parallel those of the 'insane' society the place had been designed to reject."

As to what the "insane" society actually believed, Mithers shows no more comprehension than the therapists. Ignorance here has a silver lining. For in her attempt to make sense of the fall of the Feeling Therapy Center, she helps the wary reader understand the most persistent problem in California: namely, the failure of critics to see the obvious and to draw any meaningful conclusions from what they see.

Mithers can only envision the late sixties and early seventies as a fleeting Eden, "a moment of real possibility." Whether acid flashback or honest to God nostalgia I cannot say, but she recalls a time when young people yearned "for a world more fulfilling than the one they inhabited and a way of life that was not so grim, cut-off, and lonely."

She is not talking here about the world as seen by a few disturbed youths. She is talking about the world as seen by "millions," a world chock-a-block with "poverty, war, racism, and sexism," a world that could have been "transformed" with the right mix of therapy and political action. Like so many Californians who lived too close to the sixties, Mithers pictures work and enterprise not as possible solutions to these problems but rather as forbidden fruits unwisely plucked from the tree of knowledge.

In that Ronald Reagan had yet to sow the seeds of avarice and ambition beyond his ranch in Santa Barbara, Mithers could hardly blame him for the blossoming of materialism at the Feeling Center. That much said, she interprets his election in 1980 as a large-scale expression of the same "infantile greed" that imploded the center.

Mithers errs, however, in projecting greed to the world beyond her purview. There was no "national embrace of materialism," as she and so many others claim. The burghers of a Mid-America that begins roughly in Modesto lived the same kind of grounded lives after they voted for Reagan as they had in the decades before. These people rarely saw the world "as grim, cut-off, and lonely." They worked hard and usually ethically. They tithed at church, sold Christmas trees for the Optimists, and squirreled their discretionary income away for their kids' college. These, after all, were the people who had the kids, often many of them, the most antimaterialistic act the ordinary American gets to make.

At the Feeling Therapy Center, and at Esalen as well, there were no children. In his balanced look at the Esalen experience, Walter Truett Anderson makes not one single reference to a child on the grounds. Visitors either didn't have children or, if they had them, they came to Big Sur on the weekends their spouses had custody. Children seem to have factored in none of the therapy, none of the training, none of the healing. This was even more true in Hollywood. Writes Mithers of the Feeling Center, "The children that seemed to matter were those the patients had been, not any they had."

Who had time for kids? The humanistic solar system rotated around the individual. Jack Parsons had predicted as much a generation or so earlier. "Every man and every woman is a star," he had written. In the 1970s, that insight actually began to make sense. As Tom Wolfe shrewdly observed, the decade wasn't about anyone or anything but that shiny, stellar being in the center of the universe: "The new alchemical dream is: changing one's personality—remaking, remodeling, elevating, and polishing one's very self ... and observing, studying, and doting on it. (Me!)"

With church and children left to lesser mortals, who else or what else to spend one's money on but "me"? Reagan voters were not the ones speeding down Sunset in their Maseratis, snorting coke in their hot tubs, swapping spouses with their pals, shopping for suits at Bijan, spending multiple thousands on psychotherapy, and aborting their children lest they hurt their careers and/or their figures. It was the "Me" people. Remember, Julia Phillips and her über-materialist Malibu chums despised the "fucking mean Republican machine." Werner Erhard's mercenary, much-prosecuted tax attorney "thought of himself as a radical leftist." Marin County, America's wealthiest and grooviest, voted against Reagan. To this day, these people wander among the ruins of their imagined paradise and persist in blaming some greedy "other" for its demise. This delusion continues to warp the politics of the state and the nation.

At the time, the media saw their better selves in Hart and Corriere, the self-dubbed "Butch Cassidy and the Sundance Kid of psychology." Mainstream publishers vied for their books. *Psychology Today* chose those books for its Book Club. From 1975 to 1980, the two appeared on literally hundreds of radio and television shows, including the big ones like *The Tonight Show, Tomorrow, Merv Griffin, The Mike Douglas Show,* and *Good Morning, America.* When back in Hollywood, patients treated the pair not just like celebrities but like gods. A prayer composed by Corriere's group says just about everything: "Our father, who lives in Norwich, hallowed be thy name: Riggs."

The media didn't quite get the whole picture. While Geraldo Rivera was reporting from the Gardner Street compound that the staff and its 350 patients "coexist in what apparently is one big, happy family," these patients were being punched, kicked, stripped, humiliated, ordered to have sex, told how to think and feel, and commanded to kill their unborn. After hearing the chilling tales, administrative judge Robert A. Neher described the compound as an "almost gothic maelstrom."

On November 4, 1980, the day Ronald Reagan was elected president, the Feeling Therapy Center community collapsed in on itself like a Ponzi scheme. In a large encounter group, the beleaguered faithful somehow found the nerve to turn on the Sundance Kid. Once he fell, everything else did. "The top people—with a few exceptions—weren't inherently evil," said one former patient. "They got caught up in something they believed. And they believed, after a while, that because they were worshipped, that justified anything."

★ 13. Nob Hill ★

Do what you want as long as it's paying off for you. But
once it's become a liability, then something is wrong
and you better find out what it is.
—Anton LaVey

In early May 2006, the Episcopal Church stood on the
very brink of a precipice, and the American media were
all but urging it to jump. International attention focused on the
diocese of California, headquartered in the imposing Grace Cathedral at the very top of San Francisco's Nob Hill. For the
first time in twenty-seven years, the diocese was tasked with
appointing a new bishop.

What made this selection process newsworthy is that three
of the seven finalists for the bishopric were openly gay or lesbian.
More to the point, all of them were living in what the judgmental among us might call "sin." The judgmental in this instance
included many members of the American Episcopal Church,
and most in the world Anglican community. Three years earlier
the appointment of Gene Robinson as the church's first openly
gay bishop had almost unraveled the church worldwide. And
that was only New Hampshire.

This was California. This one really mattered, especially
since the Episcopal Church, like most every other mainstream
church, had been hemorrhaging members for the forty years
before Robinson's election. In 1960, 19 out of every 1,000
Americans were Episcopalians and 8 were Mormons. By the
year 2002, 8 out of every 1,000 were Episcopalians and 19 were
Mormons. For those forty-some years the ABETTO factor had
been at play even in the fields of the Lord, and no mainstream
preacher, past or present, had wandered more blindly through

those fields than the first Episcopal bishop to graduate from Hollywood High, James A. Pike.

The only child of a widowed mother, Pike early on developed an inner barometer of extraordinary sensitivity. He could sense a shift in the zeitgeist and adapt to it long before most people read about it wide-eyed in *Look* or *Life* or *Time*. As a student at Yale Law School in the late 1930s, he wrote his mom back in LA, "Practically every churchgoer you meet in our level of society is Episcopalian." And so he adapted, converting from Roman Catholicism in a heartbeat and persuading his mom to do the same.

In his first posting as an Episcopal priest in Poughkeepsie, Pike sensed the postwar chill in the wind before his peers did and took advantage. He scolded the faculty of nearby Vassar College for being "Unitarian, humanist, materialist, and Marxist." Likely accurate—likely accurate at any snooty college—this critique won him favor among church superiors. The positive attention helped push the ambitious Pike up the church ladder and netted him an appointment as only the fifth dean of the prestigious St. John the Divine in New York in 1952. In July 1953, a precious moment before the media herd did the same, he used his pulpit to attack the vocally anticommunist senator Joseph McCarthy. This, of course, played well to his hipper-than-thou Upper West Side congregation and even better to the New York press.

When he was elected bishop of the California diocese in 1958, his California homecoming sparked further interest in the Episcopal Church and for good reason: Pike's TV show had made him the best-known cleric in America, even better known than Roman Catholic rival Bishop Fulton J. Sheen. California loves a celebrity. The buzz around Pike inspired a surge in giving. Pike used the money to renew construction of Grace Cathedral. Left unfinished since the Depression, the cathedral's sheet metal east face had lent it all the charm of an Oakland warehouse.

Even a blind man-about-town picks a deserving fashion

every now and then, as Pike did with racial integration. At about the same time, he began to sample ecclesiastical fashions as well, just not quite so artfully. A late 1960 article in *Christian Century* put his new Sky Blue theology on public display. The prideful Pike decided that certain Episcopalian notions were little more than "excess baggage." The notions in question were to him trivial things like, oh, the Virgin Birth and the Trinity. When challenged by his colleagues, he blundered forward, denying any special insight to Christian revelation and dismissing the Bible as "a sort of *Reader's Digest* anthology." The *New York Times* reported regularly on his bluster and urged him to continue plunking his Magic Twanger.

With a home court media as referee, Pike could strike back at his colleagues with near impunity. One passive-aggressive strategy he improvised was a riff on the zone of decency. When certain Georgia bishops dared to criticize his theology, he wielded his integrationist credentials like the then-popular Gardol Shield and lobbed verbal grenades from behind it. "It would be interesting for the *New York Times* to inquire of this [Georgia] clericus as to how many of their churches are racially integrated," Pike told the *Times*.

Back in California, he devised still another decency zone. Speaking at the diocesan annual convention, he congratulated himself for his early opposition to McCarthy and imputed McCarthyism to those who would challenge his cut-and-paste theology. Lesser mortals have been employing these tactics ever since, but few with the ingenuity or panache of this winsome little man.

Episcopalians, rich or otherwise, like their traditions. That's exactly why they are Episcopalians and not Shakers or Quakers or Kabbalists. The more publicly Pike and others jacked with those traditions, the more dramatically they reversed the growth curve in church attendance and giving. Yet this was a truism that Pike refused to see. When he discovered in mid-1965 that tithing was down in the diocese more than 15 percent from a year earlier, he was shocked. He did not have a clue to why.

Joan Didion, who was there, describes mid–1960s California as a time and place "when no one at all seemed to have any memory or mooring." Traditional Christianity, in particular, was under siege. The attack came not only from satanists like LaVey, and humanists like Maslow and Rogers, but most destructively of all from its own grandees, like Pike and those who emulated him. It should come as no surprise then that Pike made more than one pilgrimage to the American Tibet. He first spoke at Esalen in the fall of 1965 on a subject close to his heart, "Christianity in Revolution." So enamored was he with the Esalen mix of pop psychology and philosophy that he volunteered Grace Cathedral as a site for a San Francisco branch.

With his 1967 book, *You and the New Morality,* Pike explored the brave new world of "situational ethics." The timing was inauspicious. Son Jim, who had thought it cool to toke up with pop, took cool to a new level when he offed himself with a Savage 30-30 hunting rifle. Then Esther, his second wife and the mother of his four children, filed for divorce. Then his mistress killed herself. Then a co-ed took his "New Morality" class at Berkeley to heart by moving in with him. Finally, on his fifty-fifth birthday, he ignored his daughter Connie's call of distress, and she proceeded to overdose on sleeping pills to the point of coma.

It was the fourth act in this twenty-four-month sequence from hell that proved Pike's gift for situational ethics. In the way of background, Marin County divorcee Maren Bergrud had taken some uncivil liberties with the married Pike soon after he had addressed her ACLU chapter. Partly as a result, Esther Pike threw the bishop out, and he and Bergrud discreetly moved in together. When, however, Bergrud learned of Pike's new dalliance with Berkeley student Diane Kennedy, she objected. As Pike could see, all of the Esalen training in the world wasn't about to soothe a woman scorned.

In the early morning hours of June 14, 1967, after still another hair-raising dispute, Bergrud threatened suicide. Tired of arguing, Pike dared her to do just that. He tossed her a bottle of sedatives and said dismissively, "Take your pills and go." Bergrud was as good as her word. She swallowed fifty-five of them and slumped into a coma.

Here commenced Pike's Chappaquiddick moment. Lest he jeopardize all the revolutionary good he was doing, the ever-ingenious cleric moved quickly to salvage appearances. First he dragged the comatose Bergrud from the apartment they shared to a second apartment down the hall, which was in her name. That accomplished, no easy task for the soft and shapeless cleric, he called her physician, who promptly summoned an ambulance.

While awaiting the ambulance, Pike went back to work, mussing her bed, hoisting Bergrud into it, then artfully arranging her body to suggest a dramatic swan song. As a pièce de résistance, he ripped off the bottom part of a suicide note that implicated him and placed the top of the note bedside her. With the time remaining, he breathlessly carted her toiletries and other personal items from their shared apartment to this second one. This, of course, would have made for one rollicking French farce were it not for one quibbling detail: Bergrud died.

The police saw through Pike's scheming in a San Francisco minute. Still, given his place in society, Pike suffered no greater legal consequence than Ted Kennedy would two years later, which was essentially none at all. Two days after Bergrud's death, Pike presided over her funeral. He attended his daughter's wedding a week after that. Two months later still, he moved Diane Kennedy into his now half-empty apartment, but then again this was August 1967, the "summer of love."

For all of his personal foibles, a *Time* cover story in the midst of this two-year sequence featured Pike in a flattering light. By this time, he had come out in favor of the ordination of women, the unfettered use of birth control, abortion on de-mand, the so-called New Theology, and the uncritical extension of the communion to active homosexuals. How could *Time* not love him?

Only on the issue of the war in Vietnam did his cultural ba-rometer betray him. As unfashionably late as 1966, Pike was call-ing the war a "righteous conflict." Once he got his personal life in order, however, he self-corrected with a vengeance. By April 1968, he was preaching from Park Avenue pulpits that "Jesus was a revolutionary like the Vietcong." Personally, I can't recall Jesus setting punji sticks or beheading reluctant villagers, but those tales must have been in the gospels that the Church has notori-ously "suppressed."

David Robertson argues in his recent Pike bio, *A Passion-ate Pilgrim,* that Pike's "one great effect upon the church" was his introduction of the colloquial and the secular into Episcopal liturgy, an example being the "jazz mass." If this be so, then Pike also has to bear some responsibility for the "hootenanny mass."

In contemporary San Francisco, no church has more boldly advanced the Pike flair for the innovative than the Ebeneezer Lutheran Church on Portola Drive. "Our Christian/Lutheran feminist prayers and liturgy reach back into the storehouse of tradition," reads the church literature, "to bring forth names as Mother, Shaddai, Sophia, Womb, Midwife, Shekinah, She Who Is." The services are more entertaining still. If Martin Luther knew what was being done in his name, he'd sue.

Of arguably more consequence than his liturgical innova-tion was Pike's trailblazing work in the hunt for the "histori-cal Jesus," a project not nearly as benign as it sounds. If Pike could have found a Jesus as loopy as he was, he would have been thrilled. What motivated Pike was his desire to undermine traditional Christianity, in his mind a "sick—even dying—insti-tution." This search led him to a near obsession with the Dead Sea Scrolls, which, Pike believed, would one day show how far

Christianity has strayed from its roots or, in his piquant phras-
ing, "where the trolley went off the track." Pike, in fact, helped
to create a generation of academics who seem to have no more
pressing mission than *The Da Vinci Code*'s Dr. Robert Langdon.
That is, to expose Christianity as some kind of fraud. An amusing dust-up at Kansas University this past year showed just how
deeply the anti-Christian bias has penetrated academia even in
the heartland. Although the details don't bear repeating here, an
indiscreet online posting by the chair of KU's Religious Studies
Department, Paul Mirecki, deserves a little air.

  "The majority of my colleagues here in the dept [*sic*] are
agnostics or atheists, or they just don't care," wrote Mirecki to
a student atheist and agnostic discussion group. "If any of them
are theists, it hasn't been obvious to me in the 15 years I've been
here." He added, "As I often tell my students in the first day of
class, 'If anyone gets converted in this class, its not my fault!'"

  I have got to think that the irreverent Pike and the irreligious Mirecki would have hit it off marvelously. Unfortunately,
Pike never got the chance. A month after the Manson murders
in 1969, he and Diane Kennedy wandered off into the Judean
desert to walk the ground where the Dead Sea Scrolls were
written. That they did in spades after getting lost and driving
into a mudhole. Kennedy proved the better walker, as she made
it out alive. The less hardy Pike did not. Left unfinished at the
end was a book about the historical Jesus that Pike had immod-
estly described in an Esalen brochure as "a revolutionary study
of Christian origins." That brochure also announced an Esalen
program that Pike never got to lead, "Theological Reflections
on the Human Potential." One can only imagine.

  Not all California Protestant churches were flailing during
the Pike years. In the southern end of the state, the Reverend
Robert Schuller was taking a wonderfully American and perfectly Californian tack to success. In 1955, the same year that
nearby Disneyland opened, the young minister and his wife left

the Midwest for Garden Grove, just about five miles down the road from Frontierland. Unable to find affordable space, Schuller opened a new frontier of his own by renting the Orange County Drive-In Theater for Sunday morning services. To recruit parishioners he humbly went door to door in the new neighborhoods of this quickly developing area.

The message he developed was not altogether different from that being brewed in the human potential movement. Schuller called it "Possibility Thinking," which has evolved over time to "Possibility Living." In his recent book of the same name with Douglas Di Siena, Schuller mixes a pinch of scripture and a dash of spirituality with a cup or two of natural health advice in the hope that his readers remain "open to the voice of God in your life as you nurture your whole being." Schuller, however, has deviated from the human potential movement in one fundamental way: He built upon the Judeo-Christian tradition he inherited. He had no Jacobin urge to tear it down.

Schuller's message obviously resonated in Orange County. His congregation grew even more quickly than Pike's dwindled. In 1970 he helped launch the *Hour of Power*, which soon enough became the most popular church service in the world, with some 30 million weekly viewers. In 1980, he opened the dazzling Crystal Cathedral in Costa Mesa, one of the first of the so-called megachurches. In that same year, inspired in no small degree by Schuller, Rick Warren opened the Saddleback Valley Community Church about eight miles down the 405 from the Crystal Cathedral in Lake Forest. Like Schuller, Warren focused on reaching the unchurched with a message equal parts Christianity and can-do Americanism. Warren's 1995 book, *The Purpose Driven Life,* spent forty-five weeks on the *New York Times* bestseller list and has sold 11 million copies so far.

Although both Schuller and Warren have been criticized for sugarcoating Christianity to make it palatable, they have both sensed something that their critics, left and right, have failed to see, namely the world-class anomie of Orange County. In 1980, the year the two pastors opened their respective churches, the county's population stood at nearly 2 million. In 1950, it had barely topped two hundred thousand. The population had grown ninefold in just thirty years. People in an area this freshly minted were less concerned about finding the pathway to heaven than they were about finding the entrance ramp to the 405. What they yearned for was a spiritual lodestar, a fixed point of reference in this uncertain new universe. Schuller and Warren have provided just that. From the beginning of his pastorate, for instance, Warren had a specific goal in mind. He hoped to create not just a church but a home, a loving one for what he describes as the "hurting, the depressed, the confused." If he couldn't find these kind of folks in the OC, a northern Californian might say, he couldn't find them anywhere.

14. La Jolla ★

In Christianity truth is not a process but a state, not a becoming but a being.
— Marcello Pera, *Without Roots*

The Episcopalians got off easy. Not since Sultan Mehmed the Second and his Ottoman buddies stormed Constantinople has anyone rained such holy hell on the Roman Catholic Church as the human potential folks did.

Dr. William Coulson tells this sad saga well. Coulson came to work under Carl Rogers at the Western Behavioral Sciences Institute in La Jolla in 1964. He had recently gotten his doctorate from Notre Dame, where he had written his dissertation on Carl Rogers's theory of human nature, such as it was.

Coulson had first hooked up with Rogers in Wisconsin for a study of nondirective psychotherapy with normal people. Rogers believed that if this therapy worked for neurotics, it would work just as well with mentally healthy people. The people of Wisconsin, however, proved their good health by refusing to participate. "Nobody wanted any part of it," Coulson relates in a lengthy confessional interview. "So we went to California."

As the resident Catholic on the staff, Coulson had as his mission the recruitment of Catholic religious orders. To launch the program, he spoke to a gathering of mother superiors and showed them a film of the amiable Mr. Rogers doing psychotherapy. This appealed to the Sisters of the Immaculate Heart of Mary (IHM). Headquartered in Hollywood, a mistake for any group of women not organized as a "stable," the nuns listed to the progressive side of the sisterhood to begin with.

Soon Coulson, Rogers, and fifty-eight other facilitators

on a three-year grant from the National Institutes of Mental Health—our tax dollars at work—inundated the order with a humanistic psychology program called "Therapy for Normals." Coulson was alive with the spirit of Vatican II as strained through the "Me" filter: "I thought, 'I am the Church; I am as Catholic as the Pope. Didn't Pope John XXIII want us to open the windows and let in the fresh air? Here we come!'" As to Rogers, he was mostly just "anti-Catholic."

The IHMs were ready to change as well. In the wake of Vatican II, they had been asked, like all religious orders, to reassess their mission and to realign it with the unique spiritual gifts of their founder. The architects of Vatican II, however, never imagined that the primary realignment tool would be the encounter group. This being the sixties, more than a few of Rogers's free-wheeling Sky Blue realignment specialists zoomed in on the order's commitment to chastity—now seen as a sexual "hang-up"—and a few of those took a hands-on approach to the zooming.

The more ethical of the facilitators encouraged the participants to explore their sexual feelings on their own. In a not atypical case, an older nun in one group, "freeing herself to be more expressive of who she really was internally," decided that she wanted to have sex with a younger nun. The younger nun obliged, but soon regretted it. Guilt stricken, she went to consult a priest.

Alas, the IHM community, like the Santa Mira of *The Invasion of the Body Snatchers*, had been imperceptibly transformed. The facilitators had already been to see the priest and snatched his judgment. Although he looked and dressed like a priest, the advice he gave the sister was alien to their shared two-thousand-year-old tradition. He refused to hold her to any standards. He encouraged her instead to look within and decide for herself if her actions were right or wrong. Recalls the sister, "He opened a door, and I walked through the door, realizing I was on my own."

This young sister was not the only one to walk through that door. Within a year after Coulson and his colleagues arrived, 300 of the 615 nuns were petitioning Rome to undo their vows. "They did not want to be under anyone's authority," says Coulson, "except the authority of their imperial inner selves."

Readers are free to see this mass exit as a good or bad thing. Inarguable, however, are the material consequences. Within just a few years the 615 IHM nuns dwindled to a handful. Their college closed. Their sixty schools were reduced to one. And thousands of their students were thrown back into the public education system. The Sisters of the Immaculate Heart of Mary "were ready for an intensive look at themselves with the help of humanistic psychologists," regrets Coulson. "We overcame their traditions, we overcame their faith."

Had the damage been confined to the IHMs, Coulson's story might not be worth inclusion. But he and his colleagues lent their order-wrecking assistance to the Jesuits, the Franciscans, the Sisters of Providence, the Sisters of Charity, and the Mercy Sisters. The Jesuits, in particular, began to see not Jesus as their ultimate authority but Carl Rogers.

In addition, these missionary humanists counseled with dozens of Catholic religious organizations eager to get with the times following Vatican II. "We offered a way for people to renew," says Coulson, "without having to bother to study." The results were nearly as unsettling wherever they went. As Coulson explains, a participant in a humanistic psychology program achieves "authenticity" by rejecting societal expectations as "phoniness" and by yielding to what is deepest within. "We provoked," he acknowledges, "an epidemic of sexual misconduct among clergy and therapists." As a result, Church funds that once went to schools and the poor now go to attorney fees.

The humanists might have been able to justify their intervention if they had somehow made the Catholic Church more appealing. This did not happen. The Church changed too much for the traditionalists and not nearly enough for the modernists. As is evident in the Pike case, the Episcopalians did much the same. So did many of the other mainstream faiths.

More than a few times in his six-volume *Tales of the City* series, San Francisco's Armistead Maupin underscores the futility of trying to reconcile traditional values with contemporary ones. The keenest of all observers on late-century California manners, Maupin lets his resentment bleed through the humor in this scene from the fifth volume of the series, *Significant Others.* As the scene unfolds, the swishy Father Paddy offers to solemnize the relationship between two gay men.

"It's not a marriage, mind you," he quibbles. "The Holy Father will have none of that." When the one gay fellow, Michael, protests that he is not even Catholic, the comically indiscriminate Father Paddy answers, "Picky, picky." Michael relays the offer to Thack, his more politically aware partner. The very offer unravels him. "Why should I keep kissing the Pope's ass," Thack storms back, "when he doesn't even *approve* of mine." Thack's will prevails.

Although Thack misrepresents the Church's position on homosexuality, as does Father Paddy for that matter, Maupin captures well the gay take on the same. Maupin's work provides a touchstone for that reason. He knows whereof he speaks. No one has chronicled the change over time of Bay Area culture as shrewdly as he has. The reader will hear more of him.

Despite the best efforts of the humanists, not all priests and nuns yielded to the siren song of the here and now, for which Steven Nary is eternally grateful. In the spring of 1996, the eighteen-year-old U.S. Navy apprentice airman found himself in the San Francisco County jail, charged with a crime he did not fully comprehend, restrained under a bail his parents could never meet.

"I felt my life was over, nonexistent," he tells me. "I was an eighteen-year-old kid who was scared, alone, and hopeless. I had no contact with my parents or anyone else. The military at the time just abandoned me."

Nary recalls his constant struggle to check his tears lest the hard cases in the jail sense a weakness. One morning, which started as grimly as any other, several nuns walked by his cell and others asking if anyone wanted to attend church services. Although not Catholic or particularly religious, Steven "couldn't resist their precious, happily glowing nature." He attended the service, which he found to be "beautiful." At this service, he learned that these were Sisters of Charity, Mother Teresa's group, working out of San Francisco. Impressed, Steven started going every Saturday. To this day, he credits those sisters not only with his newly found faith but also with his sanity. One suspects that California would have been better off in every which way if the psychotherapists had consulted the sisters, and not the sisters the psychotherapists.

California served as a beachhead in the humanistic war on faith, and once established, the humanist troops soon fanned out across the nation. Wholesale assaults were rare after the California experience. More typically, the psychologists settled in as something of a fifth column.

In his regretful look at the contemporary Catholic priesthood, *Goodbye, Good Men*, Michael Rose laments the consequences of what he calls the "gatekeeper phenomenon." According to Rose, priestly orders contract with psychologists to perform the initial interviews with candidates for the seminary. For the presumed sake of objectivity, these orders do not necessarily hire Catholics or even Christians. Given the humanistic bias of the profession, these psychologists tend to see flexibility and open-mindedness as virtues and traditionalism as a vice. As a result, some of the most pious applicants get nixed for being uptight while the Father Paddys of the world get high fives for being open-minded. Once the Father Paddys reach critical mass in a given community, all hell can break loose. Ironically, the media forces that have encouraged the Church's liberalization—the *Los Angeles Times* comes to mind—are the ones that attack the results of that liberalization most gleefully.

Like far too many people in California and elsewhere, Catholic clergy came to put more trust in modern psychology than they did in their faith or in their own common sense. The Boston diocese, for instance, sent the notorious Father John Geoghan to the very same Institute for Living that had nursed Esalen founder Richard Price years before. Therapy, however, had mellowed along with the therapists. It was good-bye electric shock, and hello assertiveness training. After a few months of "human development" and general R&R, Geoghan's therapist sent him out into the world "fit for pastoral work in general including children." He wasn't fit at all. He had to be checked much more forcefully. Now, only the therapist remains at large.

★ 15. Ukiah ★

There was only silence. . . . The incident had no usable political meaning and was therefore best forgotten.
—David Horowitz, *Radical Son*

In a mass grave at the Evergreen Cemetery, in the middle of Oakland, lie the bodies of more than 250 children, the victims of the greatest one-day murder of American young people in the nation's history.

Who are they?

I should add that this is not a trick question. These are not the discarded remains of the unborn or the unfortunate Indian victims of some European disease. No, these were walking, talking children murdered within the memory of most of the readers of this book. Almost all of them were black, and a white man murdered them. Yet their story, like the story of the twenty-seven blacks killed at Waco, is taught at no school in America, not even in Oakland. Let me add another clue: When we talk about their deaths at all, it is usually in the form of a joke.

If you do not know the answer, don't be dismayed. You're in good company. The powers that be have managed to keep the truth buried with the children. This is one chilling, cautionary tale that has not been allowed to caution anyone.

As fate would have it, these children were murdered a week before gay San Francisco Supervisor Harvey Milk was. When he heard the news, Milk had to have thought himself a bit of a prophet. "More people have been slaughtered in the name of religion than for any other single reason," he had pontificated on Gay Freedom Day just a few months earlier. "That, *that* my friends, is true perversion."

As all the world was learning, these very children died "in the name of religion." So opined the *San Diego Union* in just those words, and a hundred other papers nationwide echoed the sentiment. "Radical religious cults," the *Union* editorial continued, were the price that America paid for its "tradition of religious tolerance." For all its weighty introspection, the *Union* overlooked one rather salient fact. The children did not die "in the name of religion." They died for the opposite of religion. There was not so much as a chapel at Jonestown, but that hellhole displayed so much obvious reverence for Lenin, Mao, Che, and Fidel that one might have thought it an extension campus of Santa Cruz U.

Not surprisingly, it was while at college—Indiana U—that Jim Jones got his first injection of Marx, and he was hooked from the beginning. Given that promoting communism in 1950s Indianapolis was about as sane as promoting Florida Orange Juice in 1970s San Francisco, Jones took another tack. "I decided how can I demonstrate my Marxism," he would recount years later. "The thought was 'infiltrate the church.'"

In 1955 he and his wife Marceline did just that, opening the Peoples Temple Christian Church in Indianapolis. Here, Jones embarked on a second strategy, this one a proven winner in communist circles: Exploit America's Achilles' heel, racial injustice. This he did as well, recruiting hundreds of Christian blacks and then subtly shifting their focus from Jesus to Marx, all the while reinforcing their fear of white America. In 1965, he moved the whole shebang to Ukiah, about a hundred miles north of San Francisco up Highway 101.

Seventeen-year-old Debbie Layton joined the temple in 1970, the same year Jones started to shift the operation south to San Francisco. The child of a German mother and a West Virginian father, she and her family had moved to the Bay Area in 1957 as fully deracinated as any of the millions of postwar "new people."

"I believed I was unfairly forsaken," she writes of her troubled family life in the late 1960s, "and began to search for attention elsewhere, at any cost." To the reader, Layton's story must sound almost suspiciously familiar: unshackled child of an unmoored family finds spiritual solace in a freshly contrived godless "religion"—this one, socialist. But such is the never-ending story of an influential chunk of contemporary California.

By 1970, the Peoples Temple had shed all but the illusion of Christianity. "We are not really a church," one of the leaders confided to Layton, "but a socialist organization. We must pretend to be a church so we're not taxed by the government." In meetings, Jones himself made no bones about his distaste for religion. Layton remembers him explaining "how those who remained drugged with the opiate of religion had to be brought into enlightenment—socialism." In his own reminiscences, Jones called religion "a dark creation" of the oppressed. Salvation would come through other channels. "Free at last, free at last," he led his temple comrades in prayer, "thank socialism almighty we will be free at last."

A skilled subversive, Jones helped nurture zero-sum multiculturalism, then still in its larval stage. At Jones's request, for instance, Debbie took the name of "Solano Layton." In her Chicano studies classes at San Francisco State, "Solano" routinely attacked the class's beleaguered Caucasians. Layton found sanctuary from her whiteness in the zone of decency that Jones had constructed for the good white people around him. Remembers Layton, "I had come to believe that all white people, except the few under father's tutelage, were bad." Jones was the "father" in question. "We called him Dad," reports DeDe, a Maupin character who ended up in Jonestown. "If that doesn't give you the creeps, nothing will."

To be clear, Jones had no real interest in helping black people. Although the Peoples Temple had a largely black membership, the hierarchy was almost exclusively white and female, many of whom Jones had raped, Layton and the fictional Dede included. "He fucked everything he could get his hands on," adds Dede, "including the men."

Like Manson, Jones wanted to subvert race relations in America, not strengthen them. To that end, he had his people write hateful, racist letters and attribute them to lesser white people. This mischief was right out of the KGB playbook. As Mark Shields notes in his study of the Mitrokhin files, the Soviets hoped "to weaken the internal cohesion of the United States and undermine its international reputation by inciting race hatred." One has to wonder how many of the hate letters that Hank Aaron received in his 1973–74 run on Babe Ruth's record, the majority of which had northern postmarks, came from Jones's people and other aspiring Bolsheviks. Those letters came to define Aaron's story.

By 1973, after aggressive recruiting in black neighborhoods nationwide, the Peoples Temple boasted some twenty-five hundred members, most of them in San Francisco. Better still, they voted as if with one voice, Jones's. And not only did they vote en bloc, they rang doorbells and made phone calls and hung posters en bloc. Given their affection for independent thinkers—and so many of them in one place!—the city's progressive politicians wooed Jones like a southern belle. "You could start with the governor. And half the politicians in town," said a Maupin character, listing Jones's gentlemen callers. "He was quite a popular fellow around here."

Willie Brown, George Moscone, Harvey Milk all came a-courting. So too did Rosalynn Carter, Jimmy's wife. "I figured if these people—if anybody should know, they should know," testified one black survivor about why he stuck with Jones. After taking office as mayor in 1976, George Moscone repaid Jones by appointing him to the Human Rights Commission and then to the chairmanship of the San Francisco Housing Authority. That same year, the *Los Angeles Times* named Jones "the humanitarian of the year."

"In my later years," Jones reflected near the end, "there wasn't a person that attended any of my meetings that did not hear me say, at one time, that I was a communist." In the People's Republic of San Francisco that fact bothered almost no politico of consequence. "And that is what is very strange," Jones added, "that all these years I have survived without being exposed." In San Francisco, what was strange was that he even worried about it.

In 1974, Jones leased three thousand acres of land in a Guyana jungle and began construction of a commune called the Peoples Temple Agricultural Project. Hundreds of his followers were dispatched there to work. What they discovered was a South American gulag equal parts Werner Erhard and Pol Pot, to wit—"#4, Any Socialism teacher that allows a student to go to the bathroom will go on the New Brigade." When they tried to get out of Dodge, Jones's followers quickly realized there was nowhere to go. Their relatives began to catch on, not only about Jonestown, but also about the everyday abuse in San Francisco, and they put pressure on the authorities. When the Feds started sniffing, Jones himself fled to Jonestown and took nearly a thousand people with him.

The buzz about Jonestown persuaded Democratic congressman Leo Ryan to check the place out. When Jones found out about Ryan's impending visit, he resorted to the ultimate Bay Area gambit—race baiting. He denounced Ryan as someone who had "voted sharply in racist terms and fascist terms" and began rehearsing his people for "White Night," the night when Ryan and other evil white people would come to kill them.

In preparation for visits from outsiders, Jones had earlier issued proclamation #75, "Give your original name when guest is here—do not use your socialist names such as Lenin, Che Guevara, etc." On his visit Ryan quickly saw through the subterfuge. When he attempted to fly back to civilization with inside dope on the commune, a Jonestown security team murdered him and four others on the runway. That night Jones put his well-drilled minions through a "White Night" exercise. They had been through this before, drinking the proverbial Kool-Aid and surviving. They likely presumed that this was just another test of their loyalty. It wasn't. This time the drink was heavily laced with valium and cyanide. Everyone who drank it died. Those who refused to drink it were injected with it. As to Jones, he shot himself.

Within days of the mass deaths at Jonestown people were joking about "Kool Aid drinkers"—they still do—unmindful of the fact that three-year-olds don't commit suicide. In all, 918 Jonestown residents died that day, only some of them voluntarily. Among the dead were 276 children and almost as many seniors. No matter; the media wrote off the event as a "mass suicide," a tragic case of religion gone awry. They would impose this same template on Waco fifteen years later, even though no one died willingly at Waco, not even the adults.

Only the *San Francisco Examiner* came close to getting the story right. "The truth is that [Jones] had become liberal chic here," said its editors, still mourning the loss of one of their photographers on the Jonestown runway, "and was embraced by people who wanted his support and didn't ask enough questions." The *Examiner* drew the "lesson" that political opportunists should look more closely before catering to "flaky groups," but that was not nearly lesson enough. Jones was no more "flaky" than Mao, merely smaller in scale.

With almost nothing learned from the tragedy, white political leaders have continued to do almost exactly what Jones did and get away with it: embrace minorities, alert a partisan media to the embrace, woo the minorities for their support, reward them for it but never with real power, scare them with tales of racist whites, promise to protect them from those whites, engineer societies (or school systems) from which there is no escape, and when all goes to hell, as it inevitably does, blame Ronald Reagan or some evil "other."

History rarely catches up with these good white people. They get to write it. The *Examiner* reporter who covered the story, Tim Reiterman, wrote a book on the subject as well as a commemorative piece for the *Los Angeles Times*. Twenty-five years after the fact, he remembers Jones as a "humanitarian civic leader." True, even in San Francisco, "families were systematically divided, disciplinary beatings were the norm, and sexual exploitation by Jones was a dirty secret," but otherwise the Peoples Temple was a "model of racial integration and social action." Right, and other than the Holocaust, Nazi Germany was a model of efficiency and full employment. In sum, writes Reiterman, Jonestown symbolized "the worst that organized religion, cults and madness can reap." Organized? Religion? If I harp on the ABETTO factor, forgive me. In the fifty-five-hundred-word Wikipedia entry on Jonestown there is not one single mention of the words "socialism," "communism," "Marx," or "Marxism."

In a one-party political and media environment like San Francisco's, almost nothing checks the corrupting power of this process. God help the poor man or woman who gets in its way, let alone an eighteen-year-old sailor from nowhere.

★ 16. Manhattan Beach ★

In the brutalities of actual child abuse that courts
see every day, there are no clowns, no elephants, no
butchered bluebirds or magic rooms.
—Dorothy Rabinowitz, *No Crueler Tyrannies*

The improvised priesthood of California has led the
citizenry into any number of blunders, none more
lethal than Jonestown, and none more preposterously unjust
than the one that took place in Manhattan Beach beginning
in 1983.

That year, Peggy Buckey was running a well-respected preschool that her mother, Virginia McMartin, had founded three
decades earlier. Southern California had proved fertile ground
for an enterprising establishment like McMartin's. The spiraling
cost of housing put more women in the job market, as did the
mounting rates of divorce. Few of these largely uprooted families had grandmas to help with childcare. The long commutes
kept women away from home longer than they would like.

So the McMartin Preschool flourished. The local Chamber of Commerce had named Virginia "citizen of the year." The
school developed the best reputation in the South Bay and had
a waiting list longer than Spago on a Saturday night. The school
got a further boost when Peggy's son Ray, then in his early
twenties, started work there. Many of the single moms were
pleased to have at least some male influence in their children's
lives.

The social instabilities that had led to the school's success,
however, were about to cause its downfall. Working moms may
have been good for the school, but they could be tough on
themselves. Many among them felt a deep unease about leaving

their children in the care of a paid stranger. That anxiety was soon to find an outlet.

The provocateur in this case was a not-so-gay divorcée named Judy Johnson. She showed up at the school one day and dropped her two-year-old off without so much as a fare-thee-well. The Buckeys felt sorry for the kid and let him stay anyhow. They shouldn't have. Soon after, Johnson was telling the police that Ray Buckey had sodomized the lad. She would later tell the district attorney's office that her estranged husband had sodomized her dog. No matter. Local detective Jane Hoag took the information and ran with it.

Among the women who worked outside the home, a good percentage had found careers in the helping professions, one of which was the emerging field of child abuse remediation. Others had become judges and prosecutors and police officers. Given human nature, many of these women gravitated toward child-oriented issues, but they did not always leave their maternal anxieties at the office door. In the McMartin case, the accuser, the key detective, the prosecutor, the judge, the reigning shrink, and six of the seven accused would prove to be women.

A Southern California preschool was vulnerable to crazies in ways that schools elsewhere were not. The Church of Satan had its HQ just up the road in San Francisco, and there was lots of satanic mumbo jumbo in the LA air. Los Angeles also had the most cutthroat local media in America. And finally, of course, no other spot on the planet had yielded so much moral and emotional authority to head doctors, real or pretend.

As Howard Jarvis had shown, a well-mobilized middle class plate will prevail in just about any seismic showdown, even if the media and legal/political establishment stands in the way. When, however, that plate moves in sync with the media, the state, and the therapeutic community, the combined momentum has the power to crush anything in its path, justice and common sense be damned. And damned they were. The sundry shamans of the mental health profession were about to do something no Christian clergy had done in three hundred years—namely, hunt down some witches and hang them, or at least try to.

The forces that crushed the McMartin Preschool got rolling in 1979 with the passage of the Mondale Act. This federal legislation injected too much money too quickly into "child protection" and helped spawn an absurdly amateurish industry dedicated to the same. The most visible member of that industry in LA, the stylish Kee McFarlane, had just recently descended on the town. In her late thirties when this all began, McFarlane had gotten a fine arts degree in Ohio and then switched to social work. She proved to be an adept writer of grant proposals and with that humble skill and a welder's license finessed her way up the ranks of sexual abuse experts. In Los Angeles, McFarlane reigned as the director of the Sexual Abuse Diagnostic Center for the grandly named Children's Institute International. Later, when a reporter asked a defense attorney if he was going to contest McFarlane's credentials, he snapped, "I don't contest her credentials. They don't exist." He did, of course, concede that she had a welder's license.

Detective Hoag had no more common sense than McFarlane had credentials. With an allegation from one clearly schizoid parent in hand, she called all over town and asked parents if Ray Buckey had molested their child too. The panic was on. Without any confirming evidence, the police arrested Ray and searched the homes of Virginia McMartin and the Buckeys. They found Virginia's file box full of names and addresses and seized it.

When the district attorney's office told the Manhattan Beach police to release Ray for lack of evidence, Hoag went back to work. Using the McMartin database, she sent out a letter under her chief's signature asking parents if their children had ever seen Ray Buckey molest a child. "We ask you to keep this information strictly confidential," she wrote in blissful ignorance of human nature to the *two hundred* families who received it.

"The result," Paul and Shirley Eberle write in their comprehensive book on this subject, *The Abuse of Innocence*, "was mass hysteria." The parents understandably began to withdraw their kids, and Peggy Buckey was compelled to close the school.

Meanwhile, the DA's office started to ship the school's children down to Kee McFarlane at CII. Virtually every child who arrived *chez Kee* with nothing to report left with lots to say, like, "Peggy put her vagina inside my vagina." Upon retrieving the tots, parent after parent learned the "bad news" from these official-seeming clinicians, "Your child has been molested."

Now the hysteria began in earnest. Judy Johnson continued to ratchet it up. She told the DA's office that her son saw animals being chopped up, that he rode on a lion, that Ray Buckey sliced a baby's head off and made her son stick his finger up the anus of a goat—"all the stuff that usually goes on every day at preschools," said the one prosecutor with the good sense to quit his job in disgust.

In March 1984, with the *Los Angeles Times* and the local TV stations fanning the flames, a grand jury indicted Ray Buckey and his mother, Peggy, Ray's sister Peggy Ann, his grandmother Virginia, and three female teachers on a total of 207 counts of child sexual abuse. The DA's office had tipped off Channel 7, so Ray and Peggy could be arrested live, in real time. The station promoted its coverage under the heading, "The McMartin Preschool Horror." A year later, the station's lead reporter and Kee McFarlane would take a three-week cruise together to the South Pacific. It just so happened too that the prosecutor was engaged to the *Los Angeles Times* managing editor. The defendants were in serious trouble, and they knew it. "It's an uneven struggle," one lawyer commented. "The prosecutors don't have to sell their houses and give up their life savings to stay in this poker game."

The six females arrested averaged fifty-five years of age. The feisty Virginia McMartin was seventy-nine. Four of the six were held without bail. I remember watching this from afar and thinking it all absolutely nuts: No six middle-aged women any-where would ever conspire to sexually abuse children in satanic rituals, even in Los Angeles. But I had been spared the relent-lessly one-sided coverage in Southern California. One survey showed that 97 percent of potential jurors believed Ray Buckey to be guilty before the trial, an unprecedented poisoning of the jury pool. Despite this wildly imbalanced coverage, the defen-dants were denied a change of venue.

After six years of testimony about chopped-up ponies, raped babies, giraffes beaten with baseball bats, atomic mutants, marathon molestations in car washes, and naked priests and nuns drinking blood, the prosecutors called it quits. And after nearly six years in prison, convicted of nothing, Ray Buckey finally got to go home.

As to the sorry soul who had launched it all, Judy Johnson, she had committed suicide four years earlier.

★ 17. Chinatown ★

I'll tell you the unwritten law, you dumb son of a
bitch, you gotta be rich to kill somebody, anybody,
and get away with it.
    —Jake Gittes, *Chinatown*

I do not know if Ray Buckey watched the Academy
Award show in March 2003, or know how he felt if
he did, but I can imagine. After an unendurable three hours of
peace vamping—Hollywood would willingly go to war only if
the enemy were the paparazzi—the gathered worthies surged
to their feet to applaud Roman Polanski, the surprise winner
of the best director award for the Holocaust drama *The Pianist*.
Polanski, however, couldn't quite make it to the Kodak Theater
that evening. It seems that twenty-five years earlier the widowed husband of the late Sharon Tate had driven his Mercedes
to LAX and left it in long-term parking, very long term. He has
not been back since. His new home, France, the country that
gave us the term *droit du seigneur*, has proved more understanding.

Days before the Oscars, Patrick Goldstein of the *Los Angeles Times*, the paper that had led the charge against the Buckeys, posed the question of whether "an artist's accomplishments
should be judged against his misdeeds." He used the word "misdeed" more than once to describe the act that had caused Polanski to flee. In the same article actor Warren Beatty called the
same act a "personal mistake." Goldstein concludes that "we"
always "forgive [artists] their transgressions" because, in the end,
good art trumps bad behavior. And after all, as Washington wags
might have put it, "This was just about sex."

Shortly before the Oscars someone had posted the grand

jury testimony of the victim of that misdeed, Samantha Geimer, on the Internet. Hollywood gossips were upset—not with Polanski, but with the "smear" against him. The testimony, however, is worth revisiting, and it rings entirely true. Polanski tells much the same story in his autobiography, *Roman,* though he remains shocked that "I should be sent to prison, my life and career ruined, for making love." The description that follows is not for children.

The quintessential Valley girl, Geimer artlessly tells of how Polanski approached her and her divorced mom about taking photos of Samantha for a fashion magazine. Impressed and reassured by his celebrity, the mom agreed. After a couple of outdoor shoots, Polanski and the girl ended up alone at Jack Nicholson's house. Says Polanski, "I could sense a certain erotic tension between the two of us." At the time, Polanski was a worldly forty-three. Geimer was a thirteen-year-old seventh-grader.

At Nicholson's otherwise empty house, Polanski plied Geimer with champagne and had her take her blouse off for a shot in the Jacuzzi. He then gave her a Quaalude. "Why did you take it?" asked the prosecutor. "I think I must have been pretty drunk or else I wouldn't have," Geimer answered. Now "kind of dizzy," Geimer still managed to resist Polanski's increasing demands. "I want to go home," she told him repeatedly. He would have none of it. Finally, he cornered her on a couch, put his head in her lap, and started performing "cuddliness" on her, her word.

"I was going, 'No, come on, stop it,' but I was afraid," Geimer continued. Polanski then "placed his penis in [her] vagina," but upon learning that she was not on the pill, the gentlemanly artist lifted her legs up further, "went through the anus," and climaxed therein. A "misdeed," to be sure.

In a world where the values are as shaky as the terrain, the popular and powerful get to shape the moral topography, and they can change it almost at will. Actor Cliff Robertson learned this lesson the hard way. In his neighborhood, as he discovered, there were some unexpected new hills to die on.

For those who may not remember, Robertson had won a Best Actor Oscar for the 1968 movie *Charly*. In 1976 the fifty-year-old actor was still much in demand. In that Columbia Pictures had done none of the demanding, at least recently, Robertson was puzzled to see an IRS statement arrive from the studio. Upon investigating, he learned that an employee of Columbia Pictures had cashed a check in his name and stuck Robertson with the tax due. That rogue employee just happened to be Columbia president David Begelman.

Begelman had messed with the wrong guy. David McClintick, who documents this story in his best seller *Indecent Exposure*, says of Robertson, he "seemed to live by a traditional moral code—simple and staunch—forged in his strict Presbyterian upbringing." Before the saga was through, Robertson would pay for this distinction.

In his midfifties at the time of the incident, Begelman lived by a moral code of his own devising. A classic hustler, he had worked his way up from talent agent to take over the floundering Columbia four years earlier. He did well. As the legendary L. B. Mayer was wont to say, "There's nothing wrong with this business that good pictures can't cure." Whether the pictures Begelman oversaw were "good" is open to question—*Tommy*? *Murder by Death*?—but they at least made money, and that was good enough for the board of Columbia's parent company back in New York.

Robertson, however, didn't care how much money the studio made. He harbored the quaint notion that grand theft was a bad thing and compelled the Columbia board to investigate. In so doing, the board found a second embezzlement of an even greater sum. When exposed, Begelman swore "on the life of my child" that there were no others. Not wanting to disrupt the opening of Columbia's likely blockbuster *Close Encounters of the*

Third Kind, the board overlooked the theft and kept him on as president.

Soon enough, a third embezzlement came to light—Begelman's child be damned—and the board had to face the fact that Begelman had stolen, at today's values, the equivalent of more than $250,000. In any other industry, in any other part of America, the board would have canned Begelman on the spot, if not sooner, but Hollywood played by its own set of rules.

Despite the obvious ethnicity of the players in *Indecent Exposure*—almost all are Jewish except Robertson, a fact McClintick does not shy from—the problem was not Hollywood's Jewishness. The problem was that it had ceased to be Jewish, ceased to be anything. Some of the Jewish names may have lingered, but the industry had become the single most secular in America and the least subdued by any form of internal discipline.

A public opinion survey of Hollywood's creative leaders at about this time revealed that an astonishingly high 93 percent of them seldom or never attended religious services of any kind, this in a nation where nearly half the population went weekly. Hollywood filled the spiritual void with what Julia Phillips rightly calls the "great toys," everything from est to self-actualization to the I Ching, none of which asked much in the way of good behavior. Phillips, who produced *Close Encounters*, stood proudly by Begelman throughout despite her recognition that, yes, perhaps he was "a gambler and an embezzler."

In the film industry, as at the Feeling Therapy Center, truth was what worked. Those who did their work well got to define what truth was. "I like to think of myself as a doer," Begelman told *Newsweek* in the midst of all this, "and if you are a doer you are going to make mistakes." Repeated "mistakes" like grand theft—or rape—were not a sign of sin but of sickness. True to form, Begelman's supporters on the board insisted that he "had an emotional breakdown, a temporary one," and that what was needed was not jail time but therapy.

With more therapists per capita in Beverly Hills than in any city in the galaxy, Begelman did not have to look hard to find "one of the finest doctors in the world." This doctor walked Begelman through what skeptics called the "six-week Beverly Hills miracle cure." At the end of it, Begelman pronounced himself fit.

"I have learned a great deal about the roots of my misdeeds," he told the board with a straight enough face. "The roots go deep, all the way back to my childhood and my relationship with my parents and my siblings." The multimillionaire movie mogul then broke down before his sympathetic colleagues and confessed to "an unnaturally low self-esteem." Whether the session ended with a group hug, I do not know.

Had justice been left to Columbia's moneymen, Begelman would have suffered nothing worse than a little egg on the face and a good cry. Finally, however, the local civil authorities got involved and served up a judicial wrist slap as well. Given the public exposure, Begelman oozed out of the presidency and into an independent production deal with Columbia. A year into his three-year probation, a friendly judge suspended his probation altogether and knocked the charge down to a misdemeanor.

"I understand the motivation that led me to commit the acts for which I have atoned," Begelman lied and went about his business." In December 1979, MGM lured Begelman away from Columbia's shadow and named him president and CEO. The day the news broke, the crowd at Ma Maison greeted Begelman's arrival with a standing ovation, and this was a year before Reagan had a chance to corrupt them.

More than Begelman's creepy behavior or the board's seamy complicity, the standing ovation at Ma Maison is what dismays the disinterested observer. That cut across all ethnic lines and made coconspirators out of the whole movie colony. None among them would offer the Oscar-winning Robertson a decent lead again. As to Begelman, after another two decades of mistakes, he would shoot himself in a Century City hotel room. Says Dominick Dunne of Hollywood, "Failure is the unforgivable sin here,"

Those who think a standing ovation for successful misbehavior is a phenomenon limited by place or time have not been to San Francisco's SBC Stadium in the last few years. There, just about every other day from April to October, scores of thousands of the Bay Area's best citizens pay as much as eighty-five dollars a game to watch a spectacle that one Justice Department spokesman rightly describes as "cheating the baseball immortals."

From a certain perspective, Barry Bonds's story explains no more about California than does Charles Manson's. After all, not too many black children have grown up affluent, in an all-white environment, deeply resenting the fathers who gave them their riches and their extraordinary genes. What makes his story worth telling, what explains all too much about contemporary California, is the Bay Area embrace of Barry Bonds.

Barry himself is one of a kind. The father he held in contempt, Bobby Bonds, had an equally distinct career arc from happy Riverside childhood to unstable stardom in San Francisco to angry denouement in lesser baseball towns. Bobby too had a drug of choice. His, however, was alcohol, which did nothing good for his family or his career. His extended absences and his indifference to his son help explain Barry Bonds's legendary, career-long sulk.

Barry started honing his attitude at Junipero Serra High in San Mateo, known locally as "the jock school to end all jock schools." Although the school's mission was to "foster Gospel values," those values apparently did not include humility, at least in Bonds's case. By the time major league scouts came sniffing, one of them would sum up the consensus on Barry's "Attitude/Personality" with one highly explanatory word, "asshole." In Pittsburgh, his first major league stop, the writers gave him their MDP—"most despised player"—award. In San Francisco, to which he returned in 1993 as a two-time MVP, he continued to creep out teammates and fans at a Hall of Fame level.

Unlike his future coconspirator, Victor Conte lived a text-book California baby boomer life. Born in Fresno to a working-class Catholic Italian family, Victor dropped out of the local community college right after the Manson killings and just before Altamont to join a rock group called Common Ground. Ten years later, his father would still be introducing him thusly: "This is my son Victor. He's never worked a day in his life."

Always a charmer and a hustler, Victor joined a new band in 1970. The deep irony of its name—"Pure Food and Drug Act"—would escape Victor for another thirty years. On the road in 1970's California, Victor quickly shucked his family's Catholicism and began studying Eastern philosophy, particularly the *Bhagavad Gita*. If this sacred Hindu scripture contained any "Thou Shalt Nots," Conte must have overlooked them.

In 1977, Conte arrived. He got married and joined a major funk band, Tower of Power, at the peak of its success. His constant scheming, however, got him dumped within a year or two. He and wife Audrey bounced around for the next few years in classic New Age fashion, practicing yoga, eating organic foods, and going on pseudoreligious retreats. In the midst of all this healthy living, Conte found time to deal drugs and Audrey found time to get addicted. When they split in 1995, that addiction would cost Audrey custody of the couple's three daughters.

Before that unfortunate turn of events, Conte and Audrey had opened a place called the Millbrae Holistic Health Center, just about fifteen minutes north of San Carlos where Barry Bonds had grown up. Conte dealt vitamins at the store and pot from the house. The up-and-coming young drug dealer used the health center as a springboard to his next big idea, sports medicine, and soon after launched a new venture called the Bay Area Laboratory Co-Operative, BALCO for short. From his humble BALCO offices, located in a strip mall near the San Francisco airport, Conte dispensed all manner of illegal performance-enhancing drugs to all kinds of athletes.

San Francisco Chronicle reporters Lance Williams and Mark Fainaru-Wada tell the BALCO story well and in detail in their 2006 book, *Game of Shadows*. Suffice it to say that Bonds began using steroids as a thirty-four-year-old before the 1999 season. Conte and Bonds hooked up two years later, ten years after the federal government had outlawed the nonprescription use of steroids. That year Bonds hit a major league record seventy-three home runs and won the Most Valuable Player Award for the National League. Major League Baseball banned steroid use in 2002, but with Conte's all-but-undetectable drugs Bonds felt free to ignore the ban. He would win the MVP Award in 2002, 2003, and 2004 as well.

Bonds's stats bewildered baseball historian Bill Jenkinson, who has made a science of analyzing home-run hitting. Not only was Bonds hitting more home runs as he moved into his late thirties, but he was also hitting them much farther. "This is not humanly possible," says Jenkinson. "It cannot be done by even the most amazing athletic specimen of all time . . . unless that specimen is cheating." In the twelve years before that specimen started using steroids, 1986–98, he had averaged 32 home runs a season. In his five full seasons of steroid use, Bonds averaged 52 homers. In 2006, his first full poststeroid season, Bonds hit 26 home runs. Do the math. Historically, the peak age for sluggers has been twenty-seven. Bonds just started to peak at thirty-six. The Giants management turned a blind eye to all of this.

Conte had put Bonds in the record books. And there's the rub. Baseball is a game of records, of traditions. Unlike, say, bodybuilding, baseball has meaning only in direct reference to its history. Who knows or cares what amazing hulk won the Mr. Olympia Contest from 1970 to 1974? Everyone in that world took steroids. Even if the winner did become the *governator,* he did not cheat his sport the way Bonds has. Bonds has been undermining not just the integrity of the game as played today, but the very meaning of the sport, past, present, and future. He has messed with history the way Bill and Ted and other excellent movie adventurers have. So toxic are his poststeroid statistics, in fact, that Major League Baseball may have to declare them a Superfund site and expunge them.

As Bonds lumbered shamelessly on toward Hank Aaron's all-time home-run record, he continued to cheat, and the San Francisco fans continued to cheer. This should not surprise. History and tradition—of anything other than San Francisco itself—matter less in the Bay Area than they do anywhere in America. Even after the Feds busted Conte and dragged a dissembling Bonds before a grand jury, Giants fans exulted in the team's performance. "The man is a saint," gushed a kindergarten teacher with her young son at SBC on the occasion of his seven hundredth home run. After his grand jury appearance, notes Jeff Pearlman in his Bonds bio, *Love Me, Hate Me,* "San Francisco fans hailed their star not only as a hero but as a martyr," if not exactly in the Serra tradition.

By the end of the 2005 season even die-hard San Francisco fans had to acknowledge that Bonds had scammed his way to his stats. In a random ballpark survey, 92 out of 100 Giant fans conceded that Bonds had cheated. Still, only 24 out of 100 expressed any concern that this might be wrong. The email Williams and Fainaru-Wada received from their *Chronicle* readers was just as whacked. They "passionately insisted they didn't care," but that did not deter them from attacking the pair for reporting the truth. Among the fans weighing in against these "so-called journalists" was former mayor Willie Brown.

When I talked to Lance Williams in midseason 2006, he found the fan response to be the most revealing element in the whole saga. Despite their presumed ethical superiority, Bay Area fans showed little regard for the character of the man and even less for the integrity of the game. When I talked about Barry Bonds at a gathering of adults on the Peninsula, several of those in attendance jumped on me for even raising the question. "What does this have to do with California?" one of them snapped.

Maybe more than most would care to admit. As Pearlman wryly observes, "San Francisco led the league in pregame ceremonies to bring attention to world problems." And yet as steroid abuse swelled nationwide, the organization ignored a problem that was potentially lethal and altogether local. Worse, the Giants held up as a model for young San Franciscans a man whose own abuse, if emulated, could turn their heads into pumpkins and their testicles into peas.

A twelve-year-old fan, interviewed by the *Chronicle* in July 2006, perfectly mimics the smugly amoral drift of Bay Area opinion. "I'm just glad he's not in prison," said the boy, relieved that Bonds was not to be charged with perjury. "It's pretty much all racist. They keep trying to get him, but he's never failed a drug test. They don't have anything on him. They're just going to keep trying until they do." The boy, no more deprived than Bonds himself, had flown into San Francisco to catch a four-game series with his parents. His racial hauteur was impressive even by Bay Area standards.

As to Conte, he went to jail unrepentant, threatening to write an autobiography called *No Choice*, its premise being that if everyone cheats you have no choice but to cheat too. So much for Eastern philosophy and California's "moment of real possibility." Bonds proved just as obstinate. In an historic echo of noted ethicists Warren Beatty and David Begelman, he would only admit, "We all make mistakes."

★ 18. Black Rock ★

God is dead. God remains dead. And we have killed
him. . . . What festivals of atonement, what sacred
games shall we need to invent?
—Friedrich Nietzsche, *The Gay Science*

I realized that I had seriously underestimated Burning
Man founder Larry Harvey when he pulled out a pack
of smokes, shook one out, and lit it without apology or permission sought. In other parts of the world, smoking a cigarette in
a closed space is no big deal. In California, butting a cigarette in
someone's navel would be only slightly more provocative.

Just a month or two before I met with Harvey, the upscale
San Fernando Valley suburb of Calabasas had banned smoking
not merely indoors but in all outdoor public spaces. Under the
law, residents and municipal workers are encouraged to rat out
offenders, and the city attorney then determines whether to impose fines of up to five hundred dollars or "other punishment"
as yet unspecified, although stocks or a public dunking would
suit the spirit of the ordinance. "We're putting the force of law
behind [the ban]," Councilman Barry Groveman boasted, without a peep of protest from the ACLU.

One suspects that there is much about the actual Burning
Man festival that the good councilman would find objectionable. I am thinking here less of the nude, co-ed mud dancing
than the festival's drive-by shooting range, which is exactly what
it sounds like. The clouds of firsthand smoke that come with
the incineration of a largely wooden, forty-foot-tall, seventy-six-thousand-pound "man" would probably not go over well in
Calabasas either.

No, Burning Man is not your everyday New Age ritual. Harvey shudders at the comparison. He sees the New Age movement as "callow, self indulgent, and silly." Burning Man is, as they say, something else. In the way of background, Harvey and a bunch of his more anarchic pals started Burning Man in 1986 when they carted a wooden effigy of a man down to a San Francisco beach and burned it. As tolerant as San Francisco is of odd behavior, it is less tolerant of burning stuff than just about any burg in the country. By 1990, as the crowds began to grow, and the police pressure began to mount, Harvey realized that he and his coconspirators would need a more accommodating venue. This they found in a stretch of Nevada desert as bleak as the moon and only slightly more accessible.

Little did anyone suspect that this Godforsaken landscape would become home to the nation's largest counterculture enclave, however transient. Black Rock City, as it is known, has evolved from a lonely cluster of eighty freaky people into five square miles of what Harvey calls a "civic entity" with its own fire department, daily newspapers, radio stations, department of public works, and as many as forty thousand temporarily deranged citizens engaging in any number of public, interactive arts projects over the course of a very long weekend.

Harvey has put a lot of thought into his creation. Indeed, no one with whom I have spoken in California has thought through the "What's the matter" question more systematically. He traces his earliest reflections on the subject to a childhood visit to Los Angeles. Growing up on an Oregon farm, he had missed much of the mass culture geared for baby boomers like himself, certainly the coonskin cap front end of it. Not until he visited his LA uncle had he even experienced TV, let alone Velveeta or smog, the two other California novelties that most impressed him. The trip exposed him at an early age to the perils of what he would come to call "cultural commodification," a phrase that has probably still not yet crossed the lips of an Oregon farmer.

A conceptual artist, Harvey moved to San Francisco in

the late 1970s and found a fair share of kindred spirits in the city's underground art scene. That much said, there cannot have been too many people in San Francisco quite like him, a hands-on farm boy who can casually quote William James and discuss E. M. Forster, his favorite author, without sounding like an English professor. His interests seem well integrated. The elephant-festooned tapestries in his meticulously clean and nicely eclectic Old World apartment look as if Forster himself had brought them back on a return passage from India.

When I asked Harvey the "What's the matter" question, he responded spontaneously, "a petulant sense of entitlement." As soon as I heard it, the name "Barry Bonds" leaped to the top of a mental list that grew longer the more I thought. Harvey's long answer, formulated over the years, has shaped the very destiny of Burning Man.

From his perch on top of San Francisco's Hayes Street Hill, Harvey looks down at an America whose culture has been processed and packaged like so much Velveeta. As he sees it, the nation's obvious abundance has spawned a lifeless materialism. Unrelieved, this materialism has infected us with a "moral coarsening and a growing cynicism" and a "supine passivity" that Harvey finds decidedly "unhandsome."

"We need some deep and drastic therapy to break this spell," says Harvey. And the best therapy that he can conjure is his extraordinary interactive experiment called Burning Man. In the early nineteenth century, western New York was known as the "burned-over district" for the spontaneous combustions of faith and hope that birthed one new sect after another: the Spiritualists and the Oneida Community, the Mormons and the Seventh Day Adventists. For the last half-century, as has been amply demonstrated, burned-over honors have passed to California. Harvey carries the torch forward, but with a much better sense of history, not to mention humor, and a firmer grasp on human nature than those who have come before.

Looking for a point of attack, critics have challenged Burning Man, like all of California's Nietzschean experiments, for its lack of diversity. "Inclusive is illusive for burners," reads the headline of a recent *San Francisco Chronicle* article on Burning Man.

This past spring I got a sense of the issue when I watched San Francisco's Bay to Breakers 7.5-mile run from a front porch halfway up Harvey's Hayes Street Hill. Nearly a century old, the run boasts a corporate sponsor, ING, many flamboyant costumes, and scores of local muckety-mucks among the seventy thousand runners, including, this year, the ambitious mayors of both San Francisco and Los Angeles.

Bay to Breakers also attracts hundreds of naked runners. A group of Kenyans may have led the legitimate pack, and there was a smattering of minorities throughout, but every one of the hundred-plus naked people I saw was white. Although it is hard to generalize about motive, many seemed altogether eager to call attention to "me." Minorities, on the other hand, may still be more concerned about "us."

This me-ness seemed especially apparent from my perch as most of the runners walked up the lengthy Hayes Street Hill, and some of the naked ones strolled proudly along the sidewalk or even from one sidewalk to another. Among the latter was a woman with a shaved crotch holding a sign that read "No more Bush," already a tired joke in these parts.

People of color were not the only ones missing. Despite the paradelike atmosphere, there was not a child in sight. The naked people scare parents away, as do the occasionally obscene banners and minifloats. Likewise at Black Rock City, the desert site of Burning Man, kids are scarcer than trees. Curiously, a media obsessed with "inclusiveness" never seems to factor children into the "inclusive" equation. They may not know enough to do so.

Larry Harvey, who has a biracial son, blew off the accusations of racial exclusion. "I don't think black people like to camp," he told the media with a wink they didn't quite notice. Still, as Burning Man has flourished, so have its critics. Although some of the more proudly pagan participants wish that Pat Robertson would attack them—and some imply that he has—I could find no evidence of this. Perhaps to encourage Robertson, one exhibit at the site offered fellow campers the opportunity to "have simulated sex with such intelligent, sinless men" as Robertson and the equally inevitable, if now deceased, Jerry Falwell.

If, however, Robertson had a weekend gathering for forty thousand of his followers, he would surely have fewer rules. Burning Man summarizes its prohibitions in a posted "Ten Commandments," but in fact there are many more. "Burning Man does not promote or condone the use of illegal drugs," reads the lawyerly Ninth Commandment. But this commandment, like all the others, lists several other subcommandments such as "Underage drinking is forbidden by law" and "Sex acts are prohibited in the civic space of Black Rock City and in unrestricted public environments." Say what you will about Robertson, but I don't imagine he would need a posted prohibition against public sex. Nor would he word any of his rules as severely as Burning Man's Eighth Commandment, "Violation of these rules, or violent or anti-social behavior, can result in revocation of your ticket and ejection from the event without refund."

Just about all serious protest emerges from within the hip community, not without. Harvey's need to impose external rules on the internally unruled evokes it. The most sustained yipping comes from those anarchic artists who want more primal democracy and less structure than Burning Man now offers. Not surprisingly, they also want more attention paid to themselves and what they do. "Some have thought that radical self-expression is a mandate for transgression," Harvey confided. He cannot let that be. He knows better. He believes in "civics." He remembers Altamont.

At the literal and emotional center of his "experiment in temporary community" is the burning of the Man. In fact, the Man serves the same function as the House of Congress does in L'Enfant's Washington, D.C., the ceremonial space from which radiate the streets like spokes in a wheel. Harvey sees the sacralized burning of the Man as the primal, participatory ritual that gives meaning to the community. "The bearing of witness connects us all," he argues.

Harvey deserves credit where it's due. He has taken some forty thousand of the most burnt-out citizens in this burnt-over land and eased them into a functioning community. Although some disagree, he has largely honored his libertarian instincts, consciously "steering the ship two or three degrees at a time," avoiding the Scylla of est and the Charybidis of Esalen. Harvard should do a case study.

As to the future, Harvey believes that he can do more than sustain Burning Man. He can proselytize the very concept beyond Black Rock City, and here he revealed his inner Hazel Motes. "I don't think you need a God to get there," says Harvey.

He is not the first one to think thusly. Jim Jones, Julia Butterfly Hill, Erhard, Pike, Rogers, Perls, Maslow, Coulson, Janov, Hubbard, Price, Murphy, Hart, Corriere, Parsons, LaVey, Marshall Applewhite, and even Charles Manson have all thought likewise. To his credit, Harvey thinks a good bit more clearly.

THE WEARING OF
THE GREEN

★ 19. San Mateo ★

Humanist environmentalism can be seen as one of
the last sputtering candles of the Enlightenment.
—Christopher Manes, *Green Rage*

Tom Wolfe, the most prescient of American observers, miscalled "the third great awakening." Writing in 1976, Wolfe could not know that the Sky Blue forces then budding would never quite blossom into a social and political power the way Christianity had in the eighteenth century.

The Me Decade of the 1970s, however, did produce one genuine revival of enduring significance. The revival's first major camp meetings took place on April 22, 1970, and if anything, these gatherings were antihumanist in nature. They shook up some fifteen hundred college campuses and ten thousand schools nationwide. In all, they engaged roughly 20 million people, mass enough to crystallize into a tectonic plate of considerable power. The revivalists dedicated the day not to God or even to man. No, this day belonged to the earth.

Agree or disagree with Michael Crichton, no one can deny the man his moxie. On September 15, 2003, the popular writer and producer rolled into the city where the plate's edge was sharpest, San Francisco, birthplace of the Sierra Club, Friends of the Earth, and any number of like-minded groups. There, before a full house at San Francisco's famed Commonwealth Club, the Harvard-trained medical doctor accused his orthodox fellow citizens of the one offense that could make them all wince—religious zealotry.

"Today it is said we live in a secular society in which many people—the best people, the most enlightened people—do not believe in any religion," said Crichton, taunting his audience

with a truism he knew to be false. No, even these "urban atheists" had a "religion of choice," and he identified that religion as
"environmentalism." Crichton did not merely describe the religious strains in environmentalism. He did what any enlightened
soul is wont to do when discussing religion. He made fun of it.
He mocked environmentalism as a "perfect twenty-first century
remapping of traditional Judeo-Christian beliefs." Had he accused his listeners of cannibalism or even capitalism he would
not have offended them as he did.

The new gospel has its own initial Eden, Crichton told
them, the unspoiled paradise of our aboriginal ancestors. It has
its own tree of knowledge, modern technology, whose fruit has
led to pollution and decay. It has its own day of judgment and
any number of doomsday scenarios that are hastening us there.
Eternal damnation awaits us, said Crichton, and then, like any
storefront preacher worth the rent money, he held out the great
"unless," the "unless" dearest to all their Bay Area hearts, "unless
we seek salvation, which is now called sustainability."

Other than the guys who throw McDonald's wrappers
out their car windows—they have them here too—everyone
in California is an environmentalist, and well they should be.
California is the most all-around attractive state in the union
(yes, New Jersey included). Like the Puritans in Massachusetts
Bay, however, Californians must talk and even think green to
reassure themselves that they are among the ecologically elect.
It is for this reason that, in the better circles, one hears the word
"sustainability" about as often as one hears the words "illegal
immigrants" in lesser ones. The difference, though, is that the
people who say "illegal immigrant"—the better people don't
use the phrase—know exactly what they mean. No one knows
what sustainability means.

When I checked, the first entry that came up on my Google
search—and it's not a parody—reads like this: "It is not possible
here to deal with all of the definitions and interpretations of

sustainability, including the view that in the face of an entropic universe, it is oxymoronic."

Okay, sure, that's what I thought all along. This same source then offers a consensus view that is a little closer to the graspable, namely development that "meets the need of the present without compromising the ability of future generations to meet their own needs." There is a ton of wiggle room in that definition, and most soft-core environmentalists wiggle as their wallets permit.

No county in the country is more sustainability-conscious than San Mateo County, due south of San Francisco. For ten years now it has been producing an amusing document called "Indicators for a Sustainable San Mateo County." The document evaluates thirty-one trends "that form a snapshot of sustainability." Given the political nature of the document, the county is willing to give itself a few pats on the back. So on the first page of the 2005 tenth-anniversary document, the county congratulates itself for "increased use of solar," "fewer contaminated sites," "more transit oriented development" and even "improved academic performance." It is not until page two that the county slips in a chart showing that a family of median income—higher in San Mateo than just about anywhere—can afford to buy only 12 percent of the homes in the county, down from 19 percent a decade ago, and exactly one-fourth the national average. Nor is there any acknowledgment that certain green measures—particularly restraints on building—are what have priced the middle class out of the county.

For all its vaguely socialist talk, sustainability is an indulgence of the affluent. On a routinely perfect September day, I had occasion to take an executive tour of sustainable heaven, the Kuleto Estate Vineyards in the very heart of bourgeois bohemia, Napa Valley. In 1992, Pat Kuleto, who had made a fortune in the restaurant business, bought 761 prime acres of ranch land on the eastern edge of Napa Valley and began to carve out his own

private Xanadu. This property was sufficiently large that he had
to pave a two-mile-long road to get from the highway to the
main house—excuse me, villa, as in *Villa Cucina. Cucina* means
"kitchen." It just sounds better in Italian.

At the top of the hill, overlooking the finely sculpted con-
tours of the vineyards, my group was served the most exqui-
site lunch I have ever eaten, all organic this and that, aided, of
course, by wine that even a beer drinker like myself could tell
didn't come out of a box. A young Kuleto acolyte then gave
us a walking tour of the property, never failing to remind us of
the concessions Kuleto had made to preserve the area's delicate
ecology.

In Napa Valley, however, such eco-chatter is little more
than foreplay, necessary but hardly sufficient. No, what saved the
tour from the unbearable smugness of most such tours was our
guide's enthusiastic reveling in Kuleto's excess: the thousands of
tons of rocks hauled up the twisting road by diesel-breathing
vehicles so Pat's house could fit the landscape; the re-creation
of the Loire canal on the property so Pat could cruise with his
lady friends; the helipad so Pat could fly in his poker buddies;
the pool with the soft edges that slope to the sunset where Pat
gets his nightly two hour Swedish massage in weather that is always idyllic. This was old school conspicuous consumption, and
I marveled at every indulgent detail of it.

"Ain't it great to be me?" the naked three-hundred-pounder
told the acolyte one night in the midst of his massage. Only a
Scrooge would think otherwise. Unfortunately, California has
many environmental Scrooges. To the hard-core, Kuleto might
as well have strip-mined the property.

Among the first to question man's dominion over nature
was Californian John Muir. "The world, we are told, was made
especially for humans," Muir muses at one point before adding
that this is "a presumption not supported by all the facts." Born
in Scotland in 1838, Muir moved to Wisconsin as a boy and

finally, after years of drifting, to California when he was nearly thirty. He had heard of Yosemite Valley, headed straight for it, and upon seeing it, discovered his life's purpose. A man of many talents—geologist, rancher, machinist, writer—Muir proved instrumental in preserving Yosemite, and went on to found the Sierra Club, still headquartered in San Francisco.

"All things are hitched to each other," Muir was wont to say, and this insight serves as something of a core truism for a movement that has come to be known as "deep ecology." Deep ecologists see the very contemplation of a human-centered planet, in Christopher Manes's words, as "anthropocentric arrogance."

Environmentalists come in more degrees than Masons. Like other deep ecologists, Manes has little but scorn for those paler shades of green that think people more important than plants. This includes aesthetes like Kuleto, dinner-party sustainers, backyard protectionists, philosophical humanists, Sierra Club–style "reformers," and especially the giddy New Age Gaia-worshippers, who continue to believe that "humans occupy a special place in the world."

Deep ecologists can get just as passionate about the inanimate parts of the ecosystem, such as streams and gorges and rocks, as they can about living things, such as cougars and kangaroo rats and *Limnanthes vinculans*. The last item, by the way, is the name for a quarter-inch-wide "endangered" weed. It made the news this past year when an ingenious "ecoteur" in Sebastopol, an hour north of San Francisco, reportedly planted it to stop "a controversial" $70 million housing development. What made the dwellings "controversial" was that they were to be built for humans.

The deep ecology passion does indeed take on religious dimension, and there is nothing subtle about it. Sympathizer Susan Zakin proudly likens deep ecologists to the Shakers, an eighteenth-century Quaker offshoot given to celibacy: "The women got tubal ligations," boasts Zakin of today's eco-Shakers, "and the men got vasectomies."

Given their priestly mission, children would only burden deep ecologists. "We are involved in the most sacred crusade on earth," Earth First's Dave Foreman preached to the "elect, the chosen" at the Sierra Club's International Assembly a few years back. That crusade had no lesser goal than to forestall judgment day. If we fail, said Foreman, "We'll be going down the same path of destruction that we've been on for 10,000 years of civilization."

As in all such movements, the hard-core both inspire and intimidate the soft, which is what Foreman did that day, rousing the Sierra Clubbers to a standing ovation. These are the kind of scenes that send shivers down a developer's back. When all the shades of green, or even most, fuse together, development of just about anything bogs down at the permitting phase.

What has especially troubled Crichton about this movement is its tendency to augment fact with faith and, in some cases, to disregard fact altogether. He didn't mention Paul Ehrlich by name, but he might as well have. No one in California has profited more from this indifference to facts than the good professor from Stanford. Ehrlich first came to national attention in 1968 with his breakthrough bestseller *The Population Bomb.* The book made him something of a multimedia star. He appeared no fewer than twenty times on the *Tonight Show* alone. His made-for-TV apocalyptic charm helped evangelize young Americans and bring them home to Darwin. Not surprisingly, Ehrlich was a founding father of Earth Day, the April 1970 revival referenced above.

To understand Ehrlich's continued appeal, it is useful to add a corollary to the ABETTO factor, specifically the ABATU factor. Those who disregard the obvious often compensate with *a blind acceptance of the unproven* or the unlikely or the untestable or, if one's faith is deep enough, the untrue. Ehrlich has dabbled in every which "u," and they all spell ABATU.

The Population Bomb begins with the startling claim, "The battle to feed all of humanity is already lost." Ehrlich then lays out three possible scenarios that could define the earth "in the next decade or so." In the most "cheerful" of these scenarios, Americans assume an unexpected "maturity of outlook," a new pope "gives his blessing to abortion," and only half a billion people die of famine. In the least cheerful scenario, worldwide famine leads to nuclear war, and the most intelligent creatures that survive are cockroaches. These are the 1970s Ehrlich was talking about. If my memory serves me, the most frightening plague to afflict humanity that decade was Disco.

Despite a lifetime of predictions as preposterously wrong as those in *The Population Bomb*, Ehrlich has suffered no loss of reputation among the faithful. He capped a career full of prestigious environmental awards with a $345,000 MacArthur Foundation grant and the Crafoord Prize from the Royal Swedish Academy of Sciences, the Nobel equivalent for environmentalists. Today, he is the Bing Professor of Population Studies and president of the Center for Conservation Biology at Stanford University. As Ehrlich's career bears witness, the ABATU factor has more play in environmental studies today than it does in religious studies. Academics hold the multiplication of loaves and fishes to a higher evidentiary standard than they do the multiplication of the people who ate them, and the weird thing is I am not kidding.

From Crichton's perspective, the one most critical variable that these believers have chosen to disregard is history. Almost to a person, they believe that life on the planet is less wholesome now than a century ago or a millennium ago and is getting less and less wholesome by the day. "We see ourselves," says Manes, "as men and women in a world declining towards ecological impoverishment."

The fact that technologists added thirty years onto the average American life in just one century counts for nothing among the eco-Shakers other than more mouths to feed. This empty despair Crichton finds maddening, especially when it drives policy decisions. "There is no Eden," Crichton had to remind his audience. "There never was."

One wonders whether John Muir would approve of his own followers. Although not a churchgoer, Muir brought a spiritual perspective to the environment, a deeply Christian one. Everywhere he looked he saw the handiwork of the biblical God. "The place seemed holy," he writes of Yosemite, "where one might hope to see God." Nor is he speaking in some metaphorical deistic way. At one juncture he stops to marvel at the nature around him and says, "Praise God from whom all blessings flow!"

Unlike his disbelieving heirs, Muir was not a zealot. In 1880 he married the richest girl in the East Bay town of Martinez, had two daughters, and settled down to manage the family ranch and fruit orchards. Upon his death in 1914, he left an estate valued at $250,000, the equivalent of about $5 million today anywhere except in greater San Francisco, where it would be worth about $20 million, in no small part due to the meddling of his followers in the real estate process. I don't think Muir had a pool that sloped to the sunset, but he did have indoor plumbing, which at that time was way cooler.

"The greatest challenge facing mankind is the challenge of distinguishing reality from fantasy, truth from propaganda," Crichton warned his audience. And as he made altogether clear, he had no confidence that even the go-as-you-please environmentalists bother making the effort.

★ 20. Altamont ★

We are all energy sinners, doomed to die.
   —Michael Crichton, *Commonwealth Club*

What an unhappy time 1969 proved to be in the life of California. The same year that gave us the rise of Charles Manson, the birth of the Crips, the death of James Pike, and the passage of the no-fault divorce law closed with the lethal rock concert at the Altamont Speedway.

On a gloomy December day, in that ill-omened year, Mick Jagger, doing his best imitation of a black blues singer, watched helplessly as his Hell's Angels security crew attacked a real black guy named Meredith Hunter in front of the stage. At the time, Jagger was singing "Sympathy for the Devil," an anthem of sorts.

"I've been around for a long, long year/Stole many a man's soul and faith," Jagger sang as he began to sense something amiss. "And I was round when Jesus Christ," Jagger hesitated, "Had his moment of doubt and pain." He could sing no more. "Everybody, just cool it," he pleaded, a feckless gesture captured in the film *Gimme Shelter*. It was too late. The Angels had stabbed and beaten Hunter past the point of cooling, his just one of four deaths that day at Altamont. Sixty miles east, back in San Francisco, Anton LaVey had to have been pleased.

As tragic as were the deaths of Sharon Tate on Cielo Drive and eighteen-year-old Meredith Hunter at Altamont, the Californians most widely mourned that year weren't people exactly, but birds, the 3,686 birds estimated to have died in the great Santa Barbara oil spill of January 1969. I don't exaggerate the grief. "Never in my long lifetime have I ever seen such an aroused populace at the grassroots level," observed the editor of the *Santa Barbara NewsPress*. That spill proved unfortunate not only for the state's birds but also for its boosters.

This fall from ecological grace deflated the ebullient Californian spirit. Repentant, citizens sacrificed their faith in progress for a joyless new faith. As Crichton argues, this one had little use for reason or facts—like the fact that today's high-tech rigs withstood even Rita and Katrina, or that since 1969 the existing oil rigs in California have cumulatively spilled less oil than the natural bubble-up in a week at Santa Barbara.

Locals persuaded themselves that they could enjoy the fruits of California living only if they didn't propagate, if they didn't plant little power seeds for future generation. With bipartisan support, California quickly outlawed all new offshore drilling for both oil and natural gas. The natural gas ban had something of a downside in that the state was urging that all new power plants be fueled by natural gas. The building of new hydroelectric and nuclear plants, in any case, was very nearly outlawed. The hydroelectric plants, which still produce 15 percent of the state's energy, produced it so cheaply that California once considered giving it away. The state's two nuclear plants, which produce 20 percent of the state's power, likewise do so nearly as cleanly and cheaply. None of this logic fazed the deep ecologists. The same folks who have made building subdivisions a pain have made the building of even a gas-fired plant a nightmare.

If the state's gloomy greening set it up for the traumatic 2000–2001 energy crisis—by 1995, Californians were already paying 35 percent more for energy than the national average—the proximate cause was entirely political. All observers should have been wary of a bill that passed both houses unanimously as did 1996's A.B. 1890, the so-called energy deregulation bill. To get that kind of support meant giving something to everyone, and that's exactly what the legislators did.

To please the free market people, at least those not paying much attention, the bill promised "deregulation." In fact, it didn't deregulate. It restructured. It put the market in the hands of a state-managed entity. The Stalinist name of this entity, Centralized Power Exchange, sent chills down every sentient free market spine, but the concept reassured the big-government types. To placate the consumer, the bill put a cap on retail prices. And to appease the environmentalists, it imposed an expensive and convoluted nitrogen oxide emission permitting process on producers.

For its first two years, the Central Power Exchange functioned reasonably well. In the year 2000, however, an unlikely series of events—unusually cold winter, unusually hot summer, pipeline explosion, drought-related hydroelectric reductions— put a huge demand on a diminished supply of natural gas, now the fuel behind 49 percent of California's electric power. To aggravate affairs, the nitrous oxide regulations choked supply and pushed prices even higher.

As a result, the state's private utilities were hit with severe price spikes and were unable to pass cost increases along to customers. Not feeling the pinch, customers continued to use power pretty much as they pleased. In the depth of the crisis, more than half of those surveyed by the *L.A. Times* did not plan to modify their use of heating or air-conditioning and 60 percent had no plans to limit the use of electrical equipment or appliances. 74 percent, however, were turning off their lights when not in use, the presumed Californian limit to self-sacrifice.

The results were predictably unpleasant. The utilities had to turn to the unsentimental spot market to meet the unceasing demand. In that market they play hardball, and they stuck it to the tree-squatting softballers from California. Blackouts began in June 2000 and persisted on and off, here and there, through May 2001. Energy prices stabilized by September 2001, but by that time, Pacific Gas & Electric had already filed for bankruptcy.

In any other state, a crisis of this magnitude would have inspired at least a little bit of soul searching. In California, however, environmentalism had become a faith, an identity. It would be easier to bar mitzvah Osama than to de-green a coastal Californian. At the depth of the state's power crisis in February 2001, a full 12 percent of the respondents in an *L.A. Times* poll opposed the building of any kind of power plant in the state of California. Projected out, that is roughly 3 million voters and/or protestors and/or ecoteurs.

The deep ecologists have a sympathetic ear among the not so deep. Despite the very real threat to the state's economy from crippling blackouts, 60 percent of those surveyed in that same poll still opposed the building of a nuclear plant, 64 percent opposed easing environmental regulations, and 64 percent opposed the lifting of the ban on offshore drilling. With nearly 50 percent or more of respondents "strongly opposed" to all three measures, the state would seem to be locked into energy dependency for the foreseeable future.

Nothing would dent the faith of the Greens. In their moments of doubt and pain, they could always count on Hollywood to perform a reassuring miracle or two. In his good-looking film, *Enron: The Smartest Guys in the Room,* Alex Gibney does just that. He somehow manages to shift the blame for the energy debacle from California to—where else?—Texas. This took a certain sleight of hand. Gibney concedes that "the section on California is much longer in the film than it is in the book," Bethany McLean and Peter Elkind's *The Smartest Guys in the Room.*

Since the shapers of opinion in California work largely within a closed loop of the like-minded, they can say silly things about the enemy with near impunity, Republicans especially. Gibney, for instance, singles out George W. Bush and Arnold Schwarzenegger for attack, a neat stroke of chronological jujitsu, given that President Bush took office seven months after the crisis flared up and Governor Schwarzenegger took office three years after that. And, of course, no California polemic would be complete without a poke at Ronald Reagan, this one gratuitous even by local standards. For reasons clear only to Gibney, he edits Reagan into the film saying, "Government isn't the solution, it's the problem."

"You know," Gibney gropes to explain the Reagan insertion, "because the government is a way that people have to express their will. And when you cast doubt on the government and essentially eviscerate it, then you don't really have a democracy." Huh? For those who know anything about A.B. 1890, the bill that prompted the energy crisis, Reagan's words seem altogether spot on, but Hollywood makes movies for those who don't want to know.

Freed from blame, and temporarily flush with power, green Californians went back to the work of getting more green. The deep ecologists were eager to erase the state's original sin, the Hetch Hetchy Reservoir, the creation of which in the Yosemite National Park nearly a century ago broke John Muir's heart. This idea has support beyond the fringe. The state's energy secretary first proposed it in the 1980s, and the state's Department of Water Resources recently completed a report on it. That the reservoir provides water to 2.4 million people in the Bay Area and clean, renewable power for nearly as many matters, to some, not a whit. The group that is pushing for the dam's destruction titled their report "Paradise Regained."

To replace the energy lost, the deep ecologists look to other renewable energy sources, such as solar and wind. Under current state regulations, in fact, energy producers must increase the ratio of energy pulled from these sources by 1 percent per year until 2017, when presumably 20 percent of the state's energy would be renewable. Without doubt, these regulations will be made more rigorous when plans are completed under new antigreenhouse gas legislation signed by Governor Schwarzenegger in the weeks before the 2006 election.

And this takes us all back to the scene of the crime, Altamont. The crime I refer to, however, is not the murder of some unfortunate black dude nearly forty years ago. No, who cares about that? The crime is an ongoing one. At the Altamont pass, you see, producers have installed some seven thousand wind turbines. The turbines provide the renewable energy that the state mandates. Unfortunately, the turbines kill some of the dumber or more daring of the birds that fly through the pass. In fact, the turbines kill more birds *each* year than were killed in the entire 1969 Santa Barbara oil spill. Local ecologists want the killers brought to justice. Said Jeff Miller, spokesman for the Center for Biological Diversity, "We're asking the judge to throw the book at them."

And who said government wasn't the solution?

★ 21. Eel River Valley ★

The breed of man / Has been queer from the start. It
looks like a botched experiment that has run wild
and ought to be stopped
  —Robinson Jeffers, "Orca"

In 1997, to ward off the chainsaws of the Pacific Lumber Company, the twenty-three-year-old Julia Butterfly Hill climbed into a six-hundred-year-old Northern California red-wood tree named Luna and remained there an astonishing 738 days. As it happens, she had been in a car accident a year before she began her tree sit and suffered mild brain damage. Her fellow "arboreal activists" apparently didn't notice. If environmentalism is a religion, they quickly beatified Ms. Hill by electing her to the "Ecology Hall of Fame."

Although raised Catholic, Hill's mother and father converted to Baptist and later to nondenominational Christian. Her father, in fact, became a traveling preacher of an evangelical stripe. That background, Hill believes, has helped her keep a "core sense of the sacred." Like still another Hazel Motes, she has built upon that core a wonderfully mindless Church without Christ, complete with its own origins story. "In the beginning," she declares just a bit presumptuously, "God's original intention was to hang out in a beautiful garden with two naked vegetarians. What a great vision!"

From those halcyon days in Paradise it has been all downhill. "Our choices have led us away from that Garden of Eden," says Hill, and now the nation rushes headlong "towards this pretty horrific ending." At home, she claims, America has "indiscriminately" turned old-growth ecosystems into "toxic dump lands" and handed its food needs over to "big-biz agricultural farming."

Abroad, it has created "the largest death machine humankind has ever known," one that kills innocents as indiscriminately as it kills plants and animals back home. In a nutshell, we Americans have sinned enough against the environment to deserve whatever tough love Mother Gaia dishes out.

Ms. Hill was one person I really wanted to talk to. After some finagling, I did manage to get through to a guy named Paul, her gatekeeper. As Paul explained, a whole lot of media people want to talk to Julia. She was then preparing for a new fast and tree-sit, this time in a Los Angeles walnut tree with the celebrity company of the former folk singer Joan Baez and the former mermaid Daryl Hannah. The threesome and its allies hoped to keep the property's owner, a guy named Ralph Horowitz, from building a warehouse on a fourteen-acre "people's garden" in the midst of a homely old industrial district. Horowitz offered to sell the property to the gardeners and their celebrity friends at a fair price, but they couldn't quite raise the dough, so they decided to squat instead.

Given the media demand on Ms. Hill's time, Paul established some conditions. First and foremost, I had to promise that the book at hand would be published on some esoteric variant of recyclable paper. That, I told Paul, I could not guarantee. He then asked if I were sufficiently "passionate about this issue" to demand that the publisher use this certain paper. I told him I would ask the publisher, but that I would be lying if I said I were passionate about it. He was stunned. How could I not be passionate? I told him that I spend much of my summer back east, which is more heavily forested now than it was two centuries ago and getting more so every year. I stopped short of telling him that the deer had become a royal pain in the ass.

"Those aren't virgin forests," he explained. I wanted to say that Luna is only six hundred years old in a state that has been treed and peopled for at least six thousand years, which makes it about as virgin as Madonna, but I was not in a position to argue.

I was there to wangle an interview with Ms. Hill. "Okay, Paul, sure."

Paul and I spoke for nearly an hour on all manner of issues. He told me that Julia "walks the walk," and I could not disagree. Two years in a tree was enough to convince me if not of her sanity at least of her sincerity. He also informed me that a movie was soon to be made about Julia's life "on the first ever green set." Good for her! I just hoped it had a happier ending than the last movie I saw about a self-described California "eco-warrior."

In Werner Herzog's documentary *Grizzly Man*, the grizzlies not only kill Malibu actor manqué and bear enthusiast Timothy Treadwell (né Timothy Dexter) and his unfortunate girlfriend Amie Huguenard, but they actually eat them clear to the bone. Although the audio was recorded, the bears had the good manners to consume the pair off camera.

Looking for a way in with Paul, I shared the fact that my younger daughter was a vegetarian, a vegan even. Then I made a fatal miscalculation. My daughter had joked with me recently about how nonvegan vegetarians "will never know the pain of driving by a Dairy Queen and not being able to stop." I shared her jest with Paul. He did not find it amusing. Julia does not discriminate between vegans and vegetarians, I was told. About vegetarians, "about everyone," Julia was "nonjudgmental." Even about those folks who created "the largest death machine humankind has ever known," I wanted to interject. But again I bit my tongue.

Little good did my restraint do me. I never got the interview. Paul's comments did, however, give substance to a frequent response to my "what's the matter" question. As many as a half-dozen people—most of them ex–New Yorkers, by the way—told me that their fellow Californians lack a sense of humor. "They are nice," one person added, "often too nice, but they are definitely not funny."

Not having enough experience to judge for myself, I decided to test this thesis scientifically. Admittedly, the test would have been more objective had I been able to find an official list of funny people, but absent that, I contrived a list of my own. What follows, as best I can tell, are the funniest comic actors of the last thirty years, as determined by their success in film comedies. I have also included their points of origin.

Jim Carrey	Ontario, Canada
Eddie Murphy	Queens, New York
Woody Allen	Brooklyn, New York
Adam Sandler	Brooklyn, New York
John Belushi	Chicago, Illinois
Goldie Hawn	Washington, D.C.
Bill Murray	Chicago, Illinois
Lily Tomlin	Detroit, Michigan
Robin Williams	Bloomfield, Michigan
Chevy Chase	Woodstock, New York
John Candy	Ontario, Canada
Steve Martin	Waco, Texas
Chris Farley	Madison, Wisconsin
Richard Pryor	Peoria, Illinois
Dan Aykroyd	Ontario, Canada
Burt Reynolds	Lansing. Michigan
Mike Myers	Ontario, Canada
Billy Crystal	Long Island, New York
Whoopi Goldberg	New York, New York
Michael J. Fox	Alberta, Canada

One out of every nine North Americans lives in California. Let's do some math here. With twenty people on the list, the odds of finding a Californian on the list, presuming an equal distribution of humor, are roughly eleven to one, but there are none. How worrisome is this? Well, the peevish and less peopled Canada has five people on the list. That's how worrisome.

Perhaps, the disconsolate Californian is now thinking, my fellow Golden Staters have saved their sense of humor for television, which is also based largely in Southern California. What follows is a top-of-the-head list of TV comedians whose names have gone above the marquee, also in the last thirty years.

Bill Cosby	Philadelphia, Pennsylvania
Jerry Seinfeld	Brooklyn, New York
David Letterman	Indianapolis, Indiana
Roseanne Barr	Salt Lake City, Utah
Kelsey Grammer	Colonna, New Jersey
Jay Leno	Andover, Massachusetts
Drew Carey	Cleveland, Ohio
Rosie O'Donnell	Commack, New York
Ray Romano	Queens, New York
Jon Stewart	New York, New York

With thirty names on what media types will have to concede is a reasonably fair list, the data grow convincing. The odds are more than thirty-two to one that Californians are, in fact, less amusing than their fellow North Americans. What would hike those odds even more are the two key variables that we have yet to factor in—access and nepotism. If anything, these should make it much more likely that a Californian would be among the top thirty, but such is not the case.

With a few more films under his belt, Will Ferrell of Irvine, California, will deserve a place at the table. And the case can be made that Steve Martin came of age in Orange County even if he spent his early years in Texas, but otherwise this list lends some pseudoscientific credibility to the "no sense of humor" contention. The list also suggests that nepotism only works on the dramatic side of the ledger. Hollywood parents can get their kids a job, even make them stars—Jane Fonda, Michael Douglas, Gwyneth Paltrow, and Sean Penn attest to this—but they can't make them even mildly amusing. Jane Fonda, Michael Douglas, Gwyneth Paltrow, and Sean Penn attest to this as well.

It is likely that maddening traffic, mind-rotting drugs, minifamilies, maximum divorce, and a shortage of ethnic groups that can tell jokes in English all help contribute to the irony deficiency. Then too, it is hard to be amusing when the world is coming to an end, and only eco-warriors like yourself stand in the way of apocalypse.

An already classic episode of the contrarian adult cartoon TV show *South Park* illustrates this last point. As the plot unfolds, young Kyle's father, Gerald Broflovski, buys a new hybrid car, the "Pious." Of course, he drives it endlessly around town so people can see how wonderfully green he is. "I just couldn't sit back and be a part of destroying the earth anymore," he tells one bystander. When Mr. Broflovski starts handing out "awareness citations" to SUV drivers, the town of South Park, Colorado, decides it has had piety enough.

"We need to be where everyone is motivated and progressive like us!" Mr. Broflovski tells his stunned family. "Start getting your things packed, boys! The Broflovksi family is moving to San Francisco!" Young Stan pleads with Mr. Broflovski not to leave town with his best friend Kyle in tow, but Mr. Broflovski proves to be as nonjudgmental as Julia B. Hill. "I'm sorry, Stan, but unfortunately you live in a small-minded town filled with ignorant boobs."

The show unwinds in pure *South Park* fashion. In the way of a PG summary, a "smug cloud" rising from San Francisco threatens to merge with a smug cloud rising over Los Angeles, a direct emission from the Oscar ceremony where George

Clooney has just given Hollywood "credit for the civil rights movement." These clouds threaten to form "a perfect storm of self-satisfaction" until the unlikely young Cartman saves the day. For the full scatological effect, the reader can check out episode 141.

There is something about going green that just flat-out kills a good buzz. With the exception of a few of the old-time monkeywrenchers like novelist Edward Abbey and Dave Foreman of Earth First!, hard-core environmentalists and their camp followers compose one of the least amusing sects on the planet this side of the Wahhabi. Just ask an architect or a developer.

★ 22. Mount Washington ★

These activists are really convinced that everyone is
supposed to do the same things they do and love it as
much.

—Tomas Osinski, architect

In 1999, the Self-Realization Fellowship (SRF) decided to move the body of Paramahansa Yogananda from
the famed Forest Lawn Cemetery to a soon-to-be-constructed
shrine. For those of you who may not remember, Yogananda was
the guy who brought self-realization to California, a feat as mo-
mentous, locally at least, as the introduction of air-conditioning
or oranges. This shrine was to be part of an expansion of the
SRF monastic center on the pastoral peak of LA's Mount Washington, its headquarters since 1925.

Vigilant as they are, the deeper ecologists in the Mount
Washington neighborhood asked for a slight modification of
the SRF shrine plans—namely, no shrine at all. "It's too bad
that [SRF] wants to present this as a religious issue," said activist
Clare Marter Kenyon at the time. "It's all about development."
Wanting to be good neighbors, even though they had been the
first ones in the neighborhood, the SRF people quietly dropped
their plans.

After successfully blocking the SRF expansion in 1999,
Kenyon and her allies turned their gaze on the ordinary Joes and
Josés on Mount Washington. "They started looking for other
noble causes," said Mount Washington resident Tomas Osinski,
"like taking other people's property rights." By 2006, Mount
Washington had become the site of an ecological civil war, and
Kenyon was again leading the charge. Ironies abound in such
fights. If Kenyon attacked the SRF move as a religious ploy, she

finds her own movement now being attacked as a "religion." That, at least, is what Osinski calls it. He can find no better explanation for her zeal. Ms. Kenyon, like Ms. Hill, chose not to talk to me, so I am left to interpret that zeal as best I can.

Mount Washington is one of those offbeat neighborhoods that make Los Angeles the nation's most intriguing city. Those who do not live in LA, and some who do, would have a hard time envisioning a community just ten minutes north of downtown and yet so removed that 140 contemplative yogis can live there in something like peace.

My walk with Osinski from his home midway up the hill to an undeveloped parcel he owns near the top took us nearly half an hour at a brisk pace. No cars passed us in the course of our walk. At the summit, you could still film a cowboy movie if you were of a mind to. From the top of this hill you can also see other hilltops in roughly comparable states of development to the north and east.

Osinski is one of those offbeat people who help make the neighborhood and the city so interesting. The wiry, bearded architect came to the United States, "a place of freedom," twenty-some years ago. He had wearied of spending so much negative energy just to survive the nonsense of communist Poland. "I wanted to do some positive things," he told me. Osinksi got off to a good start, going to work for Frank Gehry, who had left Ontario years before for Los Angeles, where he would become the best-known architect in the world.

Osinski's short-term objective has been to undo an "Interim Control Ordinance" passed by the city council at the insistence of the Mount's greener residents. This ordinance has threatened to impose elaborate bureaucratic restraints on building and remodeling. The effect would be to slow or stop development of all land in affected hillside areas, including the properties of the area's struggling middle-class homeowners, many of whom are Hispanic.

This slowdown would have the ultimate effect of reducing the value of many Mount Washington properties, especially undeveloped ones like Osinski's hilltop parcel. Osinski predicted that once the value dropped, conservancy groups could buy hillside property and preserve it in its presumably natural state. The ordinance pulled this veteran nonsense-fighter from an apolitical lull and forced him to the ramparts once again.

"This lunacy is spreading," said Osinski. He attributed the spread not only to the activists, but also to the politicians who like the power that comes with arbitrary regulation. "Their idea is to make the law so murky and complex," he confided, "that everything has to be done on a case-by-case basis."

Osinski has witnessed these cases up close. After nearly four years with Gehry, Osinski struck out on his own. Among his showcase projects is the home in which he lives with his wife and two daughters, a seventy-eight-thousand-dollar fixer-upper when he bought it in 1985 and now an architectural and environmental tour de force worth perhaps twenty times that much. The outward-looking home sits in an exotic wonderland of Osinki's design, abounding in tropical plant life from seemingly half the countries on the globe. This self-watering, self-cooling, fire-breaking garden creates a neat little biosphere that makes even air-conditioning unnecessary.

And there's the rub. Not only have the Mount's deep ecologists declared war on growth, but they have also declared war on things that grow, at least certain kinds of things. "They know exactly what nature is supposed to be," Osinski lamented, "and how we are supposed to interact with nature." Communities around the state are now mandating that all plants be native to California, and the pressure is building in Los Angeles to pass similar laws. "It's the same way they feel about people," joked Osinski. "Everything went to hell since Columbus landed."

An ordinance of this nature would essentially tag all of Osinski's exotic plants as illegal aliens. As Osinski pointed out, most of the vegetation we associate with California, including palm and cypress trees, comes from elsewhere. Indeed, cypress trees originated in the Triassic period millions of years before there even was a California. When I asked the motive behind the antiexotic movement, he explained that the opposition offers "no good explanation except that their way is better. Everyone knows that."

To counter the activists, Osinksi sent letters with supporting documents to the U.S. attorney general, among other prosecutors, "demanding criminal investigation of racketeering to artificially lower the private properties value." In addition to local activists, he cited the Santa Monica Mountains Conservancy and the Los Angeles City Council. Try as they might, the activists had a hard time making the ecosensitive Osinski and the modest Hispanic homeowners who supported him look like the bad guys in this seismic smackdown.

Six months after I visited Osinski, I checked in for a progress report, and the news was surprisingly good. Of course, no prosecutor plans to investigate anything, but Osinksi had put the local activists and their allies on the defensive, and they abandoned "The Project." Santa Monica Mountains Conservancy is apparently going to buy the land on the open market as any other purchaser would have to. To save face, the city council passed an Interim Control Ordinance, but just for a part of the proposed area and without any real teeth. "We'll see how it goes," said Osinski, "but it is very rewarding to bump the big guys."

It's a whole lot easier to bump the big guys if you've got big guys doing the bumping. Developers Haas & Haynie likely had this mind when they assembled a partnership group to build a new golf resort in Santa Clara County. As the partners surely expected, the county's more prominent environmental organizations objected to the very idea of the course. At a 1996 public hearing the Committee for Green Foothills, among others, warned that the development, now called the CordeValle

Golf Club, could have a serious impact on water quality, water supply, and prime agricultural soils, not to mention the general contentment of the California tiger salamander and the western pond turtle, both allegedly endangered.

The club's partners repeatedly insisted that the club had any number of "public benefits" including a minimum of 50 percent tee times available for public play. They also promised to build a series of ponds for the disgruntled turtles and salamanders. And sure enough, they got their permit. In fact, the club opened for play in the year 2000, record California time for an unwanted development. Better still, it only cost $250,000 to join, chump change for the denizens of nearby Silicon Valley at the peak of the Internet bubble.

In 2002–03, the *San Jose Mercury News* ran a series of articles on CordeValle. It seems the partners never got around to building those ponds, had filed only one of their annual environmental reports in the last seven years, and had all but eliminated public access, cutting it down to the occasional charity tournament. In a land where the law, as Osinski describes it, is "murky and complex," the powerful have a decided advantage in clawing their way through. The partners, to be sure, had hired any number of lobbyists and lawyers to do the dirty work, but it matters less who is hired than who does the hiring. Developers Haas & Haynie were prudent enough to recruit, among their handful of partners, real estate tycoon Paul Pelosi and his lovely bride, Nancy, she of congressional fame. For Pelosi, we're told, the environment is not merely an issue, "It's an ethic, it's a value." Yes, of course, Nancy, I'll buy that, but do you think John Muir would?

★ 23. East of Indio ★

We all love the environment, but we have placed
creatures above people. A rat is a rat.
    —Sonny Bono, mayor, congressman, Palm Springs

I met Gene at a swell little dinner party in Laguna Beach.
He knew why I was in town and sought me out before
dinner. "If you really want to know what's the matter with California," he confided, "give me a call sometime."

Gene is the president of a land development company. Although the group gathered was eclectic as California could be—I
met, for instance, my first right-wing, middle-aged, Jewish, artist/
surfer—Gene sensed that many of those gathered would not appreciate his message. He was right. When the question of "what's
the matter" came up, several in attendance suggested overpopu-
lation, unlimited development, indifference to the environment,
too many cars, and other greenish concerns. Gene held his fire.

I caught up with Gene later, and he made his case. He has
been in real estate for the last twenty-five years and land development the last fifteen. His company buys raw land, engineers
it, divides it, and sells it to homebuilders. In this business, time is
money. As he lamented, projects that used to take six months to
"permit"—and still do take six months in states as close as Ari-
zona—now take two to three years. This delay and the attendant
legal fees not only add cost to the homes that do get built, but
they also "choke the supply pipeline." The resulting supply defi-
cit adds more cost still to the homebuyer. "I know builders who
simply won't come to California," said Gene ruefully.

Hard to believe, but in the 1970 song "I am . . . I said" Neil
Diamond sang about a Los Angeles where "palm trees grow and
the rents are low," and no one doubted him. In fact, as late as

1973 home prices in Southern California were below the national average. In *City of Quartz*, Mike Davis witheringly details the trends that flipped the curve. These include the descent of the neighborhood associations into NIMBYism (Not In My Back Yard—another California neologism) as well as the almost universal embrace of Earth Day–inspired regulation, national and local. Davis, however, was writing in 1990. Gene insists that the situation has gotten much worse in the last ten years. He attributes the problem not so much to new regulations as to new *regulators*. As he tells it, and his observation makes sense, eco-activists have worked their way up and through agencies like the U.S. Fish and Wildlife Service and the California Department of Fish and Game.

"If you've got a wheel rut, you better hope it doesn't rain," says Gene. "Otherwise, you've got a navigable waterway." He wasn't kidding. To protect some standing water on a recent Ventura County project, the regulators forced him to give up at least six roadside acres.

To test Gene's contention, I decided to track housing affordability from a decade ago and see how it compares to 2006. The results are eye-popping.

City	1995	2006
San Francisco/San Mateo	20.8	7.8
Los Angeles/Long Beach	46.3	1.9
Santa Barbara	47.5	3.2
Modesto	70.9	3.9
San Diego	40.6	5.2
Riverside	52.3	8.4
Salinas	25.1	12.7
Bakersfield	75.4	16.5
Redding	52.3	14.6

In 1995, a median-income family could have afforded to buy nearly 50 percent of the homes in the LA metro. In mid-2006, it was down to one in fifty. Once-affordable Central Valley cities like Modesto and Bakersfield had become no more affordable than Washington or New York. This is not due in any meaningful way to population growth. Texas grew nearly 50 percent more quickly than California during this period without market malfunction. In 2006, Dallas residents of median income could still afford more than 60 percent of the area's homes.

By the time this book is published, a housing market collapse may possibly play havoc with these numbers. In fact, as of early 2007, reports were showing a flattening of at least the Bay Area market. But a flattening brings on a whole new set of worries, and a crash even more, and unless the root causes are addressed, the relief—to buyers, not sellers—is likely to be temporary in any case.

As Gene explained, the cities and counties try to help. Most have streamlined their permitting processes. Still, they fear lawsuits and the sympathetic courts that hear them, so they tend to overreact to potential problems. Nor does the state legislature do much good. The Democrats who control both houses sit on their hands for fear of offending their greenish base. That base, however, has no fear of offending the Democrats. "If they gathered to form a firing squad," said one eco-warrior of the progressive politicos, "they would assemble in a circle." The right errs in thinking that environmentalists form one big happy left-wing family. They're not a family, and they're never happy.

I had hoped to follow one large development project through the permitting process, but two factors made that well-nigh impossible. One was the length of the process, and the second was the fear of retribution. I offered Gene anonymity after I began to hear caution creep into our discussion, and he accepted it. Other developers would not talk at all. One developer, Harvey Niskala of the Glorious Land Co. (GLC), initially agreed to let me track his project but then thought better of it, and I could scarcely blame him. Still, the development in question intrigued me, and I did a little investigation on my own.

Niskala practices what he calls "environmentally sustainable" architecture. Six years ago, he and his colleagues bought a ten-square-mile parcel fifteen miles east of Indio and have made plans to turn it into a retirement community for semiactive boomers. As projected, "Paradise Valley" will house some forty thousand people in a community that irrigates with reclaimed water, protects the migration routes of the local wildlife, and, in general, "tread[s] lightly on the land."

Deep ecologists and their allies hate the project for any number of reasons, but the reason most frequently cited is its location near the southern boundary of Joshua Tree National Park. Being totally unfamiliar with this part of the world, I decided to drive out and take a look.

Indio lies about 125 miles east of Los Angeles, and about twelve miles east of Palm Springs, on I-10. Fifteen miles beyond Indio is fifteen miles beyond the end of the world as we know it. There is not even an exit for the first fifteen miles on the interstate, the only road east. This vast expanse of empty scrubland stretches more or less to suburban Phoenix, 240 miles further east.

For those people who like their scrubland packaged, the federal government has kindly set aside an area roughly two and a half times the size of Los Angeles called Joshua Tree National Park. I imagine that regulars can tell the park's twelve hundred square miles from the scores of thousands of square miles around it, but even the Park Service admits that Joshua Tree "may appear bleak and drab." On this score, I have no argument.

Curt Sauer, Joshua Tree National Park superintendent, would seem to bear out Gene's contention that the eco-activists have burrowed into the bureaucracies. Sauer has publicly argued against Paradise Valley. He has cited, among other grievances, that the project would increase the population not just of humans—bad enough—but of "human-dependent ravens." These poor corrupted birds in turn prey upon juvenile desert tortoises.

I would have thought that the tortoises might have found some other place to hang out along the equally attractive 240-mile stretch to Phoenix, but Sauer, I presume, knows more about this than I. The fact that a housing shortage pushed area home prices up 30 percent in the preceding year, however, did not seem to bother him a bit. This is a man who has his priorities in order.

Sauer has good company. The Sierra Club and five other associations have formed a coalition to block the project as well, arguing that it "violates recent federal court rulings which ordered the U.S. Fish and Wildlife Service to protect critical habitat for endangered species recovery." This nicely matches Gene's nightmare scenario of a three-front war—the associations, the courts, and the bureaucracies all allied in an axis of the litigious.

I might have been more sympathetic to the turtle's plight had I not made my first visit to Palm Springs on this same trip. What a pleasant surprise! The town's mile-or-so-long, two-block-wide town center area struck me as among the most attractive and accessible anywhere in the world, with virtually all of the eateries spilling onto the sidewalk and a ten-thousand-foot high mountain due west lending shade. I think if a desert had free will it would gladly choose to be a Palm Springs.

Helping spark the town's revival is a growing gay population, now estimated to be proportionately higher than San Francisco's. The town that once elected Sonny Bono mayor recently elected Ron Oden, who is black and gay. Despite appearances, however, local politics have not shifted much. Oden is aggressively moderate and business-friendly. From what I am told, he represents something of a norm among Palm Springs gays, many of whom have fled the excesses of San Francisco for the orderly calm of the desert. Walking the main streets of town, one does not even sense any particular gay cultural presence.

Steven Nary certainly didn't. The naïve young basketball player spent the last two years of his high-school career at Cathedral City High. Only about five miles from downtown Palm Springs, the school might as well have been five light-years for all Steven knew of local society. He would not learn about this society until his extraordinary 1999 trial in San Francisco for the murder of Juan Pifarre, the fifty-three-year-old man who had sat down next to the young sailor at the Palladium in North Beach in 1996.

"How many gay bars and gay resorts are on that street?" asked prosecutor John Farrell, referring to Highway 111, the main drag of Palm Springs and all the cities east of it, including Cathedral City.

"I couldn't tell you," said Nary.

"So it's news to you," Farrell asked sarcastically after some additional sparring, "that there are these gay bars and gay resorts in Cathedral City?"

"Very much so," said Nary honestly.

Farrell proceeded to reel off the names of one gay club after another, asking if Nary knew of it: the Villa Resort, the World Wide, the Construction Company, the Hidden Joy, Daddy Warbucks, Shades, Cuddles, the Carriage Trade, Rocks, the Little Bar. When Nary interjected at one point to ask if Farrell were talking about Palm Springs, he snapped, "I'm talking about Cathedral City, sir."

Farrell also asked rhetorically, "If you go out Dinah Shore Drive, take a left down Date Palm Drive and go two blocks you're at Highway 111, right?"

Nary did not know the town well enough to know Farrell was inventing his own geography. In fact, Highway 111 is nearly two miles down Date Palm Drive, not two blocks. Besides, Nary lived in Thousand Palms, five miles north and east of the high school, in the complete opposite direction from the 111 strip. "When I lived there," Nary answered ingenuously, "it was mainly school, go back home, sometimes stay over at trainer's house or what not." At the time, Nary didn't have a car or even a driver's license. He knew nothing of the area's discreet gay social life.

No matter. For this San Francisco jury, the picture Farrell painted of Nary was that of a devious young predator who tracked the comings and goings of the desert gay the way ravens track those of the desert tortoise. There was no record at all or even a hint of this kind of behavior in Nary's background, but the San Francisco jury had no way of knowing. Nary's public defender did not have the wherewithal to respond.

When I visited Cathedral City, I did not notice any particular gay presence. I stopped by Cathedral City High, located on the world's only street named in honor of Dinah Shore. A bright, sprawling, Mission-style school, Cathedral High is as open to the world as LA's Fremont High is closed. I talked to Gloria Hernandez, the assistant principal, and Mark Morrison, the athletic director. Both spoke of Nary as an easy-going, mild-tempered kid, who got along with everyone at a school that was perhaps two-thirds Hispanic.

Although not the most focused of students, said Morrison, Nary "ran well and played hard" on the school's championship basketball team. When I asked Morrison why the school or the town did not rally to Nary's defense, he could give me no firm answer. Reading between the lines, I sensed how intimidating a city like San Francisco could be, especially on an issue that threatened to ruffle local gay feathers. Given the charge at hand, Nary could not have picked any two less accommodating cities to have come from and gone to.

There was one man, however, whom the legal process did not intimidate. "Celebrity trainer" Artie Funair had worked with some of the biggest names in sports and show business and had served as longtime personal assistant to Frank Sinatra. On the walls of his Cathedral City den, he had a priceless collection of memorabilia, including pictures of himself with Vince Lombardi,

Joe DiMaggio, Chuck Connors, Jerry West, Wilt Chamberlain, and even O. J. Simpson. When I met Funair in April 2006, the feisty former U.S. Marine still seemed ready to hit the beaches for a good cause.

"He never got in any trouble and minded his own business," said Funair of Nary, whom he called "one of the nicest young athletes I've trained." Outraged by the so-called 1999 trial, Funair signed a sworn affidavit a year later contesting the one prosecutorial point that he believed to be pure fabrication, the contention that any number of gay bars and clubs flourished in an area within blocks of Cathedral City High School. "The nearest gay bars and bathhouses are at least TWO MILES AWAY IN THE OPPOSITE DIRECTION," he wrote emphatically, adding that Farrell's claim to the contrary was "a perjury and a fraud." By this time, though, no one was paying attention. All eyes had turned to the desert tortoise.

In October 2006, "living legend" Artie Funair died of a heart attack. Two weeks after Funair's death I received a letter from Nary. "Artie is a friend who treated me like a grandson," he wrote unsuspectingly. "If I needed anything, he would help me. He was there for so many athletes. I miss him a lot and I hope he is doing O.K." No one had yet told Nary of Funair's death. Such is life in Pleasant Valley S.P.

★ 24. Whittier ★

By 2050, 60 percent of Italians will have no brothers, no sisters, no cousins, no aunts, no uncles. The big Italian family, with papa pouring the vino and mama spooning out the pasta down an endless table of grandparents and nieces and nephews, will be gone, no more, dead as the dinosaurs.
—Mark Steyn, *America Alone*

Richard Nixon wasn't born in Whittier, California, but his daughter Tricia was. Her father moved to Whittier as an adolescent, graduated from Whittier High and Whittier College as well. He served as assistant city attorney for the City of Whittier before the war and returned afterward to live and practice law.

Although it has grown larger and older, Whittier hasn't changed that much since Tricia's girlhood. The modest homes are pretty well worn now, the trees are well grown, and the city of eighty-five thousand people has become fully woven into the fabric of metropolitan Los Angeles. More than half the residents are Hispanic, but the city seems unruffled by the change. Here as elsewhere in California, whites have not felt any urgency to move out when Hispanics move in. The two groups fuse with surprisingly little friction statewide, even in prison, and certainly in Whittier.

Michael and Deborah Grumbine live in a small house on a main street just a few blocks from one of Nixon's old ones. If Independence, Missouri, proudly points visitors in the direction of its presidential boyhood home, Whittier chooses not to. Although the Grumbines have lived in their home for twenty-four years, they weren't quite sure where the Nixon homestead was.

I had never met the Grumbines before the Sunday morning that I visited. I was looking for a large family to interview. A mutual friend volunteered the Grumbines, and they graciously consented. Michael and Deborah have raised nine children, now aged eleven to thirty-one, on what is almost exactly the LA area's median income. I was curious to know how they did it.

Although both are in their early fifties, the Grumbines each look a decade younger. With her frizzy blond hair and southwestern-style turquoise blouse, Deborah could have passed for a Santa Monica eco-warrior or a Grateful Deadhead. The half-Sicilian Michael is darker but looks just as hip in an amiable sort of way. They rent the home they inhabit, a single-level bungalow with three bedrooms—one for the boys, one for the girls—and one bath.

"One bath?" I asked incredulously. Said Deborah with a smile, "It promotes charity and self-control." I did not doubt her, at least on the self-control part. The landlord has frozen the rent at $925 because he likes the Grumbines as tenants. That helps a lot.

The reader will not be surprised to learn that the Grumbines are Roman Catholics and, as is evident from head count, take their Catholicism seriously. Christians, like environmentalists, come in degrees. To continue the parallel, the Grumbines practice what might be called "deep Christianity." They don't send their children to Catholic school because the schools are insufficiently Catholic. "Catholicism is not a class," said Deborah. "It's a life." They discipline themselves, however, to respect those whose commitment is less. When discussing the hierarchy of the Los Angeles archdiocese, like many serious Catholics in Southern California, they have to work hard to maintain that discipline.

The morning I visited, Marietta, thirteen, and Joseph, eleven, cooked up a breakfast of scrambled eggs and sausages and served it. They and two of their older sisters joined us for this good-spirited meal as well. As in every deeply Christian home I have visited, Catholic or Protestant, the family begins the meal with a prayer, usually improvised around the blessings of the day. The Grumbines' was no different. After breakfast the kids cleared the table and did the dishes uncomplainingly.

I asked the kids how their peers at public school accepted them. The ingenuously cute, well-spoken Marietta told me it wasn't a problem, "We just hang out with the good kids." That she and *Thirteen*'s Nikki Reed could share the same age, race, county, schooling, and economic class and yet live such extraordinarily different lives speaks to the diversity possible even in California's supposedly homogenized suburbs. This book, however, does not presume to measure the spiritual richness of their respective lives. That I will leave to the reader. The question of the day is how families like the Grumbines affect the material quality of California life.

In "Sustainable San Mateo" there is much hand wringing over the county's unusually large "ecological footprint." "The average county resident," admits the annual report regretfully, "consumes more than 4.5 times the world's capacity of global resources per person, contributing to the depletion of the earth's natural resources." The "depletion" part is largely nonsense, but the consumption part is probably accurate.

In Grumbine County, however, consumption of resources per capita likely undercuts the world norm. This family of eleven uses less electricity by far and no more natural gas or water than the average San Mateo family of two or three. They have not added an in-ground pool or Jacuzzi or a redwood deck. They count the square feet of their home in the hundreds. Their "second home" is an RV in the driveway, which they use for guests.

"Living simply is a virtue," said Deborah, "You realize that what you have is better than what the world could offer." The Grumbines believe that. They decided early on that they would remain a one-income family "so Deborah could be the nurturer." They have never owned a new car. They shop at thrift stores. They buy wheat by the barrel, grind it, and bake their own bread. They sew many of their own clothes. In short, they have lived the kind of genuinely sustainable life that would give the folks in Sustainable San Mateo nightmares. "One bathroom for eleven people, puhhleeze!"

When one parent stays at home, only one member of the family has to negotiate rush-hour traffic, and it is that rush that strains the infrastructure. With only one parent in the workforce, the family has the ability to live closer to the breadwinner's place of employment. Michael drives just three miles each way to and from work in his 1996 Toyota Corolla. In California, the literal millions of two-income families generate the lion's share of epic commutes. It is not unusual for the two jobs to be an hour or more apart.

The Grumbines would not impress the seriously green, not at all. Like several other classes of Californians—gays, feminists, yuppies, humanists—deep ecologists are disinclined to reproduce and have little enthusiasm for those who do. If Californians stopped having children, it would likely please the eco-Shakers. They would have all that many more desert tortoises to fret about per capita. But more grounded Californians, whatever their politics, are beginning to see that the real population problem is not too many home-grown people, but too few.

In his recent book on the subject, *America Alone*, Canadian Mark Steyn describes the increasing failure of the developed nations to reproduce as the "single most important fact about the early twenty-first century." Other than the United States, no country in the developed world is achieving the fertility rate of 2.1 necessary to sustain either its population or its typically generous social security system. Many aren't even coming close, Steyn's Canada included. Italy clocks in at 1.2, Spain at 1.1. "The progressive Left can be in favor of Big Government or Population Control but not both," says Steyn. "That mutual incompatibility is about to plunge Europe into societal collapse." For the most part, it is the deeply Christian families in the United States that keep our numbers in balance.

That said, not all families function productively. Michael Grumbine spoke to this point with obvious forethought. "The nuclear family," he told me, "is a nuclear disaster." He gradually clarified this startling observation. As he sees it, California is "a land of discontented immigrants," whether from other countries or from other states. The first impulse of the liberal politician, Michael elaborated, is to exploit their unease and build a "culture of discontent" around it.

For the nuclear family to function happily in an unsettled landscape, it needs the support of its own biosystem. This includes an active faith and ideally an extended family, both of which "corral moral behavior." Said Michael, "I was terrified of upsetting my saintly aunts even during my rebellious years." The Grumbines have stayed in Southern California because this is where their families are. The grandparents have been at every significant event in the grandchildren's lives. "They're regular party animals," Michael joked.

Michael grew up in Whittier, one of twelve kids. His mom, a high-school graduate, stayed at home. His father taught junior high. They too lived a deeply Christian life, close to the bone. Eleven of the Grumbines survived to adulthood and have had forty-seven children among them. I asked Michael to survey his siblings on a variety of relevant variables, and he was kind enough to oblige.

★ Two-parent households

Forty-three of the 47 cousins have spent their entire childhood with a father in the household, 39 of those with both parents. One of Michael's sisters suffered a long-term illness before dying, leaving four children behind. One divorce accounts for the other four.

★ Subsidization
Of the 47 cousins, two depend on welfare or other government subsidies.

★ High-school graduation
Of the 35 cousins more than nineteen years of age, 35 have graduated from high school.

★ College graduation
Of the 15 cousins over thirty years of age, 10 have graduated from college.

★ Arrests
Of the 47 cousins, a surprisingly high number have been arrested, 9. Five of those, Michael explained, were the result of peaceful protests, typically of the prolife variety. Before the Clinton administration made even peaceful abortion protests a federal crime in 1994, Michael himself had been arrested a number of times. The other four arrests were for unpaid tickets and DUIs. As Mel Gibson spectacularly proved, California Catholics are not immune—nor even averse—to alcohol.

★ Imprisonments
Of the 47 cousins, none has ever been sent to a state or federal pen. "They'd be dead before their sentencing," said Michael. "We uncles take our job seriously."

One variable that is difficult to calculate is the cousins' contribution to the service economy. In fact, they have virtually all had to work their way through school and college with little parental support and no race-based government aid. One could argue that the Grumbine cousins "do the jobs that Americans don't want to do." Historically, too, it has been large Catholic ethnic families like the Grumbines that have contributed disproportionately to the police, fire, and military services.

The Grumbines are not unique. Other large Christian families with whom I spoke, Protestant and Catholic, Anglo and Hispanic, would likely produce similar outcomes if surveyed. Although the sample is obviously small, I think I can safely venture some generalizations.

One is that material poverty does not seem to cause crime. Michael Grumbine grew up in the same metro at the same time as Tookie Williams. Tookie was the one with his own bedroom. Michael was the one with his own father. If all the materially impoverished children in California had grown up with the support of faith and family that the Grumbine cousins did, California could virtually *eliminate* serious crime.

Nor does California seem to have too many people. What it has are too many households. The people who talk the most about sustainability tend to inhabit more space and use more resources per capita— often dramatically more—than those who don't. Stay-at-home moms save the state's highway infrastructure from meltdown, especially since a "nanny" often drives to the working mom's house. Environmentally inclined on many levels, the Grumbines even describe themselves as "eco-wackos."

Of note, too, these families place a relatively light burden on the public education system. Although Michael and Deborah's children have attended public school, many kids from comparable families are home-schooled or go to parochial schools. Those that attend public schools tend not to aggravate the system with security concerns or special needs. On balance, these families may even pay more in school taxes than they absorb.

When all is said and done, the state's future depends on the Grumbines. They and similar families form the tax base of tomorrow and the one dependable source of hard-working, low-priced, legal labor today. The children of Marin and San Mateo will not become cops or firemen or—God forbid—soldiers, at least on our side. The Grumbines will.

So why then, the reader asks, does not the state or Hollywood or even the Los Angeles archdiocese encourage young people to model themselves on the Grumbines? Hard to answer, but it has at least something to do with those arrests, and I'm not talking about the DUIs.

THE BENNETON
COLORS DISUNITE

★ 25. Gold Mountain ★

They are quiet, peaceable, tractable, free from
drunkenness. A disorderly Chinaman is rare, and a
lazy one does not exist.
—Mark Twain

The University of California, Davis, was not the first university in the California system that I visited, but it was the one where the system-wide transformation visually overwhelmed me.

A relatively new campus on a semiarid plain about seventy-five miles northeast of San Francisco, UC Davis lends itself well to the bicycle. As I watched the thousands of students whizzing by, I found myself impulsively humming "Nine Million Bicycles," a mesmerizing song that had been popular in Europe during my last visit whose opening line instructs us that there are "nine million bicycles in Beijing."

Last school year, Asian-Americans made up 44 percent of UC Davis's American population—nearly four times their percentage in the state, ten times their percentage in the nation—and nearly half of those were Chinese-Americans. Whites made up 41 percent of the campus population, nearly equal their 44 percent representation in the state as a whole. Blacks, who represent 7 percent of the state's population and 13 percent of the nation's, made up less than 3 percent of the student body. Indeed, there were more Korean-American students on campus than African-Americans. Hispanics make up 35 percent of the state's population but not quite 12 percent of the campus's.

Davis is not unique. In 2006 for the first time, the incoming freshman class of the ten-campus UC system had more students of Asian descent than white, with UC Irvine, UC Berkeley, and

UCLA all hovering around 50 percent of total enrollment. The fact that whites outnumber Asian-Americans five to two at UC Santa Cruz is a testament to Santa Cruz's lack of seriousness.

Asian-Americans owe their dominance on UC's better campuses to one man above all others, the marvelously incorrect Ward Connerly. In 1996, Connerly, an African-American and UC regent, led the drive to prohibit discrimination on the basis of race, sex, or ethnicity. He did so first on the UC campuses and then statewide through Proposition 209, which passed by an impressive 54 percent to 46 percent margin. Before Connerly, the UC campuses openly discriminated on the basis of race, almost always to the disadvantage of the state's high-performing Asian-Americans. If not for the people of California and the initiative system, the legislature never would have had the nerve.

Such discrimination made no sense on any level. If groups were to have been repaid for lumps meted out to their ancestors in California over the years, Chinese-Americans would have stood second in the queue behind only American Indians. Until Connerly intervened, the Chinese had been getting hit upside their head, figuratively and otherwise, since the Gold Rush.

Given the state of transportation in the mid-nineteenth century, the news out of Sutter's Mill reached China more quickly than it did New York. Soon the Chinese came to know California as *Gum Shan*, Gold Mountain, a much more effective, if less accurate, marketing pitch than, say, Laundry Mountain. In the early days of the Gold Rush, Americans received the Chinese and other Asians reasonably well, and not just in California. The eponymous "Siamese Twins," for instance, Chang and Eng Bunker, invested the fortune they had made with Phineas T. Barnum in a North Carolina plantation. There they both married local girls, eased into local society, bought themselves a parcel of slaves, sired some twenty-one kids between them—I'll leave that to your imagination—and sent their oldest off to fight in the Civil War on the side of the South.

In California, as late as 1851, the San Francisco *Daily Alta California* would cheerfully predict, "China boys will yet vote at the same polls, study at the same schools and bow at the same Altar as our own countrymen." This more or less happened as predicted, but a long time would pass between the "will" and the "yet."

As their numbers swelled in California—and at the time the world held twenty times more Chinese than Americans—the locals began to fret. They objected less to Chinese vices than to Chinese virtues. The Chinese worked hard, stayed sober, and rarely shot each other. They were busting the curve even then. When it came to justice, however, the Chinese enjoyed little more than a "Chinaman's chance"—a California neologism that pretty much summed up the state of affairs in the gold fields. Not surprisingly, some Chinese returned to the homeland. Among them was Yung Win, the first Chinese student to graduate from Yale. Soon after his arrival, viceroy Yeh Ming Hsin set up an execution grounds just a half-mile from Yung Win's house and proceeded to behead some seventy-five thousand of his countrymen, most of them innocent. At this point, Yung Win decided that perhaps a Chinaman's chance was better than no chance at all. He would go on to launch an exchange program in which other young Chinese could journey to America to be educated. Unfortunately, authorities eventually shut the program down because students were returning not only with American wives—bad enough—but with nervy new concepts like freedom and democracy.

Over the years, the resistance to the Chinese in California stiffened. As often happens, it served a larger political purpose. In this case, the presence of Chinese workers gave unorganized labor something to organize around. In 1877, Denis Kearney—not the guy they named the street after—led some ten thousand potential members of the Workingmen's Party on an anti-Chinese pogrom. The rioting left a trail of death and destruction in its wake, the greatest man-made mayhem San Francisco would ever suffer. It took the National Guard, the U.S. Navy, and four thousand volunteers to suppress it.

There followed a series of uninspired laws, at both the state and national levels, that made it progressively more difficult for the Chinese to live, work, and buy land in America. In a useful turn of events, no one thought to ban the Chinese from owning their own businesses and hiring their own employees. This would pay dividends down the road. So, oddly, would the gender disparity. With at least ten men for every Chinese woman, only the best and brightest of the men got to procreate.

As our valiant allies in World War II—my own favorite movie as a kid was the inspirational *China's Little Devils*—the Chinese image improved, and the various exclusionary laws began to fall away. In the years following the war, after the Nationalist government moved to Taiwan, the brightest and most ambitious of the Nationalist Chinese came to America, and the collective Chinese gene pool continued to fill with high-quality DNA. By 1959, the Chinese in America had passed the American norm in family income.

In the last two decades, the influx of Chinese immigrants has shifted to Southern California, particularly the San Gabriel Valley just east of Los Angeles. Today, no fewer than seven of the towns in the valley have a majority Chinese population, including the city of San Gabriel, which has a mayor of Chinese descent. As a group, the Chinese are doing better than all right. Only the continued infusion of new and less affluent blood keeps the Chinese from being the single highest-earning ethnic group in America.

I have heard it said that the Chinese ideogram for "crisis" is composed of equal parts "opportunity" and "danger." Though not exactly true, this still makes a useful metaphor for the discussion that will follow. As it stands, the Chinese, who are now arguably California's most respected ethnic group, have the potential in the very near future to be its most suspect. Much of their future—and California's as well—hinges on America's relationship to the People's Republic of China.

To illustrate this conundrum, let me turn to another branch of the University of California system, the Los Alamos National Laboratories in New Mexico. In 1978, a young Ph.D. from Texas A&M found his way there to work on America's nuclear program. A native of Taiwan, Wen Ho Lee had gotten his American citizenship in part, as he himself admits, because it allowed him to seek employment at a national lab. To start, Los Alamos paid him $50,000 a year, the equivalent of $133,000 today. Twenty years later, by his own account, Lee was making $82,000 a year, which may or may not explain his undoing.

For those twenty years, Wen Ho Lee seemed very much the "model minority." He and his Taiwanese wife worked hard, obeyed the law, and raised two good kids. Well liked by colleagues and neighbors, Lee indulged in nothing more superficially provocative than trout fishing, classical music, and computer code. In 1999, however, Lee's American idyll came to an indecorous end. The FBI shocked Lee's friends and colleagues when they arrested him on suspicion of espionage.

Notra Trulock, the Department of Energy intelligence chief who helped bring the Lee case to light, admits that even he does not know whether Lee had actually betrayed his country. "I do know," Trulock elaborates in his fair-minded book, *Code Name Kindred Spirit*, "that he was a walking security nightmare who violated every security rule in existence at Los Alamos National Laboratory."

It is possible that Lee was, in fact, a bumbling innocent. It is likely that he understood why he had to be investigated. Left to his own devices, he might never have dreamed of playing the race card. Trulock claims, in fact, that Lee did not believe himself to be the victim of racial profiling. The Lee that I will be talking about, however, is the politicized Lee that the reader meets in his memoir, *My Country Versus Me*.

Given the limitations of Lee's English, coauthor Helen Zia almost assuredly drove the content of the book. Although superficially patriotic in tone, it oozes anti-American agitprop. Zia had to know what she was doing. This second-generation Chinese-American and first-generation radical feminist lesbian has been at play in the fields of the left since she quit medical school to work as a labor organizer in Detroit. On a Bay Area promotional website, Speakout, she tellingly describes the Wen Ho Lee affair as the "worst case since the Rosenbergs."

Much depends on what she means by "worst." As history has shown beyond question, the Rosenbergs did pass nuclear secrets to the Soviets. They were executed for their mischief. In Zia's world such facts are irrelevant. Propaganda trumps truth. It has since the Comintern first discovered Sacco and Vanzetti and realized how absurdly willing are the media, both here and abroad, to portray even the guiltiest of non-Anglo felons as innocent victims of a racist society. If Zia's goal were to undercut America and to cause her fellow Asian-Americans to question their national identity, she succeeded marvelously.

Lee first fell afoul of the authorities in 1982 after he called a Taiwanese scientist at the Lawrence Livermore Laboratory near San Francisco. Lee had never before talked to this guy. In his book, Lee claims that he called to learn if Livermore had terminated the scientist's employment as he had read and, if so, why. Lee was unaware that the scientist was under court-ordered FBI surveillance for passing nuclear secrets to Beijing. When the FBI questioned Lee about the call, he denied making it. Later, he would deny the denial. Says Lee obliquely, "I don't agree with the FBI version of the story."

This was the first of perhaps six flaming red flags in Lee's career. What he takes away from this misadventure is this typical bit of ethnic posturing, "I didn't know that the FBI monitored Chinese American scientists." In truth, the FBI did not profile Chinese, despite the fact that it made sense to do so. The People's Republic was emerging as America's leading nuclear rival, a hostile one at that, and its agents were conspicuously targeting Chinese-Americans scientists. Besides, the building of a nuke on the federal dime was not exactly the founders' idea of a constitutionally guaranteed right.

In 1988, a year before the Tiananmen Square massacre, Lee visited Beijing with his wife. While she just happened to be out shopping, two Chinese scientists visited Lee in his hotel room and asked some pointed questions about nuclear warheads. Lee knew that he had an absolute obligation to report such contacts. He did not. Says Lee unconvincingly, "I was afraid that if I reported their visit, I would be subjected to the kind of FBI questioning I'd received before."

By the late 1990s senior scientists at Los Alamos had become convinced that the Chinese had acquired—"probably by espionage"—vital data on the W-88 nuclear warhead, the most modern in the U.S. arsenal. By this time, too, with the collapse of the Soviet Union, the People's Republic loomed as America's most serious potential enemy, and its leaders were not afraid to say so. In 1996, a Chinese military officer had warned American ambassador Chas Freeman, "If you hit us now, we can hit back. So you will not make those threats [about Taiwan]." The officer then proffered the following not-so-cryptic caveat: "In the end you care more about Los Angeles than you do about Taipei."

As one might expect—hope, actually—authorities moved to plug the presumed leak at Los Alamos. On an initial list of a dozen possible suspects, six were Chinese in origin, including Wen Ho Lee. When the FBI asked Lee during a polygraph exam if he had worked on the W-88, he denied it. "With what I now understood," wrote Lee later, "my answer might have been 'yes,' but I wondered if it was *really* a 'yes,' since I didn't know I was working on the W-88." Young readers should be aware that, in the age of Clinton, answers like this made more sense than they do today.

Whether guilty of espionage or not, Lee clearly deserved the FBI's scrutiny. To be sure, its agents botched the case. Given the various China influence-peddling scandals then engulfing it, the Clinton administration overreacted to cover its own butt. Lee ended up in prison, without bail, and was indeed treated badly.

His skilled legal and PR teams quickly turned the imprisonment to his advantage. To arouse public indignation, they portrayed Lee as an "American Dreyfus," a dedicated patriot persecuted only because of his race. This strategy may have frayed the bond between the nation and its citizens of Asian origin, but from Lee's perspective, it worked beautifully. It inspired all manner of his fellow Asian-Americans to rush to his defense, as well as those enlightened whites seeking a fresh new zone of decency. His guilt or innocence mattered not a whit. No one could possibly have known.

"Asian American/Arrest me too," read a fairly typical sign, carried in this case by a young woman at a pro-Lee rally. The pressure built as planned. No one likes to be called a racist. After nine months in prison, Lee was allowed to cop a plea to just one of the fifty-nine counts against him and walk away a martyr, his halo dimmed only by the fact that this all happened on a Democratic watch. Major book deals and lawsuits followed.

Lee's book is dishonest from front cover to back. Lee, for instance, often compares himself to Caucasians who had run afoul of the authorities on security breaches. "They were all excused," he writes, "because they were assumed to be good Americans." Contemporaries like Aldrich Ames, Robert Hanssen, and Jonathan Pollard might take exception. Dying in prison on spy charges is probably not their idea of being "excused."

Team Lee repeatedly cites former CIA director John Deutch as one of these charmed Caucasians. "Nobody even whispered that John Deutch 'stole' the many CIA files he downloaded," Lee/Zia gripes, adding sarcastically, "He was a 'real' American." As with Lee's performance in the lab, it is hard to tell here whether he is being subversive or merely sloppy.

The "real" American Deutch was born in Brussels to a Russian father. He was the first Jew to head the CIA. When Deutch quit the agency, he left classified material on his unsecured laptops. Once discovered, Deutch's dereliction triggered a huge, embarrassing investigation by the Justice Department that led to permanent revocation of Deutch's security clearance and a criminal plea deal with Justice. A day after Deutch signed the deal, President Clinton shocked his prosecutors by pardoning him. Despite the pardon—perhaps because of it—Deutch's reputation suffered considerably more than that of the multimedia star Lee, and yes, there has been a whole lot of whispering going on about his motives ever since.

None of this would matter much were the People's Republic to elect Arnold premier tomorrow and invite the Franciscans in to open a string of missions, but this is not about to happen. More likely, China will focus its internal unrest—especially from those 20 million or so excess males—on external aggression. The Pentagon has worked out any number of scenarios to confront this possibility, none of them very cheerful.

If America ever does go to war with China, even a proxy war abroad with terrorism and sabotage at home, all other California problems will melt away. The majority of Chinese-Americans live in California. China will have surely planted a fifth column among them to incite the alienated, Asian and otherwise.

Were these agents to raise hell in the state's people's republics—Berkeley, say, or Santa Monica—half the home-grown crazies would join in. The other half, the too old and too rich Jane Fonda half, would stage candlelight vigils and sing surly renditions of John Lennon's "Imagine," a musical testament to the brain-sapping effects of primaling. Whether the saner Californians would have the will or the wherewithal to resist is open to question. If they tried, the ACLU would likely denounce them as vigilantes and haul them over to the Ninth Circuit. San Francisco would be of even less help. Its supervisors would be tempted to capitulate preemptively. They could then negotiate a separate peace, declare San Francisco an open city, and dust off those old Maurice Chevalier records.

The Chinese in America deserve better. It's too bad they didn't settle in Kansas.

★ 26. Maywood ★

There can be no divided allegiance here. Any man
who says he is an American, but something else also,
isn't an American at all.
—Theodore Roosevelt

As jittery and unstable as the cultural tectonics of California tend to be, only rarely does a plate break the surface. And never before had one broken through with such noisy bravado as "La Gran Marcha" of 2006. On that spring day in Los Angeles no other force in California could have countervailed.

The LAPD had expected maybe twenty thousand people for the march, but it must not have been monitoring Spanish-language radio. I counted no fewer than seventeen stations that broadcast in Spanish in Los Angeles alone, and many of these had been abuzz with the march for weeks. As a result, some five hundred thousand people, maybe more, surged through the streets of downtown LA that day—happily for all, in good order.

"The size of the pro-immigrant march and rally surprised the world and the nation," wrote Ernesto Cienfuegos in the web journal *La Voz de Aztlan,* and this time he did not exaggerate. Cienfuegos argued that "Mexicanos" and other "Latinos" now have the "political will and organizational skills to direct our own destinies." Although no one doubted the will or the skill, the "our own" part was a little trickier.

The five hundred thousand marchers had come downtown with nearly as many different agendas. Some actually came to protest the Sensenbrenner Bill on illegal immigration, though hardly spontaneously, as the bill had been passed the previous November. Some had come to be part of history and show a little solidarity. Some wanted to hook up with relatives and friends. Some were playing hooky. Some were playing politics. And some came to hijack the plate and roll it out and over the entire Southwest.

The radical plate-jackers tried hard to get their message out. They made their signs, waved their Mexican flags, and posted their warnings on their websites. Cienfuegos, confusing the Los Angeles rally with Nuremberg's, promised that his people would no longer "be subservient to the White and Jewish power structures" and asked why so many Jews got involved in school politics if not for the sake of "enriching themselves and their cronies through crooked deals."

The Mexica movement headlined its website with an all-cap, red-on-black declaration: "The only illegals on this continent are the criminal Europeans who have invaded our continent from 1492 to the present day." In their passion, movement leaders likely forgot that those post-1492 Europeans had bequeathed the marchers their culture, their language, much of their blood, and all of their freedom. I don't think Montezuma would have provided his protesters Johnny-on-the-Spots.

"One of the more negative parts of the march," according to the Mexica site, was the waving of American flags. Organizers had given these out so that marchers would be seen as part of "America." Declared the site boldly, "We should be looked upon as the Indigenous people of this continent returning to their land." Evidently, the Los Angeles Unified School District teaches neither logic nor history. The Mexica movement also posted photos of its followers making provocative signs and carrying them at the march. Given the Germanic names of Sensenbrenner and Schwarzenegger, there were lots of mock-ups of the pair in Nazi gear. Bosche-baiting never goes out of fashion.

As hard as these aspiring Pancho Villas worked to get their message out, the major media worked just as hard to screen them. With the *Los Angeles Times* in the lead, these news outlets showed their fellow citizens the PG-rated march, the one with the smiling babies and American flags. As recently as ten years ago they might have succeeded in controlling the message. This time, they merely looked foolish.

Unlike the majors, the samizdat media had no interest in sanitizing the festivities. With the help of talk radio, cable TV, and particularly the Internet, the politically engaged on the other side of the debate picked up the Mexican flags and "This Is Stolen Land" signs and distributed them far and wide. Not surprisingly, this bifurcated image stream aggravated the divide among non-Hispanics on this critical subject. As I learned in my California travels, illegal immigration was not a polite issue to put on the table if there were more than a few people in the room.

Sentiments seem to split along class lines. The affluent tend to have more regular contact with undocumented Hispanic workers—gardeners, pool boys, cooks, nannies. They "love" them in an only slightly more democratic way than Miss Scarlett loved her Mammy, and they won't hesitate to tell you that either. For some, the telling is the most important part, as it places them in a zone of decency, apart from and above the Minutemen and other such "bigots," the word of choice for those who insist that immigration laws be honored.

"Why should we punish people just because we don't manage our borders properly?" one LA publisher asked me. He had just hired a two-man crew from the Home Depot lot to move his belongings from a Malibu tear-down to his new home next door. What surprised him was that the pair wanted five hundred dollars for one day's work. The fellow had expected to pay minimum wage. They settled on twenty dollars an hour per worker—cash. Still, they put in a good day's work. No one ever complains that "they" don't.

The 2004 James Brooks movie *Spanglish* gently ridicules

the ethos of the affluent while at the same time propagandizing for illegal immigration. In the film single mom Fior Moreno—the last name of Helen Hunt Jackson's Ramona as well—and her daughter Cristina illegally enter the United States, hitch a ride north, and find themselves "right back home" in a fully Mexicanized section of Los Angeles. Only after six years does Fior get around to "entering a foreign land" when she accepts a job as housekeeper *chez* Clasky, a comically uptight, white, yuppie family. In due course, as the audience fully expects, Fior helps show the family its way out of its sterile self-absorption.

Paz Vega, who plays Fior, is drop-dead gorgeous. She has a tentative romantic interlude with John Clasky, played by Adam Sandler, but other than the near adultery, there is nothing forbidden about it, no implied crossing of racial lines. Why would there be? In real life, the Spanish-born Vega is one of those "criminal Europeans." Like most actors who play Mexicans in the movies or on TV, she comes from someplace other than greater Aztlan.

Adam Sandler has written an amusing "Hannukah Song" in which he proudly outs Hollywood's more subtle Jews, for instance: "David Lee Roth lights the menorah/So do James Caan, Kirk Douglas, and the late Dinah Shore-ah." A useful challenge for a popular Hispanic comedian like Carlos Mencia would be to out those non-Mexicans who play Mexicans. What follows are the origins of some of the more prominent Hispanic screen presences in America of the last generation:

Actor	Birthplace	Ethnicity
Paz Vega	Spain	Spanish
Antonio Banderas	Spain	Spanish
Penelope Cruz	Spain	Spanish
Jennifer Lopez	The Bronx	Puerto Rican
Rosie Perez	Brooklyn	Puerto Rican

Jimmy Smits	Brooklyn	Puerto Rican
Benicio Del Toro	Puerto Rico	Puerto Rican
Andy Garcia	Cuba	Cuban
Carlos Mencia	Honduras	Honduran
Lou Diamond Phillips	Philippines	Filipino-Caucasian
Freddie Prinze	New York	Puerto Rican
Salma Hayek	Mexico	Lebanese-Mexican

The only Mexican-American actor to receive acclaim in recent years is Edward James Olmos of East Los Angeles, and his name is hardly a household word. Anthony Quinn also grew up in East LA but with an Irish father. Antonio Banderas meanwhile has played Zorro, Pancho Villa, and El Mariachi in *Once Upon a Time in Mexico*. Jennifer Lopez played Selena Quintanilla-Perez, a Texas-born tejano singer, in the movie *Selena*. Lou Diamond Phillips has played Mexican-Americans at least twice, including a star turn as Richie Valens in *La Bamba*. Freddie Prinze played the classic *pachuco* in TV's *Chico and the Man*. Rosie Perez starred as Gloria Clemente in the provocative LA tale *White Men Can't Jump*. All-around TV star Jimmy Smits has played any number of Mexican-American parts. And today's hottest cinematic Mexican, Benicio Del Toro, was born in Puerto Rico.

Even that ultimate "beaner" comedian, Carlos Mencia, comes from Honduras. To his credit, Mencia does more to reinforce his audience's American identity than the entire California educational system—or Hollywood, for that matter. Although blacks often complain of being shut out of the entertainment industry, Mexican-Americans have a much better case. They outnumber blacks five to one in California and have a dramatically lower profile in American film and TV, especially in TV commercials.

Unlike their more affluent fellow citizens, middle- and working-class whites tend to favor immigration law enforcement. Their motives are partly economic as well, in that they find themselves competing for jobs and contracts. That much said, they too have a largely positive attitude about the Hispanics in their midst and a much easier relationship with them than they do with blacks. They work alongside Hispanics, hang out with them, date them, marry them. The quintessential cookie-cutter town of Lakewood, now nicely matured, is roughly one-quarter Hispanic, and there is no barrio. It is these everyday whites, not their betters, who see assimilation as the answer. They like a good burrito as much as the next guy, but they have more of a stake in preserving American institutions, such as the rule of law.

Caught in the middle are American citizens of Hispanic descent. Before the illegal immigration flare-up, most had come to see themselves as just another ethnic group. Now, increasingly, they are being asked to choose sides in a potentially devastating tectonic clash.

To read about the city of Maywood is to get the impression that it's a radical stronghold. The dusty, low-slung industrial city of nearly thirty thousand nestles tightly in the right underarm of the city of Los Angeles no more than fifteen minutes southeast of downtown. It gained some minor prominence in the 1960s as the home of auto finisher Big Ed Roth, the designer of the Kandy Kolored Tangerine Flake Streamline Baby made famous by Tom Wolfe. In the forty years since, it has slowly turned Hispanic. By the 2000 census, the city registered 96 percent Hispanic origin and 55 percent foreign-born.

In 2006, Maywood secured its fifteen minutes of fame by declaring itself a "sanctuary city" for illegal immigrants, so I decided to pay it a visit. I was both disappointed and reassured. Maywood looks less like Mexicali than it does Mayberry RFD. As in much of East LA, its neighborhoods are lined with neat bungalows and trim lawns. Old-timers might notice a little more

orange and purple paint on the homes and stores than a generation ago, but otherwise the difference seems minimal.

When I strolled the streets on my two visits or stopped at
the local McDonald's, I got no sense of being somewhere alien
or hostile. I presume there are multiple thousands of the undocumented underfoot as advertised, but if so, they are impressively
well concealed. I saw no Hoovervilles or tent cities, no sprawling
encampments Okie-style. Since both sides in the illegal immigration debate have a vested interest in inflating numbers—one
to threaten with and one to be threatened by—a certain caution
is in order in calculating the number of illegal residents. Even
the Mexica movement concedes that the great majority of its
membership has been born in the—quote—"U.S."

I met with Maywood's Anglo city manager, Ed Ahrens, who
shared with me the charming book he had written on the city
that has employed him most of his adult life. The transition in
group photos from nearly all Anglo to nearly all Hispanic strikes
the reader as very nearly seamless. The two groups belong to the
same clubs, watch the same kids' sporting events, attend the same
Chamber functions. One typical photo from the 2004 Fourth of
July parade shows three local celebrities—one black, one brown,
and one blond—riding in a car together, each of them waving
an American flag. At Maywood's art deco City Hall, the only
language I heard spoken was English.

A deft politician after twenty years as a minority city administrator, Ed Ahrens just smiled and shrugged when I asked
him about the "sanctuary city" folderol. Under prodding he did
admit that, yes, there was a little "political grandstanding" going
on and that a councilman or two who used to speak in English
at the council meetings now insist on speaking in Spanish, a language that Ahrens does not speak. "It makes for long meetings,"
he joked, but Ahrens does not take the radical turn seriously.

Many of the city's more settled Hispanic residents do. "I'm
afraid we're testing the limits of the law, and that's dangerous,"

longtime resident J. Luis Ceballos, fifty-two, told the *Los Angeles Times.* "I think there is a danger of people thinking that they can do whatever they want." The more radical activists may not sense that danger, but local homeowners and businesspeople seem to. What the savvier among them understand is that push can lead to push back.

In late August 2006, for instance, an anti–illegal immigration group called Save Our State came to Maywood to protest the city's self-declared sanctuary status. Although the group was roughed up and its cars vandalized, the images that went out over the Internet were far more inflammatory. They showed radicals pulling down the U.S. flag over the United States Post Office and running up the Mexican one. One of the edgier groups headlined its photo of that Mexican flag, "Buy your Aztlan postage stamps here." The Marines stormed the Halls of Montezuma for less provocation than that.

For all the talk of white resistance, there are more than two sides in California's ethnic tectonics. The Hispanic plate is beginning to mash up against another plate, equally formidable, but oddly ignored. The tension increases daily along the fault lines, especially during the school year, and an upheaval is inevitable. This is just one more story the major media choose not to see, and more on this later.

There is much the media miss. If they were paying attention, the "Gran Marcha 2006" would not have surprised non-Hispanic America as much as it did. There had been omens. The most obvious were the various protests surrounding Proposition 187. This 1994 initiative would have denied those without papers all social benefits except deportation—and that with the help of local police. To protest, some seventy thousand people or more marched through the streets of Los Angeles. In that march, however, the protesters flourished Mexican flags so prominently that even the *Los Angeles Times* could not help but show them. The public reaction to those flags likely aided the bill's 59 percent to 41 percent passage three weeks later. The "our own" did not include the 40 percent of Hispanic voters yanking the "yes on 187" lever. Not surprisingly, the judiciary scuttled 187 as it does—or tries to do—just about every Red- or Beige-plated initiative.

A more troubling display took place at the Los Angeles Coliseum in February 1998. On that day more than ninety thousand fans, the great majority of them local residents, turned out to watch the Mexican national soccer team square off against the United States. It was not a pretty sight. The pro-Mexico fans blew horns and booed loudly enough to drown out the U.S. National Anthem. They held American flags upside down. They punched and spat on the seeming handful of U.S. fans in the crowd. They threw beer and trash at the U.S. players.

"The garbage covered the U.S. team like an ugly blanket," wrote sports columnist Bill Plaschke in the *Los Angeles Times.* "It was accompanied by a chorus of words screamed in Spanish." Had the Mexican team not won the scene might have been less seemly still. Said U.S. coach Steve Sampson, "This was the most painful experience I have ever had in this profession."

America has always had immigrants. What's new, says Victor Davis Hanson, a fifth-generation Californian and Fresno State classicist, is the "growing despair and uncertainty over how—or even whether—to assimilate the arrivals into the fabric of the United States."

Hanson is not your ordinary academic. When not teaching or writing highly acclaimed books on subjects as diverse as immigration and military history, he runs the family farm in the Central Valley, where he grew up. Few Anglos know Hispanic culture in California as intimately as he. When I caught up with him, he was hopeful, but not optimistic about the state's future. He posed the obvious question that after the various marches and protests the *Los Angeles Times* should have asked long ago but dared not: "Do we really want unassimilated, angry radicals coming up to tell us what our laws are?"

★ 27. Army Street ★

Preservation of one's own culture does not require
contempt or disrespect for other cultures.
—César Chávez

San Francisco had witnessed its own tectonic clash on the
Hispanic front a few years before. In early 1995, activists prodded their plate forward when they urged the Board of
Supervisors to name one of the city's streets in honor of the late
farm organizer César Chávez.

It was not as if San Francisco had ignored its brief Spanish
heritage. Indeed, the area has almost as many streets named after
Mexicans as Mexico City. Early explorers Gaspar de Portolá and
Francisco de Ortega have streets bearing their names. So too
do Juan Bautista de Anza, who landed at the Presidio in 1776.
His soldiers and settlers included Moraga, Peralta, Pacheco, and
Castro, who were honored with streets as well. So too were
Father Junípero Serra and Father Palóu. Spanish and Mexican
governors and army *comandantes* didn't do too shabbily either, as
Argüello and Sanchez streets bear witness.

By contrast, the city has yet to name a street after Italian-
American mayor George Moscone, who was assassinated in
1978, or its all-time favorite native son, Italian or otherwise, Joe
DiMaggio. Bush Street, to be sure, is named after neither of the
Georges. And no street in the city bears a Chinese name, not
even in Chinatown.

For the young and restless, however, history does not count.
"Most of the Spanish names in the city are of saints or con-
quistadors," said San Francisco state administrator Ed Apodaca.
"It's hard for the kids to relate to that. César Chávez was a real-
life, flesh and blood hero." In contemporary California, "hero" is

code word for a guy on our side of the political fence. The fact that Chávez's outfit ultimately failed due to what Victor Davis Hanson calls "its corruption and misappropriation of workers' funds" seems to have troubled no one.

Had the activists chosen to rename Peralta Street or Pacheco or just about any street other than Castro Street—they knew better than to mess with Castro—the move would have met with negligible resistance. But they didn't. They went after the three-mile-long "Army Street." Said activist Eva Royale, "It's fitting that a military name be replaced by a name dedicated to peace."

Always eager to make a show of its peacenik airs and ethnic enlightenment, the Board of Supervisors blew off the protests of the affected businesspeople and voted eleven to none to approve the change. Unexpectedly, at least for San Francisco, the citizens fought back. Certainly, the businesses on Army Street had economic reasons to resist the change, but they alone did not have nearly the clout to do what happened next.

"San Franciscans to Save Army Street" recruited eighteen thousand of their fellow citizens—twice the needed number—to sign a petition and forced an election to undo the name change. Although the military presence had dwindled in the area, there remained if not a respect for the Army itself at least a respect for a San Francisco tradition stronger than anyone would have anticipated. The campaign that followed was brutal.

Among those leading the charge for the name change was Juan Pifarre. An Argentina native, Pifarre came to the United States in 1968 as a twenty-six-year-old on a student visa, and he never looked back. According to probate records, Pifarre married a San Francisco activist, a female actually, "purely out of convenience." The sham marriage allowed Pifarre readmission to the United States after a return trip to Argentina and eventually legal residence. The couple stayed technically married so that his American bride "could receive health care benefits" through Pifarre's employers.

In February 1987, the forty-five-year-old Pifarre, then San Jose's affirmative action officer, acted a bit too affirmatively in the presence of an undercover officer in the restroom of San Jose's Bernal Park and was promptly arrested. Being both Latino and politically wired, Pifarre never feared for his job. According to the *San Jose Mercury News*, he took several days' sick leave to recover from his ordeal, requested a job reassignment, and remained on the payroll. In 1995, Pifarre was still working for the City of San Jose, now as a senior analyst in its Finance Department.

By 1995, Pifarre had established himself as something of a mover and shaker in San Francisco politics. As publisher of *Horizontes*, a Spanish-language paper that he had launched a decade earlier, Pifarre had real presence in the Latino community and serious pull at City Hall. According to San Francisco supervisor Susan Leal, Pifarre frequently took his beefs about Latinos in general and the Mission District in particular to the supervisors. "He often held very strong opinions," said Leal, "but I think that people, even when they disagreed with him, knew that what he was saying was definitely heartfelt." This seems to a very nice way of saying "petulant sense of entitlement," a San Francisco trait.

In the Bay Area, few citizens seemed as royally entitled as Pifarre. Somehow he managed to juggle his publishing and protesting with an aggressive social life, a cocaine jones, and that full-time job in San Jose, a tough fifty-mile slog south of his Potrero Hill home. According to a spokesperson for the city of San Jose, he was considered "a very valuable employee." According to probate documents, Pifarre was the sole proprietor of a newspaper "worth a considerable amount money," into which he had poured "ten years of his time, sweat, money and knowledge." Busy guy.

Although Caucasian, as were many of his fellow protesters in the Army Street campaign, Pifarre and chums had no prob-

lem charging the opposition with bigotry and racism, charges
that cut deeply in this almost comically race-conscious region.
By 1995 this tactic had become standard operating procedure in
such urban battles, even where race wasn't an issue. Chávez had
helped pioneer this strategy when he actively sought out what
Hanson describes as "the opposition of an easily caricatured ra-
pacious, racist, wealthy, white enemy."

Speaking for many, Carlos Solomon, a senior fellow at
San Francisco State's César Chávez Institute, called the move
to block the name change "a huge slap in the face to the Latino Community." In the weeks before the election activists
imported thousands of farm workers from Salinas, Napa, Santa
Rosa, Delano, and Bakersfield to do whatever farm workers do
before an election, which is mostly just make San Franciscans
feel even more guilty than usual and perhaps do a little voting
on the side.

The strategy paid off. The Chávez name change held. But
in a city where George Bush would get only 15 percent of
the vote, the pro–Army Street forces had gotten 45 percent. "It
would be a terrible embarrassment to the city, and to the name
of César Chávez if it had gone the other way," said Apodaca. But
the 45 percent was embarrassment enough. The city's Latino
activists had prevailed, but they were not pacified, and the city's
nabobs knew it. A largely unseen and seemingly dormant plate
had rumbled into the tectonic mix.

Four and a half months after the election, with emotions
still raw, an unexpected event unnerved Hispanic San Francisco.
An unknown assailant killed activist Juan Pifarre. "Latino Publisher Found Slain in S.F." read the headline of the *San Francisco
Chronicle*. The story focused almost entirely on Pifarre's work
in the community as "a vocal advocate for Latino issues" and a
"champion of the poor."

San Franciscans had to read between the lines to infer Pifarre's prominence in another politically powerful community as

well. But that wasn't hard. The *Chronicle* dropped obvious clues. "Pifarre was last seen Saturday night when he went to visit a friend's Castro District home," the text signaled. Pifarre's Latino friends may have reacted "with disbelief" at the news of his death, but his Castro friends did not. They knew Pifarre's habits. The lack of a forced entry, as the *Chronicle* pointed out, told them all they needed to know.

If Pifarre had indeed been murdered, the person who had left his Navy-issue socks and T-shirt behind could not have picked a more politically inopportune victim or a more politically inappropriate time, and he would pay dearly for it.

★ 28. Downtown LA ★

God isn't compatible with machinery and scientific
medicine and universal happiness. You must make
your choice. Our civilization has chosen machinery
and medicine and happiness.
—Mustapha Mond, Aldous Huxley's *Brave New
World*

Little did I expect to find myself in the midst of the battle
for the Hispanic soul, but Providence apparently was feeling mischievous. On an April day in 2006, I was in Los Angeles
with an hour to kill between appointments. Being downtown, I
decided to check out the city's controversial new $200 million
cathedral, a clunky modernist structure with all the spiritual allure of a grain elevator. Given the cathedral's three-dollars-per
twenty-minutes parking fee, I had cash enough for only about
three "Our Fathers" and a "Glory Be."

I emerged from the parking garage right in front of a press
table. "Are you here for the press conference?" asked the woman
manning it. "Yea, sure," I answered. Dressed as I was in a sport
jacket, and looking semirespectable, I aroused no suspicion as I
wrote "World Net Daily" on the press sheet and got my press
pass. I still had no idea what the press conference was about.

I walked up another flight of stairs to a courtyard and saw
about a dozen TV cameras arrayed in a semicircle around a po-
dium. "What's going on?" I asked one of the cameramen, a generally more trustworthy media breed than the producers and
reporters.

"Cardinal Mahony is going to speak on illegal immigration,"
he said. "When?" I asked. "In about ten minutes." Okay, I thought.
I can hang around. As it happened, the cardinal did not speak. He

sent instead Auxiliary Bishop Gabino Zavala. The good bishop surrounded himself with a few union organizers and about twenty chubby, confused-looking workers, most of them wearing T-shirts that read "Justice for janitors, SEIU local 1877." They were all part of what was called the "We Are America Coalition."

The bishop explained that on May 1, "International Workers' Day," the Archdiocese of Los Angeles would instruct its parishes to ring their church bells at 5:00 PM "as a symbol of solidarity" with workers and immigrants. On that same day Catholic schools throughout the diocese would stage various "teach-in" activities to help students "gain an understanding" of immigration issues. Church leaders meanwhile would march down Wilshire Boulevard to "demand" that Congress pass "just and humane" legislation. Although the bishop did not say so, the LA rally would likely be the greatest gathering of Hispanics on International Workers' Day outside Havana, May 1 being the Marxist Fourth of July.

The star speaker was one Dolores Huerta, cofounder of the United Farm Workers. She railed about "death and destruction" in Iraq, the need for universal health care, a higher minimum wage, and a smorgasbord of other happening causes. The other union organizers followed Huerta with their take on "just and humane." To them it meant "genuine legalization now." These folks knew full well that they had not a prayer of getting the whole legal enchilada, but that was just the point. The hard-core hoped to create from the discontent a permanent revolutionary cadre. The soft-core would satisfy themselves with millions of new Democrats. "Today we march," declared the banners. "Tomorrow we vote."

If nothing else, the LA Catholic Church managed to stir up a new wave of anti-Catholicism in Southern California and beyond. More than a few people with whom I spoke discerned a pecuniary motive in the Church's position. They argued that the Church needed to recruit new Hispanic troops to help pay for the cathedral and for the legal costs stemming from sundry sex scandals, real and imagined.

Motives, however, are rarely as simple as money. The afternoon before the press conference I had found myself stuck in traffic on the 405, listening to Larry Elder's excellent, LA-based talk radio show. On the question of the Church's motives, a caller did a good job of explaining how the noisy "peace and justice" cliques within the Church have seized a new opportunity to lure the Church leftward. As she explained, these cliques are attempting to negate the rightward drift of practicing Catholics on life issues by elevating workers' rights to a comparable status. In the 2000 election, she noted, they tried the same tactic with the death penalty.

The problem for the P&J crowd is that the Catholic Church considers abortion "always morally evil"—"murder," in fact— but has no official position on immigration, legal or otherwise. One can read all four gospels and every encyclical ever written without encountering a single "undocumented immigrant" swimming across the River Jordan. Serious Catholics treat the LA hierarchy's showy preference for immigration issues over life issues as some sort of Joblike test of their fidelity.

I had absolutely no intention of saying anything at the press conference. But with the caller's lucid argument still resonating in my head, I could not resist the urge to inject a note of realism into the Q&A happy talk that followed the speeches.

"Bishop," I blurted out, "what do you say to those Catholics troubled by your alliance with these left-leaning groups, given their historic affection for abortion rights?"

The bishop looked at me as if I had just peed on his shoe. "What are you talking about?" he scoffed. As respectful as I try to be to my Catholic clergy, I did not appreciate the public dissing. "Let me tell you what I mean," I answered and elaborated on what I had already said.

"This isn't about left or right," he finally answered. "This is about justice."

"Bishop," I said, smiling, "May 1? International Workers' Day?"

I had expected the other reporters to give me the evil eye, but they did not. My question seemed to remind them of the role that reporters used to play. "Bishop," said the next fellow, "you keep saying that the Church is supporting immigration. Isn't this really about illegal immigration?" I did not have time to listen to the answer. I had a twelve o'clock appointment across town, and I had already spent nine dollars on parking.

A few months later the unions repaid the Catholic Church for its support in a way that left me feeling much more insightful than I actually am. The *Los Angeles Times* summarized the issue succinctly enough: "California's leading union organization, bucking organized labor's long-standing neutrality on the issue of abortion, is for the first time taking a strong stand in favor of abortion rights." Specifically, the union asked its 2.1 million members to reject Proposition 85. This initiative would merely have required abortionists to honor the standards of ear-piercers and aspirin dispensers and get parents' permission before going to work on their underage daughters.

Spearheading the union assault on parental rights was none other than Dolores Huerta, star of the press conference I had attended at the cathedral. As the *Times* noted, Huerta, "a Roman Catholic," had persuaded a prochoice group to put its many interns to work passing out proabortion propaganda to the union delegates before the vote was taken. The union support proved crucial in defeating Prop 85 by a fifty-three to forty-seven margin.

Said Tod Tamberg, an archdiocesan spokesman, "It doesn't preclude us from working together on those areas where we do share common concerns." The "it" in question is the union's decision to sanction what the church considers *murder*. In the battle for the Hispanic soul, the LA Church hierarchy has already surrendered, and God only knows why.

★ 29. Glendale ★

We have become not a melting pot but a beautiful
mosaic. Different people, different beliefs, different
yearnings, different hopes, different dreams.
—Jimmy Carter

What follows are, in my humble estimation, the twenty
best movies *about* California life, ranked in the order
of quality. In one case I list the presumed real setting first followed by the actual location.

Movie	Setting
1. *Chinatown*	Los Angeles
2. *The Graduate*	San Fernando Valley
3. *Crash*	Los Angeles
4. *American History X*	Venice
5. *L.A. Confidential*	Los Angeles
6. *American Graffiti*	Modesto (San Rafael)
7. *Sunset Boulevard*	Los Angeles
8. *East of Eden*	Salinas Valley
9. *Pulp Fiction*	Los Angeles
10. *Boyz N the Hood*	Los Angeles
11. *American Me*	LA, Folsom, Chino
12. *House of Sand and Fog*	San Francisco
13. *The Player*	Los Angeles
14. *Clueless*	Los Angeles
15. *Rebel Without a Cause*	Los Angeles
16. *Grand Canyon*	Los Angeles
17. *Thirteen*	San Fernando Valley
18. *The Day of the Locust*	Los Angeles

Of the twenty films, the one that tells us the most about the cultural tectonics of contemporary California is the entirely deserving 2006 Academy Award winner, *Crash*. Other than the fact that writer director Paul Haggis limits the many conflicts in the film to ethnic ones, the "crash" metaphor mirrors the theme of this book. In a state that has unwisely scrapped its road signs, cultural collisions, from minor sideswipes to massive head-ons, now constitute the grist of California news. Shattered parts of Jimmy Carter's "beautiful mosaic" litter the highways and byways.

Most of these collisions, including the most potentially violent, occur *within* the greater Blue plate. For all the talk of rift in the Red plate, the California Blue is the San Andreas of political coalitions. Blacks and feminists collide over the O. J. Simpson trial. Blacks and Koreans physically clash in the Rodney King riots. The unions glibly rear-end the Catholic hierarchy on the issue of parental notification for underage abortions.

In 2002, a grand jury in the dog-loving city of San Francisco indicted attorney Marjorie Knoller for second-degree murder. Despite Knoller's best efforts to intervene—she had a bloody shirt to prove it—her Presa Canario had fatally attacked a neighbor, Diane Whipple. Knoller's attorney Nedra Ruiz shocked the city by citing the obvious reason for such prosecutorial zeal: "Maybe [the DA] wants to curry favor of the homosexual and gay folks who are picketing at 2398 Pacific [the site of the attack] and demanding justice for Diane Whipple." Oops! She wasn't supposed to say that out loud, even if her name is Ruiz.

The Los Angeles jurors convicted Knoller because she was a head case. The San Francisco DA tried Knoller for murder, the first time ever in a dog mauling, because Whipple was a lesbian. In San Francisco the gay plate, the Rainbow, is the Presa Canario of cultural forces. By comparison, even the Green is a poodle, and the Red is just raw meat.

Gay concerns, however, do not much faze deep ecologists. "If radical environmentalists were to invent a disease to bring human population back to ecological sanity," wrote Christopher Manes of Earth First!, "it would probably be something like AIDS." Manes later described AIDS not as a problem but a "necessary solution." To be fair, Manes was probably unaware of his comment's Mein Kampfish overtones, history not being the deep ecologist's long suit.

Greens and Browns are on an even more serious collision course. Softer Greens think of themselves as both antigrowth and anti-anti-illegal immigration. They don't exactly argue *for* illegal immigration. They just argue against those who argue against it. It is all very complicated. I asked one fellow how he reconciles his pro-illegal position with his antigrowth one. He looked at me askance and said, "You can't understand. You don't live here."

Orwell understood. He called the phenomenon "Doublethink." Each of the dueling positions reinforces the virtue of the one who holds it. By turning a blind eye to the obvious side effects of illegal immigration, the shallower among the antigrowth crowd can feel doubly smug. The deeper ecologists, however, have moved beyond conventional virtue. Eco-novelist Edward Abbey and Earth First! founder Dave Foreman caused no small amount of discomfort among their peers with their outspoken opposition to illegal immigration. So has Stanford's population guru, Paul Ehrlich. The fact that immigration raises the living standard of immigrants is, from his perspective, exactly what's wrong with it. "The world," he argues, "can't afford more Americans."

As long as the Browns live like third worlders, they will not disturb the sleep of the Greens. But they did not move north to live as they did south. Once here, if they can ignore the Aztlan siren song, they will continue to assimilate and buy property. As is evident on Mount Washington and elsewhere, the Brown plate has already started to bump up against the Green. This movement has the very real potential of fracturing the fragile Blue coalition that now drives California politics.

The effort to secure the Oscar in the year of *Crash* revealed some underlying seismic stresses as well. The pro-Rainbow forces in Hollywood were pushing hard for the gay caballero film, *Brokeback Mountain*. The Purple—Blue socially, Red economically—were pushing back.

"I'm for gay marriage, gay divorce, gay this and gay that," wrote *Seinfeld* producer Larry David in a bold *New York Times* op-ed piece. "I just don't want to watch two straight men, alone on the prairie, fall in love and kiss and hug and hold hands and whatnot. That's all." David and others in power could see that an Oscar for *Brokeback* had the potential of fully alienating an already estranged Middle American audience.

The opposition to *Brokeback* coalesced around "Trash—excuse me—Crash," wrote *Brokeback* author Annie Proulx in a *London Guardian* piece so sour in its grapehood that it had me actually defending Hollywood. According to the eastern-born and -bred Proulx, "the somewhat dim LA crowd" was no longer progressing as progressives, by definition, are expected to progress. Unable to grasp "what was stirring contemporary culture," these "conservative" yahoos were stuck on race movies, which, to Proulx, were about as relevant as "a debate over free silver."

What Proulx fails to see is that *Crash* is easily the more iconoclastic movie of the two. *Brokeback* merely dandifies the minority-as-victim template all but mandatory since *Black Like Me*. *Crash* shatters it. Haggis takes victimology off the table. Like the literary naturalists of old, he drops his characters in the ethnic studies lab called LA and lets them have at it. In *Crash*, no group has a lock on power or the guilt that goes with it. None has a lock on morality. Haggis even gives his white "racists" credible motivation, much as director Tony Kaye did in 1998's equally provocative *American History X.*

Haggis, however, avoids the deepest ethnic fault in California, the one that has 8.0 potential on the cultural Richter. In *Crash*, there are good reasons to steer clear of the conflict. It would consume the whole movie. The major media lack any such excuse.

To explore this fault line up close I took the 101 to the 134 on out to a radio studio in Glendale, a shiny city of two hundred thousand that I had scarcely known existed. There I met the inimitable Terry Anderson, the one black man on air in LA mad enough to say what others—black and white and yellow—only think. Said Anderson succinctly about his brown brethren, "They don't give a flying fuck about us." Anderson hosts a Sunday night radio program that focuses on one subject: illegal immigration. When he started, the experts told him a one-subject show would never last. That was seven years ago.

Anderson is one of those fascinating California hybrids. Although black in language and culture, he has more than a little Cherokee in the veins. This multiracial mix may be what gives him a clearer perspective on race in California than most of his peers. The day I met him he had just come from a rally of African-Americans against illegal immigration in South Central LA's Leimert Park. In attendance, in addition to Anderson, were the Black Minutemen and the Mothers Against Illegal Immigration. "The anger was unbelievable," Anderson told me, and I did not doubt him. We talked about what I was hearing on the subject of immigration, and I responded as best I knew how. When he asked me what white people were saying about blacks, I answered, "Nothing at all." That did not surprise him. Like many other blacks, Anderson believes that the noisy Hispanic events of recent years have drowned out whatever voice the black community had.

Blacks and browns tend to meet at the roughest edge of their respective colliding plates—the streets, the schools, and the prisons—and sometimes those edges blur. "For those that don't know," observes one insider, "the streets of Los Angeles are ruled by prison politics." To listen to Anderson and his callers, you get the sense that blacks feel they are getting the raw end of the rub, especially now that there are five browns in the state for every one black. Anderson has a theory that once Hispanics outnumber blacks sixty to forty in a given institution, violence soon follows. Curiously, right after I met with Anderson, a riot broke out in the East Bay's San Leandro High School. The ratio of Hispanics to blacks in the school proved almost exactly what Anderson had predicted. The school's white and Asian students were not involved.

"There are big fights between blacks and Mexicans at my high school every year," wrote one student at San Leandro. "The reason I participated was because I know I have to get down with the black people because I'm black and that's just the rules."

In March 2006, a hundred-student-strong interracial melee erupted at LA's Fremont High, once the legendary spawning ground of the Crips but now predominantly Hispanic. Shortly afterward, I finessed my way through security at Fremont—the LAUSD had ignored my requests for a tour—and took a walk through the controlled chaos of the school's corridors. One image sticks with me. It was of a bookish black girl, her head pulled into her shoulders like a turtle, walking meekly down the hall as two boys talked noisily in Spanish over the top of her.

A Hispanic principal in Oakland whom I talked to described these big inner-city schools as "warehouses," and that is exactly what this one seemed—a place to store children for six or seven hours a day in the hope that nothing terrible happens while they are there. The growing tension between blacks and Hispanics may soon make even warehousing impossible. Says one ex-con, "Lunchtime in the Los Angeles high schools has become something you can compare to yard release in the state prisons system."

It was not until early 2007 that brown on black violence caught the eye of the national media. What prompted the attention was not so much the murder of fourteen-year-old Cheryl Green by Hispanic gang members in LA's Harbor Gateway neighborhood, but the killing's gratuitous nature: The gang had been looking for a black person—any black person—to shoot. Despite the horror of the shooting, it took weeks of concerted pressure by LA's black community to break this story out of Southern California.

As tense as the schools and streets are, the prisons are the real flashpoint. Hispanics, many of them illegal immigrants, now outnumber blacks in the state prisons and county jails and tend to be better organized. They also ally with the white prison gangs like the Aryan Brotherhood. This power shift has led to chronic "brown-on-black" violence and numerous lockdowns throughout the state.

"What's weird is [that] whites and blacks were separated by the racial issues of segregation and slavery," Steven Nary wrote from Pleasant Valley during one of the prison's frequent lockdowns. "However, it's apparent in this state that Hispanics have a dislike towards blacks. Why? I am not sure." Racial battles in the LA County jails in early 2006 lasted more than two weeks, involved more than a thousand prisoners, and left several hundred injured and at least two dead. Black prisoners have had to ask the authorities for protection from their brown brothers. Such flare-ups have become as common statewide as wildfires. "It is often volatile to mix black and Hispanic inmates," says the black ex-con referenced above. "There is bound to be a racial explosion." One hears the expression now that "brown is the new black." If so, the corollary may be that "black is the new white."

Terry Anderson senses this metamorphosis. He talked about the Hispanic incursion into South Central the way whites talked about the black incursion a generation or so ago. He has, however, a more valid gripe. To illustrate it, he used the example of Anthony Quinn and the roles he played in war movies during World War II. Blacks didn't get to play in those movies, Anderson reminded me. They didn't get to serve in those units. To him, Hispanics are just another ethnic group, posing as a racial minority. "When black folks asked them for help," said Anderson, "Mexicans said they were white." Likewise, there was scarcely a black face in the great Hispanic demonstrations of 2006.

Today, Hispanic commerce has pushed west on LA's Florence Street all the way to Normandie, the epicenter of the 1992 riots. These Hispanic businesses have had pathetically little black commerce to displace. Postintegration, blacks failed to develop a retail culture that would have helped root them in place. Now, they are being squeezed out of these neighborhoods before they ever really arrived. The fact that these Hispanic businesses, and mainstream businesses as well, reward or even require bilingualism embitters young black workers still struggling with English.

For all of their dominance of world culture—music, sports, dance, fashion—blacks have not been able to mature as a culture on the local level. White attention has not helped. For the past forty years whites in power have treated blacks the way divorced dads do their children—sporadically, guiltily, indulgently. While denying blacks their larger faiths—in God, in country, in family—they have tried to fill the void with material things. It hasn't worked.

No amount of money was going to save the faithless and fatherless Tupac Shakur. As a kid in Baltimore he had attended the School for the Arts and landed the role of the Mouse King in the *Nutcracker.* He moved with his mom to Marin County as an adolescent and flourished there as well. By twenty-one, he was a multimillionaire hip-hop artist. He made his millions, however, by imagining racial slights more grievous than his grandparents had ever endured and selling them to an empty-headed audience, black and white.

Literary wunderkind Ben Shapiro recalls "little on this planet weirder than watching a white suburban kid driving an SUV, putting on a bad 'nigga' accent, pumping up the subwoofer until the car shakes—and then walking into the school to study Hebrew." Such pop nihilism passes through affluent white kids like a bad cold, but a hip-hop anthem like Tupac's "I Don't Give a F**K" can hit vulnerable young black men like the Ebola virus. Bakari Kitwana, author of the insightful *Hip-Hop Generation*, foretells the future when he describes rap as "the primary vehicle for transmitting culture and values to this generation, relegating Black families, community centers, churches and schools to the back burner." This thought is not terribly reassuring.

Believing his own raps, Tupac willed himself to gangsterhood. By twenty-five, the one-time Mouse King had been shot and wounded, convicted of sexual assault, and finally gunned down fatally in the streets of Las Vegas. His murder—as well as the retaliatory murder of rapper Biggie Smalls in Los Angeles—remains unsolved in no small part because an aggressive investigation would invite other hip-hoppers to memorialize that investigation in song as police harassment.

This bloody nonsense could change and should change, and California has a unique opportunity to make it change. This is the first state in which Blue theorists have so busied themselves with other movements—Green, Brown, Rainbow—that they have ceased to indulge or even care about the Black. African-Americans like Terry Anderson are now finding common cause with what Tupac would call "all you redneck prejudice mutha fuckas." They are finding common cause not only in their complaints but also in their language, in their culture, in their very American-ness. A suburban San Francisco woman confided to me her relief in calling a plumber and having a black guy show up. "It was good to be able to explain the problem to someone who speaks English," she told him when finished. He just smiled and said, "I hear that a lot lately." The plumber was going to the bank on references like this one.

This transaction suggests why race relations in California still work much better than they do in countries like France. Stripped of a shared belief in faith or country, Californians—from the most cynical Blood to the most humble *bracero*—all still want to get ahead, and most think they can do it. This urge to succeed—what comedian Carlos Mencia calls "the drive and the heart to be superior"—propels the sundry ethnicities forward in more or less the same direction. Only after the riots in France did at least some European intellectuals begin to appreciate the cohesive power of this drive, the core virtue of what their peers deride as "America's money culture."

In *Crash,* Haggis smartly picks up on this theme. He gives the film's critical punch line to young thug Anthony, played by rapper Ludacris. After a vanful of Thai stowaways fall into his lap, Anthony chooses not to sell them into servitude. Instead, in his moment of personal redemption, he sets them free in China-town and gives them forty dollars to buy "chop suey."

"Come on now!" he tells them knowingly at film's end. "This is America. Time is money. Chop, chop!"

★ 30. Oakland ★

No student can be a complete failure at American
Indian Public Charter School. You can always serve
as a bad example.
        —Ben Chavis, principal

Just as I finished writing about the dispiriting, self-inflicted
mayhem on the racial and ethnic front, I got an uplifting
letter from the all-around coolest guy I met in California, Dr.
Ben Chavis, principal of the American Indian Public Charter
School (AIPCS) in Oakland. He sent along a copy of his school's
most recent results in the California's Academic Performance
Index test.

Year	API Score
2000–2001	436
2001–2	596
2002–3	732
2003–4	816
2004–5	880
2005–6	920

"My students continue to kick the trend and outperform
all the other schools in the East Bay," Chavis wrote. The maximum score on the test is 1,000, the minimum 200. When Chavis
took over the school, it was blithely preparing its students for a
life of welfare, low wage service jobs and/or prison. To maintain
its rankings in the academic cellar, the school had to squan-
der the freedom allowed in the charter school system. "They

were playing Indian when I got here," said Chavis, a Lumbee Indian himself, this despite the fact that the student body is almost exactly equal parts African-American, Hispanic, Asian, and American Indian. "The school was total chaos." Now, they play American, as in success story, and the results affirm it.

In one of those only-in-California experiences, the good kind, I met with Lance Izumi and Xiaochin Claire Yan at the Pacific Research Institute, a free market think tank in Sacramento. I had asked if it was possible to succeed within California's public school system, and they surprised me by saying yes. They referred me to Chavis and a protégé of his, Jorge Lopez. In one fell swoop, the four of them showed me how little ethnic stress there can be when all plates move in the same direction.

Chavis has a story to tell, and no one can tell it better. One of ten children of a single mom, Chavis grew up without electricity or indoor plumbing among the Lumbee in North Carolina. "Isn't Kelvin Sampson a Lumbee?" I asked. Sampson is the basketball coach at Indiana University. Yes, Chavis affirmed. In fact, they are cousins.

I raised the issue because Sampson and Chavis look something alike. The Lumbees intermarried with blacks and whites generations ago, and one can see all three strains in Chavis, a lithe, vigorous, middle-aged guy with caramel-colored skin, close-cropped graying hair, a smart goatee, and dazzling bright eyes. Lacking a reservation, the Lumbees grew resourceful rather than dependent and emerged, according to Chavis, as "the Jews of the Indian world." Chavis believes in free enterprise and put its principles into practice even in the multiculturalism courses he taught at San Francisco State. For those with an urge to revolution, he counseled, *"Buy* America back and lease it out." When not teaching, Chavis has done very well himself in real estate and donates his salary back to the school.

The American Indian Public Charter School sits modestly in a tough, humble neighborhood in Oakland's flatlands. Leased from a small church next door, the school building still has a large cross on the front. "How do you get away with that?" I asked Chavis. "I tell [the authorities] that it represents the four directions of the wind," he joked, "and I haven't gotten around to putting the feathers on yet."

If he kept the cross, he did not keep the teachers he inherited. "I got rid of every last one of them," he boasted. Using the personnel freedom inherent in the charter system, he began to hire smart, ambitious people who did not have an education degree. Given the unhappy state of teacher training, he sees the education "credential" as a liability. He also paid the teachers five thousand dollars more to start than they would get in other public schools. Since this figure would disrupt the union pay scale, the unions don't want his teachers, which is fine with Chavis. Although a charter school gets less money per pupil than a regular public school, Chavis saves money by avoiding all the trainers and consultants and assistant what-nots that clutter up public-school payrolls.

"Squawkers, multicultural specialists, self-esteem experts, panhandlers, drug dealers, and those snapping turtles who refuse to put forth their best effort will be booted out," reads one of the sixteen rules posted on Chavis's office door.

"Chavism" works pretty simply. Along with the teachers, he got rid of the computers. Every class, every day, begins with ninety minutes of no-nonsense language arts. Nothing preempts it. The math is just as serious and intense. Every eighth-grader, including the special-ed kids, takes algebra. "I have high expectations," said Chavis. "I don't want excuses."

"Our staff does not subscribe to the black swamp logic of minority students as victims," reads another of the sixteen rules. "We will plow through such cornfield philosophy with common sense and hard work."

Chavis believes strongly in punctuality and attendance. A student who arrives a minute late gets detention. A student who completes a year without missing a day gets a monetary reward.

There are many such students. In an eighth-grade classroom I visited in May not one student had missed one day the whole year. In reviewing the literature, I see other inner-city schools actually boasting of 8 percent daily absentee rates. The inner-city norm runs at least twice as high. At AIPCS the daily absentee rate runs at about 0.33 percent.

I had the chance to visit with Chavis at his nicely restored home in the pleasant China Hill neighborhood above Lake Merritt in the heart of Oakland. I met his wife, who comes from Central America, and his two young children. It seemed a likely setting to talk about family, a subject to which Chavis has given a lot of thought.

Chavis sees the breakdown in family as part of an ongoing California tragedy that a school has to address if it hopes to succeed. Like Michael Grumbine in Whittier, however, he too believes that the nuclear family cannot stand alone, especially given its current fragility in the inner city. "I create an extended family for my class," he told me. He involves the kids' grandparents and aunts and uncles and doesn't hesitate to call whomever it takes to get a rogue kid's attention. "I'm big on embarrassment," he said. He laughed, but he meant it.

To reinforce the sense of kinship, the students stay together as one class for three years with the same teacher, no rotation among classes. "At this school, we are like a family," wrote one of the students proudly in a charter school publication. "We work through things because we care for each other." When challenged by outsiders about the Indianness of the school experience, Chavis shrewdly points to this, the shared "tribal" experience. He just shakes his head when he sees school districts trying to buy their way out of societal problems far too basic to be papered over, even if the paper is green. "Money's not the problem," he said. "Schools have too much money."

Chavis could have been referring to South LA Area High School in Los Angeles. In July 2005, this model school opened with a heated swimming pool, a rubber track, a ballet studio, a fully equipped chef's kitchen, and enough new Macintosh computers to buy some enterprising thief a year's supply of Pakistani black. By March of its first year, the school led the district, not exactly in test scores, but in police reports, an astonishing 218, including shootings and stabbings. Discussion in the *Los Angeles Times* of what went awry focused almost exclusively on the school's *location*. The ABETTO-rich conversations are too numbingly dumb to bear repetition.

Charter schools, however, are not in and of themselves the answer to California's problems. Marcos Aguilar, the principal of LA's La Academia Semillas del Pueblo—The Seeds of the People Academy—has proven this point in spectacular fashion. Indeed, Aguilar has done the Hispanic cause in LA more harm than anyone since the Menendez brothers. To paraphrase Chavis, what prevents him from being a complete failure is the impressive talent he has shown as a bad example. Talk radio hosts in LA thank God for the day he came into their lives.

Aguilar claims to be teaching his primary-school students how "to analyze the world in several languages," including English, Spanish, Mandarin, and Nahuatl, an Aztec dialect. By learning Nahuatl, the students are expected "to understand their relationship with nature" as well as the "customs and traditions that are so imbued in the language." Given what they actually do learn, these kids better hope that the Aztec Denny's has pictures on the menu, or they are going to starve to death.

On the upside, the kids at Seeds Academy do plenty of math. On the downside, they do Nahuatl math, which works on a base 20 system even though the rest of the world works on base 10. The fact that California also tests on a base 10 system helps account for Seeds' rank as the 458th best elementary school of the 463 in the LA Unified School District. Reportedly, Seeds beat out those schools that calculated in Ebonics, Esperanto, and Pig Latin.

Under the leadership of people like Aguilar, once-proud California chalked up a "bottom six states" ranking in 2005 in every single National Assessment for Educational Progress (NAEP) test its students took. Only Mississippi sends a smaller percentage of high-school students to four-year colleges than California, a trend that, according to one typical study, results from "too few counselors, teachers and college preparatory courses." As if.

When Jorge Lopez took over the 92 percent Hispanic Oakland Charter School in 2004, it was nearly as deranged as Seeds in LA. In his visits, Lopez saw the educators forcing this "culture crap" on the kids and mixing in enough "liberal jargon" to turn them against their parents. Lopez responded by firing the entire staff down to the janitors and starting over with the Chavis model. "Culture is a job for the parents," said Lopez. "My job is to educate the kids." This past year, with 100 percent of his students taking the API test, Oakland Charter scored an 857, second in Oakland only to Chavis's school.

The first of his family born in America, Lopez grew up hard on the mean streets of Richmond. In the tenth grade at Richmond High—"Gladiator School" he calls it—he got jumped on the first day of school and pistol whipped on the second. On the third day, he called it quits and went to work with his mother cleaning houses. Only the intervention of an attorney client of his mother's redirected him into the safer confines of Berkeley High, from which he finally graduated. With the help of an older brother and his girlfriend, now his wife and mother of his three children, Lopez abandoned a not-so-promising career dealing guns and drugs and made his way to and through college and grad school.

Even more than Chavis, the affable thirty-five-year-old Lopez has an epic struggle on his hands. On this small battlefield in Oakland, he is fighting the Aguilars of California for the soul of Hispanic America, the soul of the nation, for that matter, and he knows it. He says of Aguilar, "We're enemies." As he reminds his students, "The reason our parents moved to the United States is because their own countries were so screwed up." He pushes not Mexican culture but what he calls "first-generation ideals," namely hard work, family, and conservative values in an American context.

To make Lopez's life just a little more difficult, however, the Blue establishment is pulling for Aguilar. "School Regenerates Immigrants' Pride," reads one headline. "Charter School Fighting Back," reads another, and they are not talking about the Oakland Charter Academy. As is his wont, Chavis cut right to the chase in explaining why many in authority want people like him and Lopez to fail. "The liberals hate [us]," he told me, "for proving their method does not work with us 'darkies.'"

THE RAINBOW LOSES
ITS LUSTER

★ 31. Potrero Hill ★

She was enough of a Californian to resent being
called an American.
  —Armistead Maupin, *Babycakes*, 1984

In the sixty-plus postwar years literally millions of fathers
have walked away from their California homes. Of all
those acts of abandonment, few have proven more consequential
than the flight fifty-some years ago of a gent known as "Sweet
Jimmy." Although he could not have dreamed it at the time, his
departure from his San Francisco home lit a slow fuse that, when
finally consumed, would damage race relations in California for
a generation.

At the time, Sweet Jimmy and wife, Eunice, and their four
kids lived in the city's eclectic, multiracial Potrero Hill district,
unfashionably far south of Market Street. "Potrero" is the Spanish word for pasture, which the hill was during its Mexican era.
It is far enough south of the fog-drenched bay that the various
cows and sheep and what-not could graze happily in the sunshine. Today, neighborhood guides still boast of the sunshine. As
to the sheep, it's strictly BYO.

In the American years, the hill itself has been home to one
generation after another of immigrants and still is. The flatlands
around the base of the hill have historically been given over to
industry and, today, to the various mixed uses that clever developers have concocted for the postindustrial era. For all its
conventional uses and for all its proximity to the heart of San
Francisco, Potrero Hill seems oddly remote, oddly off-kilter, especially at night when, unlike most of San Francisco, life seems
to disappear.

Sweet Jimmy craved the nightlife of the city down below.

Given its Gold Rush beginnings, San Francisco has long been a city of the night, and a more tolerant one than most. Ministers were calling it "Sodom by the Sea" even before that phrase implied a certain sexual proclivity. During the Spanish-American War, the city served as home port for thousands of sailors and soldiers. They sensed immediately the difference between where they were and where they had come from. A century later, that difference could still dazzle an innocent from the inland empire as it did U.S. Navy apprentice airman Steven Nary, the Billy Budd of our story.

For some sailors and soldiers and other passers-through, that difference captured their imagination, as they were "different" themselves. Many of them stayed behind when the war was through or returned when they had settled accounts elsewhere. In the years after the Spanish-American War, as AIDS historian Randy Shilts observes, "Resourceful gays staked out Market Street, the city's main thoroughfare, as a cruising zone and there shopped among the always numerous sailors for satisfaction." The eastward-looking World War I may have bypassed the city, but World War II sealed its destiny. San Francisco served as disembarkation point for hundreds of thousands of men who fought in the Pacific. Many stayed or returned.

It was easier to be who they were in a distant city. It still is. Juan Pifarre had come all the way from Argentina to San Francisco for that very freedom and eventually settled, like countless immigrants before him, in Potero Hill. As fate would have it, his was the last home that sailor Steven Nary would ever set foot in.

To be gay close to home back then could be more than uncomfortable, especially for an African-American. And yet, if you lived in Potrero Hill, just a streetcar ride from this *soi-disant* Sodom, where else would you steal away to? So Sweet Jimmy shrugged off his befuddled wife and bawling kids for the bright lights down below. Nor does Jimmy seem to have been shy about his orientation, as he left openly for another man and would soon gain a local reputation as a drag queen. One can only imagine the shock waves this sent through family and community.

Jimmy's two daughters seemed to have survived the shock well enough. They had their sweet mother for a role model and adapted reasonably well, both marrying and raising families of their own. The sons were another story. The younger one got involved with gangs before moving on to more productive ventures. The older one turned to drugs and stayed there.

Given the lack of data, I can only speculate on the impact that a dad's homosexual epiphany might have on an impressionable son. There is nothing close to consensus even on the most public and dramatic case in the Bay Area in recent years, that of the Lindh family of Marin County.

When young attorney Frank Lindh and wife Marilyn moved to Marin in 1991 there was little to distinguish them from their neighbors save perhaps for their three children, a huge family in an area where the average fry cook can speak knowingly about ZPG. By contrast, Johnson County, the most affluent in Kansas and the boyhood home of Thomas Frank, has, per capita, nearly 30 percent more children under the age of eighteen than Marin.

I have not spent enough time in Marin, right across the Golden Gate Bridge from San Francisco, to know whether it deserves its old reputation as a haven of aging hippies in hot tubs. I suspect, though, that in a county where the *median* price for a single-family home was $960,000 in 2006 and the *average* price more than $1.2 million, not a whole lot of people have the time to laze around in tubs of any sort. That's a shame actually. So many of the homes nestle nicely in Marin's hills and have dazzling views of the bay beyond. If there is a more attractive suburban community in the world I have not seen it.

The Lindhs lived in the hills above San Anselmo, one of the

county's perfect little towns. The two main streets of the town flank a perfect little creek. Along the creek is a scenic little park dedicated to "the children of our community"—precious few that there are—"as a symbol of support for this and other generations." The streets are lined with perfect little shops like Toys & Antiques, Books Bought and Sold, and my favorite, the porn flick–inspired Debbie Does Dessert. Unfortunately, I did not get to sample Debbie's wares as the shop was "*fermé*."

I did go into Bubba's Diner, which is not at all like the gritty, workaday diners back in New Jersey, the "Diner State." No, Bubba's reminded me of nothing so much as the diner in Pleasantville, a perfectly pristine, 1950s-movie-set diner, this one with a PC upgrade, to wit, "Our leftover fryer oil is used for biodiesel fuel." If they are doing any such thing in New Jersey, they certainly don't brag about it at the front door.

I had hoped to wander the streets anonymously, but when I pulled up to the curb in my rented Ford Taurus—okay, okay, I drive one at home, too—the natives knew I was not one of them. As far as I can tell, other than the occasional service vehicle, there are no American cars in Marin. None. This is not a stereotype. This is a symptom.

I got a sense of the larger problem when I wandered the streets of Berkeley in the year after September 11—not the student radical end of Berkeley by the way, but the halfway sane, home-owning upper half, the half that more or less matches Marin in its basic psychographics. As I walked I decided to start counting American flags. After a five-mile jaunt, I had counted a grand total of, drum roll please, *one*. In the Castro, San Francisco's iconic gay neighborhood, the *only* flags one sees are the ubiquitous rainbow flags, 9/11 notwithstanding.

A week after my Berkeley stroll, I took a walk in Cranford, my sister's comparably affluent New Jersey suburb—home, by the way, of the first-rate Cranford Diner—and I counted roughly 150 flags in the same stretch. So when the Lindhs's son, John, started having trouble at home he wasn't about to head down to the Marine recruiting office on Sir Francis Drake Boulevard, because there is none. The people of Marin leave the fighting of wars, at least on our side, to other people's sons.

There was, to be sure, trouble at home. Although Frank and Marilyn divorced in 1999, when John was eighteen, Frank admits that they had effectively separated six years earlier. More problematic still, Frank, like Sweet Jimmy before him, left Marilyn for another guy. Marilyn was cool with Frank's reorientation, this being Marin in the nineties and all, but son John seems to have taken the news rather hard. One indication of this is that he dropped the old man's name and started calling himself "John Walker."

As we have seen, guys changing names is a California kind of thing, and not just in Hollywood. Philadelphia car salesman Jack Rosenberg reinvented himself as Marin's Werner Hans Erhard. New York's Timothy Dexter transformed himself into Malibu's "Grizzly Man" Timothy Treadwell. Angeleno Ron Everett invented Kwanzaa, assaulted two women, went to prison for four years, and came out the other end as Dr. Ron Karenga, chairman of black studies at Cal State, Long Beach. But the precocious John Walker Lindh had changed his name by sixteen, and it was merely the first of many name changes to come. Something was going on here.

Lindh changed schools even more often than he changed names, ending up finally at Tamiscal High. This uniquely Marin kind of educational experience opened its doors in 1991 to the weird and restless. Although humbly situated in a series of high-end doublewides, the school looks beyond a parking lot of Lexi, across a lake, and onto what may be America's most gorgeous suburban development. When not admiring the view, the school's "lifelong learners" grow to "develop a positive self-image and high level of integrity" and "assume personal responsibility for their learning and time management." I don't know about positive self-image, but you can't fault Tamiscal on the personal responsibility end. Young Johnny was about to concoct a program for lifelong learning that would impress even the most creative curriculum designer.

There is some debate about where the inspiration came from. Frank Lindh traces it to the movie *Malcolm X*, which Marilyn took John to see at age twelve. Apparently, he was moved by Malcolm's transformation at film's end from a Muslim who believed that white men were mutants created by the big-headed evil genius Yakub to one who espoused more traditional beliefs like "jihad." John also read the book on which the movie is based and likely discussed it one-on-one with a teacher at Tamiscal, actual classes there being strictly *infra dig*.

Even beyond Tamiscal, the state's otherwise secular public schools serve as Islamic propaganda mills. In the absurdly ambitious seventh-grade world history and geography course mandated by the California State Board of Education, students are treated to several weeks of uncritical Islam. They are required to "trace the origins of Islam and the life and teachings of Muhammad" and to "explain the significance of the Qur'an and the Sunnah as the primary sources of Islamic beliefs, practice, and law." If this Islamic enthusiasm was offset by some comparable study of Christianity, it might be more comprehendible. It is not. Although the students study Rome and medieval Europe, there is no mention of either Christ or the Bible in the state's content standards.

Given the state's multicultural mania, some schools take Islam almost as seriously as they take Ebonics or Nahuatl. Students in Byron, an hour east of San Francisco, had to adopt Islamic names, memorize verses from the Koran, recite them, pray to Allah in class, and simulate Ramadan fasting by going without some food item for a day. From what I can tell, however, the students did not quite get around to the simulated stoning of a pretend homosexual, death being the officially recommended punishment for what Islam considers a "depraved practice."

Marin educators are nearly as hip to Islam as those in Byron. Melanie Morgan, the popular host of a KSFO radio show in San Francisco, told me that her son had to make a field trip to the same Mill Valley mosque where Lindh was first indoctrinated—and this in the year after 9/11. Morgan accompanied the kids on the trip, and her tough questions to the imam made her son a "pariah" among the school faculty. "He was the kid with the crazy mom," said Morgan. When Morgan asked the teachers if the students would make a comparable trip to a church, almost as rare in Marin as a mosque, the teacher dismissed the suggestion as "Eurocentric."

As to Lindh's education, one of John's cousins cites the "pseudo-Muslim murmurs within hip-hop music" as John's original inspiration. His email name, the timelessly adolescent Hine E. Craque, was a Marin stab at hip-hop nomenclature. At one point, John even claimed to be "hip-hop's Christ," whatever that means. John also trailblazed the nether regions of the then-novel Internet, wandering through the cyber-haunts dedicated to UFOs, the Illuminati, and ultimately Islam. He slipped into Islamic chat rooms and asked trenchant questions about the faith like "Is it O.K. [for a Muslim] to watch cartoons on TV?" When he began to sign on as "Brother Mujahid" and wander around San Anselmo in his flowing white *thobe* and matching *taqiyah* headgear, the folks down at Bubba's knew that Johnny had finally found his thang.

Given the range of vices available to an alienated Marin County adolescent, Frank and Marilyn were not displeased by his Islamic drift. They did nothing to discourage John's visits to the nearby Islamic Center of Mill Valley and allowed him to journey, when barely seventeen, to the Middle East hellhole called Yemen, there to pursue his Islamic studies, now as Suleyman al-Faris.

Although it would be reassuring to blame Yemen for John's radical turn, the Yemenites throw this one right back at us. John's

Yemenite language teacher told *Time* magazine that Lindh "came from the U.S. already hating America." His correspondence seems to bear that out. In a letter to his mom soon after the 1998 bombings of the U.S. embassies in Africa, he argues that these attacks were "far more likely to have been carried out by the American government than by any Muslims."

Young John didn't have to go to Yemen to pick this stuff up. Several Bay Area kids I talked to told me they get a steady stream of anti-Americanism from the teachers at their local public high. One East Bay student complained that his history teacher, who also happened to be the union shop steward, a scary combo, has the Communist Manifesto prominently posted in his classroom, almost as a lesson plan. "He's not abusive," the student told me. "Just constant." In speaking to California parents, I heard this same story over and over again, with the anti-American, anti-Republican, prounion indoctrination beginning as early as the third grade. Said one mom, "I would object formally, but I honestly believe it would hurt my sons' chances in school."

The ideological imbalance in the schools is obvious, undeniable, and reinforced by a teacher's union that hasn't endorsed a Republican, if memory serves me, since John C. Frémont. In 2002, a union spokesman unabashedly showed his hand by arguing against a California assembly bill that would have required testing students on the essentials of American history like the Declaration of Independence and the Constitution. The union was of the opinion that the Declaration and the Constitution, unlike the Koran, were "nonessential materials." In the movie *Thirteen*, the one good teacher we see proudly wears a big Bush-bashing button to class.

The state's academics make the schoolteachers look like John Birchers. So loopy are the universities in the area that Berkeley is not even the most radical. Now, the kids at UC Santa Cruz openly mock the Berkeley kids as right-wing sticks-in-the-mud. The Pentagon made Santa Cruz's rep by placing the university on "surveillance," an honor denied Berkeley. The Santa Cruisers caught the brass's attention by their creative harassment of military recruiters, including such parent-pleasing strategies as "a queer kiss-in."

"Berkeley may have the reputation for having a lot of anti-war activists," said one teaching assistant proudly, "but I feel like Santa Cruz has had a lot more going on." Of course, not all Santa Cruz students are Marxists or Maoists or Kim Jong-Iliputians. I met one such student, in fact, who is downright conservative. "Why Santa Cruz?" I asked him. "Great surf," he answered without missing a beat. Ah, California!

If only the newly christened Suleyman had been a surfer, he sure as hell would not have ended up in Afghanistan, a country without any running water, let alone surf, and one where the phrase "hang ten" has some truly ominous overtones. On the way to Afghanistan, young John fired his first Kalashnikov, filled his notebook with phrases like, "We shall make jihad as long as we live," recorded passages from the Koran detailing battles with the Jews, and, in general, acclimated himself to the religion of peace.

Following the 2000 U.S. presidential election, the nineteen-year-old emailed his mother with a mocking reference to "your new President" before adding, "I'm glad he's not mine." This was not exactly an act of rebellion. George W. Bush pulled a whopping 28 percent of the Marin County vote in the 2000 election and 25 percent in 2004. This represents something of a trend. Walter "Fritz" Mondale carried the county against native son Ronald Reagan during a 1984 election in which Mondale carried not one single state other than his own. Given Marin's 2 percent black population, it is unlikely that Mondale carried any other county in America nearly this white. And as for the notion that the Republicans are the party of the rich, please note that Marin has the highest per capita income of any county in America.

In Afghanistan, John went by still another name, Abdul Hamid. There he hung out at the training camps, shook the hand of the great Osama bin Laden, and headed for the hills with pop's permission. The next time his folks saw him was on TV as the instantly celebrated "Teen Taliban." An incident just before his final capture sealed his fate. The video of the encounter shows CIA agent Johnny Spann attempting to interrogate the surly Abdul Hamid.

"Do you know that the people you're here working with are terrorists?" Spann asked him. "They killed other Muslims. There were several hundred Muslims killed in the bombing in New York City. Is that what the Koran teaches?" Young Abdul refused to answer. When Spann asked, "Are you going to talk to us?" he again refused. Almost immediately afterward, his fellow prisoners erupted in a revolt that left Spann dead. This is the reason John Walker Lindh, or "Hamzah" as he is now known—his sixth name?—is spending a hard twenty at the Federal Correctional Complex at Victorville, California. There, his supporters are already lionizing him as the "new Malcolm X," the Eminem, as it were, of black nationalism.

After the Teen Taliban's capture, publicity descended on Marin County like acid rain. The county and the parents were widely rebuked for their indulgence and indiscipline. George Bush *père* reflected the gist of the criticism, if not the rage behind it, when he described John as a "poor, misguided Marin County hot-tubber." This criticism led not so much to reflection on how a John Lindh could possibly have become a Teen Taliban but to angry reaction from those who resented the inquiry.

The *New York Times'* Frank Rich led the rush to the cultural ramparts, chastising the Lindhs' critics for "knee-jerk" cultural profiling. The *Wall Street Journal* and editorialist Shelby Steele particularly irked him for daring to suggest that the Lindhs exemplified "a certain cultural liberalism" of the sort likely to be found in Northern California.

Rich countered with the competing idea that Lindh and

his family had been "regular Catholic churchgoers." Although others had made the same point, Rich took this gambit a misstep further and linked Lindh to FBI traitor Robert Hanssen, "a rigorous member of the conservative Catholic sect Opus Dei." Thus, it made as much sense to blame the Lindhs' Catholicism for their son's fate as their cultural liberalism, never mind that Robert Hanssen used his wife's Catholic faith as a cover for his sundry sexual kinks.

After this brief dabble in anti-Catholic sophistry, Rich simply dismisses the Lindh affair as an anomaly, one "that cannot be pinned on any particular cultural influence, family constellation, religion or sexual history." One sees few acts of ABETTO this ham-handed. The fact that the Lindhs *subsidized* John's descent into mujahideen madness moves Rich not a tick. The case obviously threatens his worldview. Rich not only refuses to analyze it but also scolds those who do.

Meanwhile, much of the debate in the gay press and in the San Francisco press—no, I'm not being redundant—focused on the impact of Frank Lindh's apparent homosexuality, a nuance that was largely downplayed elsewhere. The public debate started when *San Francisco Examiner* columnist P. J. Corkery first revealed the gay angle, noting, "Sources close to the family say the father's turn of life from married man to modern gay man startled and flustered the 16-year-old."

In high ABETTO dudgeon, Rob Morse, one of the *San Francisco Chronicle*'s liberal, progay columnists—now I am being redundant—charged Corkery and the *Examiner* with "taking attacks on [Walker's] family to a new and disgusting level."

Morse had unwittingly stepped in the poop from an easily angered sacred cow. Michelangelo Signorile, a gay columnist for the *New York Press*, took him to the progressive woodshed for doing so. Why, he asked, does a San Francisco liberal still think it "disgusting" to talk about Lindh's homosexuality, especially when Frank Lindh was well out of the closet? "If what Corkery says is true," adds Signorile, "that events surrounding the break-up of the marriage affected John Walker, then it is absolutely relevant to the story of Walker's journey and his actions."

If Signorile had stopped here, he would have chalked up a minor victory for common sense. But no Rainbow fable is complete without "Jerry Falwell and his pack of wolves." Signorile accuses them of gnarling their way through Marin County, up the hills of San Anselmo, and into the unformed brain of John Walker Lindh. Now infused with America's "ingrained, religion-based hatred of homosexuality," young Lindh embraced the most "rigid, homophobic religious philosophy and regime" he could find. Signorile won't even entertain the possibility that a dad's dumping Mom for Tom might just naturally whack a kid out.

If guys like Rich and Morse and Signorile were not so willfully myopic, they could see the obvious pathology at work here. First, the Lindhs uproot their sensitive ten-year-old son to the opposite coast. Two years after moving to Marin, the Lindhs effectively separate. Some time after that, Frank leaves home for another guy, not that there's anything wrong with that, and soon afterward, the Lindhs finally divorce. Welcome to California, John.

Young Lindh's behavior on Christmas Eve, 1997, speaks to the mess his life had become. According to sympathetic biographer Mark Kukis, Lindh turned up at the Mill Valley mosque, "saying he had to get out of the house." Kukis suggests that he left home because his family was celebrating Christmas, a holiday the sixteen-year-old had righteously rejected. That hardly explains, however, why he spent the night at the mosque. Something is clearly amiss here.

In splitting, the Lindhs sacrificed their moral authority to guide John's life, not that they had much to begin with. The Lindhs' idea of Catholicism, one that tolerates Marilyn's dabbling in "native rites" and Frank's dabbling in native Califor-

nians, cannot be taken seriously as a guiding force. Nor can a liberal tent big enough to shelter an ambitious power attorney for a large utility company. No, in an area that mocks patriotism and trivializes even liberalism, and in a home where faith and family have no real meaning, the radically unmoored Lindh had nothing to hang on to. In this regard, he has much more in common with a Monster Kody Scott or Susan Atkins than he does a Robert Hanssen. With all of its order and discipline and group cohesion, the Taliban became his Crips, his Manson family.

True to form, Kukis refuses to confront the obvious. He rejects the notion that Lindh's quest represented a "troubled search for identity" or that it "reflected issues in his upbringing." "I don't see it that way," says Kukis in the book's preface. "Lindh, like many young people, explored religion." Yes, and the Manson girls were "idealists and social rebels and spiritual seekers" exploring cult living. That explains everything.

Like Frank Lindh, Sweet Jimmy Simpson did his greatest act of disservice to his children not so much by coming out—although that could not have helped—as by going away. His wife, Eunice, managed as best she could, but by age thirteen her younger son had become unmanageable. He was running full-time with a gang called the Persian Warriors and increasingly falling afoul of the law.

But my, how he could run! His athletic talents attracted the attention of Giant baseball great Willie Mays. Mays took young Orenthal James Simpson under his wing and provided a stabilizing father figure through the remainder of his high-school years. For the next twenty years of his life O.J. prospered in the patriarchal world of the locker room, where coaches provided at least temporary discipline and colleagues insisted on performance. It was when that world fell away that O.J. was thrown back on resources that he had never fully developed.

In one of the very few analyses of Simpson to dare mention Jimmy's gay ways, Dr. David Gutmann, a psychology prof at

Northwestern University, makes a powerful case for the role of a "true patriarch" in a boy's life. As he sees it, the patriarch provides a steady hand and an occasional kick in the butt to move a son away from the dominion of his mother and fully into the world as a self-disciplined male. Tookie Williams, among others, traces his own descent to the lack of a patriarch. "In my life," he regrets, "the natural progression from maternal weaning to paternal guidance was absent."

Boys with no dad or an ineffectual one often find "less trustworthy ways" to establish distance from their moms. "Physical distance," adds Gutmann, "they achieve by flight: from the mother's home to the streets, to the fighting gangs that rule them and, at the end of the day, to the all-male fraternity of the penitentiary." As to social distance, that they achieve "by moving out of the mother's cultural world, and off her scale of values." John Lindh did both. O.J. ultimately did the same—and with a vengeance.

Gutmann makes the case that O.J. only gave the appearance of having matured. When he lost the artificial discipline of pro sports, he had little internal discipline to fall back on. As a way of asserting his masculinity, O.J. divorced his first wife, repeatedly abused wife Nicole, cheated on her, divorced her, and almost assuredly killed her in a jealous rage. "The troubles of a poorly fathered son," says Gutmann, echoing Judith Wallerstein, "can afflict not only his childhood and adolescence, but his later years as well."

Worse, the troubles of a person like O. J. Simpson can and did afflict an entire society. No one documented O.J.'s cultural impact more lucidly than *Vanity Fair* reporter Dominick Dunne. For the length of the judicial process in 1994–95, Dunne was the most sought-after dinner guest in all of California. He dined almost nightly with some contingent or another of America's elite opinion makers, from Norman Lear to Nancy Reagan. He did not hide from them his conviction that O.J. was guilty. Nor

did they hide theirs from him. This seemed to be the one transcendent passion in all of California, the rare force that pulled the Red and Blue plates together and likely every other plate save one.

On October 3, 1995, the illusion of transcendence came to an abrupt end. The "not guilty" announcement set off a seismic storm from which California has yet to recover. The verdict horrified white California, froze it in place. Says Dunne, speaking for many, "A terrible evil had been done." The Black plate, however, surged forward in a burst of enthusiasm that fully discombobulated white California—white America, for that matter. In assessing O.J.'s legacy, Dunne says flatly and knowingly, "He's divided the races."

Although, as Dunne reports, a West LA matron or two did fire their overly gleeful cooks, the tectonic damage was not obvious in the way that it was after the "not guilty" verdicts in the Rodney King case, three years earlier. No, "the rage of white citizenry" would take different forms, none more powerful than indifference.

To be sure, indifference is hard to calculate. A year later, Proposition 209, which outlawed affirmative action, carried the state easily, winning majorities in every county in California save for LA and those in the Bay Area. Ten years later the state executed Stanley "Tookie" Williams without riot or protest from anyone more serious than Susan Sarandon or the Swiss whack job who had kept nominating him for the Nobel Prize.

Oddly, though, it is this indifference that may lead to the ultimate liberation of black California. The kind of attention African-Americans have received these last forty years has not done the culture—or California—a whit of good.

★ 32. The Castro ★

"In this town," he thought, "The Love That Dares Not
Speak Its Name almost never shuts up."
—Armistead Maupin, *Tales of the City*

Social historians trace the birth of the gay liberation
movement to 1969, the year of Manson, Altamont, the
Crips, Bishop Pike's death, no-fault divorce, and the Santa Barbara oil spill. On June 22 of that year, in London, singer Judy
Garland took a few dozen seconals too many and ended her
confused life at age forty-seven. On June 27, her funeral was
held in New York City. More than twenty thousand fans filed
past her open coffin, many of them a "friend of Dorothy," code
for "gay" in those preliberation days.

That night, the New York City Police just happened to raid
an after-hours mob joint in Greenwich Village, the Stonewall
Inn. They picked the wrong night and the wrong joint. Still dis-
tressed over Judy's death, the club's resident drag queens threw
a collective fit, and that bitchy show of defiance sparked several
days of high-spirited protest and rioting.

In New York, at the time, few took the flare-up seriously.
The *New York Daily News* headlined the incident, "Homo Nest
Raided, Queen Bees Are Stinging Mad." Even the usually insur-
rection-friendly *Village Voice* dismissed Stonewall as the "Great
Faggot Rebellion."

As much as New York City may want to take credit for the
birth of gay liberation, the movement's rolling front edge has always been in the streets of San Francisco, often literally. As early
as 1961, a drag queen had run for the Board of Supervisors—the
city council equivalent—and gotten a respectable seven thousand votes. By 1969, the city had emerged in the estimate of

gay historians "as the capital and mecca of gay America" with at least fifty thousand gays among its seven-hundred-thousand-plus people. On recalling his move to San Francisco in this era, Armistead Maupin's gay protagonist Michael enthuses, "I had never seen so many faggots in my whole godamned [sic] life."

I should caution the reader that historians of gay culture often write with unsparing candor about the movement and/or themselves. This includes not only Maupin but the others referenced herein, including *San Francisco Chronicle* reporter Randy Shilts in *The Mayor of Castro Street* and *And the Band Played On*, *New York Times* writers Dudley Clendinen and Adam Nagourney in *Out for Good*, culture critic Daniel Harris in *The Rise and Fall of Gay Culture*, Eric Marcus in *Making Gay History*, and Gabriel Rotello in *Sexual Ecology*.

That much said, the ABETTO factor rules the mass market with an iron fist. "Boosterism has largely displaced real discussion about gay culture," Harris rightly complains. The result, he laments, is that gays are now expected to achieve self-worth "by consuming the propaganda our political leaders disseminate in such vast quantities." In California today, certainly in the major media, nongays write about the gay movement as gingerly as non-Muslims write about Islam in Islamabad.

Propaganda, however, is what makes a cultural plate cohere, especially in the political sphere, and in San Francisco, the gay plate had begun to rumble long before it did anywhere else in the world. By 1969, aspirants for the Board of Supervisors felt compelled to show their ideological wares before the gay-organized Society for Individual Rights, or SIR, on its candidates' night. Among the candidates to audition that year was a good-looking thirty-six-year-old housewife running for supervisor, her first shot at political office. The folks at SIR liked her. If they had not, it is unlikely that Senator Dianne Feinstein would have gotten beyond the local PTA.

In 1971 the city's gay community came into its own politically when it all but recruited a young maverick police officer named Richard Hongisto to challenge a crusty old incumbent in the sheriff's race. Although straight himself, Hongisto did not shy from advancing gay issues. His victory solidified San Francisco's reputation as gay Mecca. Now scores of thousands of eager gay men would make their hajj to this "Baghdad by the Bay," and each year, many would stay. By decade's end, a Maupin character would claim "one hundred and twenty thousand practicing homosexuals" in the city, "conservatively speaking." The number is too high but not absurdly so.

Typically young and well educated, the new gays replaced the retreating ethnic working classes and transformed the very heart of the city. One neighborhood proved particularly opportune, a fading Irish enclave with cheap rents centered on Eighteenth and Castro. Within a decade, the neighborhood had become *"the* Castro," the sanctum sanctorum of gay America.

In the way of clarification, the Castro is not a gay and lesbian neighborhood. It's a gay neighborhood. To further clarify, just as the word "man" can mean either a male or all mankind, so too the word "gay" can mean either a male or all homosexuals. Often, the meaning is unclear. In this case, I mean "male." You'll see only a few more women in the Castro than you would at a Promise Keeper rally. For all their political alliances, gay men in general don't seem to care much for gay women. "The truth was," admit Clendinen and Nagourney, talking about LA politics, "that gay men didn't like spending time with lesbians."

In California and elsewhere, one gets the sense that gay men don't take the "gayness" of their female counterparts very seriously. Maupin is a case in point. The three main lesbian characters in his *Tales* change sexual identities almost as easily as they change hairstyles. Of the character Mona, he writes, "Lesbianism had simply been the logical follow-up to macrobiotics and primal screaming." Later, someone asks her, "Are you off men completely?" D'orothea meanwhile "felt that being a socialist was more important than being a lesbian." And DeDe, the least convincing lesbian of the three, had been married until a noon-time coupling with a Chinese delivery boy blessed her with a set of twins undeniably not her husband's. These *Tales* began as a series in the *San Francisco Chronicle*. Were a *Chronicle* writer today to even suggest that male homosexuality is a matter of choice, he'd be on the streets before the paper was.

Among those who made their way to the Castro in these early years was a hyperactive, wannabe hipster from New York with the Dickensian name of Harvey Milk. Having turned forty with little to show for it, Milk quit his gig as a financial analyst and opened a small camera shop right on Castro, the emerging Main Street of gay America. Something of a "spoiled child," even in the eyes of friends, Milk would demand attention and get it.

He was not alone in needing it. Looking for big cosmic hugs and get-out-of-guilt-free cards, many gays came west to test the waters of the human potential movement, then just cresting. For a good percentage, the wells turned up dry. The psycho-therapists did not want to "celebrate their diversity"—that bit of moral preening had yet to be invented. They mostly just wanted to set them straight. The gay patients balked. They wanted room to maneuver. Some would find it not in group therapy but in guerilla theater.

In May 1970 the American Psychiatric Association (APA) happened to stage its annual meeting in San Francisco. Bad choice. As the unsuspecting shrinks quickly realized, local gay activists had prepared a show of their own. Provocateurs hounded the shrinks throughout, shouting insults, disrupting meetings, snatching mikes from trembling hands, all the while insisting that they be heard. "Psychiatry has waged a relentless war of extermination against us," shouted one activist. In confusing these timid docs with the SS, he was hardly unique. From the beginning of the insurrection, gay activists would undermine their foes' defenses with Nazi allusions until they skulked away or surrendered.

The shrinks were not remotely man enough to fight back. They were keening for their own private Vichy before the San Francisco meeting was halfway through. By December 1973, they had fully capitulated. The APA's Board of Trustees voted overwhelmingly that month to remove homosexuality from the *Diagnostic and Statistical Manual*. With the upward thrust of a few wrinkled hands, they opted for collaboration, declaring gayness to be something other than an illness. The pols, in San Francisco at least, had already declared it to be something other than a crime. Soon the churches would declare homosexuality to be something other than a sin—and, if not, there would be hell to pay.

★ 33. Roseville ★

Selfishness is not living as one wishes to live, it is asking others to live as one wishes to live.
—Oscar Wilde

On June 7, 2006, I received an email from Peter Verzola, headlined "Today is his 28th birthday." The "his" refers to Steven Nary, whose case Verzola and a handful of supporters have kept just barely alive for the eleven years of Nary's imprisonment.

In his own odd way, Verzola himself embodies the quirkiest and most original of San Francisco's multiethnic eccentricity. As dark as the average American black, the gray-bearded, shaggy-haired Verzola defies easy ethnic identification. I had to ask. He told me his father was Asian and his mother Sioux with a little Cherokee, Scotch-Irish, and Jew thrown into the mix. As a kid in Illinois, he passed himself off as a "Hawaiian" because it was a lot easier than explaining his roots. Then as now, he refuses to hyphenate his Americanism. People who look like Verzola or the African-American Terry Anderson or the Lumbee Indian Ben Chavis represent something of a new norm in California and likely will in America a few generations hence.

In the late 1960s Verzola had been among the thousands of young people to go "clean for Gene." When Senator Gene McCarthy's quixotic run for president flamed out at the spectacularly chaotic 1968 Democratic convention in Chicago, Verzola, like millions before him, headed west to soothe his soul. He landed in San Francisco, but not exactly on his feet. He would spend a total of three years living on the streets—in two separate sidewalk sabbaticals—before he got his act together as a legal investigator and freelance journalist. Now semiretired, and still digging up dirt from a squirrel's nest of an apartment in the Hayes Valley neighborhood, Verzola knows the underside of San Francisco life better than Sam Spade ever did.

Curiously, the usually precise Verzola got both the date and the year of Nary's birthday wrong. In fact, Nary turned *twenty-nine* on June 8, 2006. He was born not on the day of—that would have been too perfect—but on the day after "Orange Tuesday," June 7, 1977, a day that rubs gay activists as wrong as the Orange Order parades of July 12 do Irish nationalists.

The seeds of this most lamented of days had been planted in Miami, Florida, in late 1976. There, two activists—one, a gay bathhouse mogul and the other a bisexual encounter group leader—had gotten together to draft an ordinance banning discrimination based on "affectional or sexual preference." They had the support of a sympathetic Dade County Metro Commission. After the commisssion held a public hearing on the matter, usually a formality, the ordinance would have become law.

Former commissioner Robert Brake read the ordinance in mild shock. This wasn't about decriminalization. The live-and-let-live Catholic attorney had no problem with that. This was about one set of rights crunching up against another, specifically his right of free association and freedom of religion. If passed, the ordinance could have forced parochial schools like his children's to hire openly gay teachers.

The then spokeswoman for Florida Orange Juice, the former Miss Oklahoma Anita Bryant, felt the same way and much more fervently. When Brake met Bryant, a Southern Baptist, he knew he had found the person to lead his campaign. They and their allics gathered more than sixty thousand signatures and forced the commission to schedule a public vote.

In the halcyon days of the 1970s, gay activists, for all their smarts, had not yet learned lesson one about cultural tectonics: namely that, for every push, there is sooner or later a push back. On June 7, 1977, the push-back proved aggressively opposite and more than equal. Some two hundred thousand Floridians turned out to vote against the ordinance, a stunning 70 percent of the total vote. The political pros took away one lesson that activists would continue to forget: "Homosexuals should avoid taking their case to the public."

In Miami, gay activists were crushed. "The Lord will see us through some day," they sang, appropriating the civil rights hymn to help cope with defeat. In San Francisco, gays coped by taking to the streets and demanding that the very same Lord be banned from politics: "Two, four, six, eight, separate the church and state." In reality, the churches had less to do with Bryant's movement than they did with Martin Luther King's. No matter. For progressives up and down California—in cities named after Saint Francis, Saint Barbara, Saint Rose, Saint James, Saint Monica, the Holy Cross, the Blessed Sacrament, the angels—the defeat offered one more excuse to drive Christianity out of the public square. During those same ill-starred early morning hours of protest, Steven Nary was born in Biloxi, Mississippi.

If nothing else, the enemy now had a face. A few weeks after the vote, when 250,000 marchers paraded in San Francisco's annual Stonewall commemoration, one of them held a large picture of Bryant while others in his row held pictures of her presumably like-minded fellows: Adolph Hitler, Joseph Stalin, and Idi Amin. Just in case the point was missed, another person in that row carried an image of a burning cross.

The Florida vote agitated even Maupin's apolitical Michael. In the second volume of the *Tales of the City* series, the reader learns that Michael had grown up, conveniently enough, in Dade County. After the Dade vote, he decides to come out to his mother, a Bryant fan. "I never needed saving from anything," he writes her, "except the cruel and ignorant piety of people like Anita Bryant." A few sentences later, he adds, "Being gay has taught me tolerance, compassion and humility." Tolerance? Compassion? The usually observant Maupin fails to see the paradox in the character closest to his heart. Like so many of his amigos, Maupin expected people of faith to shuck their nearly four thousand-year-old belief system as meekly as the psychiatrists shucked theirs and could find no words, certainly not the right ones, to express his dismay.

Despite what gay activists might think, the Judeo-Christian plate has not pushed forward on any significant front in California since Father Serra reached San Francisco Bay. In 1977, the year of the Orange, an initiative that would have denied gays the right to teach in California public schools went flamingly down to defeat by a three-to-one margin. Heck, Ronald Reagan came out against it. No one cares or remembers. Christians of the Anita Bryant variety still loom as large in the gay psyche as Hutus do in the Tutsis'.

These Christians scare so because they are the only force of consequence that refuses to yield. This refusal leads to a seemingly endless series of rumbles along a statewide fault. In May 2006, for instance, the State Senate, with but one Democrat dissenting, voted to mandate in all public schools "discussions of the contributions of gay, lesbian, bisexual and transgendered people."

"All we're saying," said the bill's author, Senator Sheila Kuehl of Santa Monica, "is let us also be reflected in history." As the homely Zelda Gilroy on TV's *Dobie Gillis* show, Kuehl had sparred weekly with the lovely Tuesday Weld for Dobie's attention. Tuesday won. Sheila became one of "us." Only Governor Schwarzenegger's promise to veto the bill quelled a determined resistance.

The resistors are sometimes surprising. That same month the bill passed the Senate, I drove to the unpretentious city of Roseville, north of Sacramento, to check out a *Russian* resistance movement at the town's Oakmont High School. To protest a state-sanctioned, school-based "Day of Silence" in support of "tolerance," thirteen Slavic-American Christian students had worn T-shirts to school that said, "Homosexuality is a sin." The school chose not to tolerate the protest and suspended the thirteen kids. The principal chose not to talk to me. The Russians gave me a highly accented earful.

In March 2006, when twenty-five thousand evangelical youths rallied in San Francisco to protest TV porn, the Board of Supervisors greeted the kids about as warmly as they would a new Wal-Mart on Nob Hill. Even before the kids got there, the board had condemned their harmless protest as an "act of provocation" by an "antigay," "antichoice" organization. How dare those little scamps try "to negatively influence the politics of America's most tolerant and progressive city!"

Tolerant? Progressive? The organizer of the protest said it was the first time any city had officially condemned one of his events. He was amazed and perhaps a little proud. That same month, when the San Francisco archdiocese complied with a Vatican reminder to not place adopted children in gay households, the Board of Supervisors pressed its "negatively influence" boilerplate on the Vatican.

"It is an insult to all San Franciscans," the board declared unanimously, "when a foreign country, like the Vatican, meddles with and attempts to negatively influence this great city's existing and established customs and traditions." Not too long afterward the legislature of Pakistan voted unanimously to condemn the same pope when he suggested that winning converts by the sword was not such a swell idea. In the Midwest, the attempt to influence one's representatives, negatively or otherwise, goes by the name "democracy." In San Francisco and Pakistan, it's considered heresy, as is just about anything that challenges the prevailing orthodoxy.

Back in the day, Harvey Milk had enjoyed this kind of rumble. After losing three consecutive bids for office—and antagonizing the gay Democratic establishment in the process—the theatrical Milk rode the angry energy of Orange Tuesday to a seat on the Board of Supervisors. In-district voting made his victory possible, as it did that of another maverick, a troubled young Irish-American cop named Dan White. A year later, in November 1978, White abruptly resigned from the board. On Milk's advice, Mayor George Moscone refused to reinstate White when he petitioned to get back on. White snapped. He shot and killed them both and promptly turned himself in.

No reputation has swelled more in martyrdom than Harvey Milk's. When he was alive, even his friends and family didn't much like him. "Harvey left a lot of fractures in his life," an estranged lover consoled Milk's estranged brother at the memorial service. "He was rash and left a lot of things behind. We're just some of the fractures."

The murder cases went to trial the following May. The White team had no defense to speak of. They just lined up a swarm of psychotherapists and hoped that something someone conjured up would stick. One famously argued that White had eaten too much junk food—Twinkies in particular—and this caused homicidal surges in his blood sugar. On May 21, 1979, the jury came back with its verdict: voluntary manslaughter on both counts. White would likely be out of jail in less than five years. When asked what the verdicts meant, one gay activist answered, "This means that in America, it's all right to kill faggots." What it really meant was that in San Francisco, at the height of the human potential movement, people still took psychotherapists seriously. In Kansas, no one would have ever bought the Twinkie defense, even if Dan White were an old cop buddy.

After the verdict, the anti-death-penalty coalition organized a protest march. It quickly went south on them. How far south? How about thousands of angry gay men marching down Market Street chanting "Kill Dan White" south. When the marchers reached City Hall, their behavior shocked San Francisco as much as the Stonewall drag queens' had shocked New York. They broke windows, burned police cars, and injured sixty-one cops. To be sure, the video of the "White Night Riot"—a cold-blooded pun on the recent Jonestown carnage—wasn't about to make the anti-death-penalty highlight reel.

That night, however, gays finally did establish themselves as a serious force in the state's cultural tectonics. They had the power to influence, to elect, and now to intimidate. From that time forward, in any case of controversy involving a gay, no judge or jury in the city could fully forget the White Night Riot, especially if that gay were also a prominent ethnic leader like, say, Potrero Hill's Juan Pifarre.

★ 34. The Creative City ★

I mean five years ago you could have caught these
turkeys down in the Fillmore, chowing down on
chitlins and black-eyed peas with the Brothers and
Sisters. Now they're into faggots.
—Armistead Maupin, *Tales of the City*

When I first visited San Francisco twenty-five years ago,
the city dazzled me. Having grown up in Newark, I
had presumed that the inexorable fate of cities was decay. San
Francisco had reversed the process. And as I deduced, it was the
gay in-migration that had caused the reversal.

I returned home with the idea that Kansas City should try
to attract gays for the same reason. The *Kansas City Star Magazine*
commissioned me to write an article on the subject, in which I
argued that gays pay more in taxes than they take out in services,
buy into fringe neighborhoods that middle-class parents would
not dare to, and, all stereotypes aside, do a great job redecorating
their houses. The *Star* rejected the article for being "too positive." My progressive friends had yet to see how fabulous they
could feel by merely assenting to gay rights.

Beyond San Francisco, politicians were likewise slow to discover their passion for the gay cause. Just ten days after Orange
Tuesday, for instance, Democratic vice president Walter Mondale
gave a speech in San Francisco on "human rights" without a
passing nod to "gay" anything. Dismayed by the speech's drift,
a gay onlooker shouted, "When are you going to speak out on
gay rights?" Mondale would have none of it. He walked off the
stage in a snit, and the state Democratic chairman scolded the
gay guy.

Just five years later, in 1982, Mondale was championing

gay rights before a thousand gay men and lesbians at the newly organized "Human Rights Campaign Fund" dinner. "Tonight I pledge to you to continue the fight against all forms of irrational discrimination," Mondale thundered with a convert's zeal. He was hardly alone. In that five-year period, all the leading Democrats had managed to put their irrational fears behind them.

Pundits attribute this mass conversion experience to the effect of AIDS on the national conscience, but in truth, the top dogs had softened their bark even before they knew or cared about AIDS. Mondale would not even mention the disease when he ran for president in 1984. Nor would the media ask him to. Besides, if the media mentioned it, Reagan might, and then they would have no one on whom to blame AIDS. As reporter Randy Shilts shrewdly observes, "For Democrats AIDS was a Republican epidemic." Let's see, there was Roy Cohn and, uh, others, I'm sure.

The virus did not move Democratic politicians. Votes did. What boosted the cause immensely was the widespread belief that every tenth guy was gay. That number derived from Alfred Kinsey's fanciful 1948 study, *Sexual Behavior in the Human Male*. Drawing far too many samples from prisons, gay bars, and frat houses, Kinsey proved—to his own satisfaction at least—that 10 percent of white males are "more or less exclusively homosexual" for at least three adult years. As should have been obvious even at the time, Kinsey skewed his stats to normalize his own masochism and homosexuality. His numbers proved to be three to six times higher than those gathered in any serious study, but ABATU—a blind acceptance of the untrue—had struck again, especially since Kinsey's work had a veneer of science about it. The 10 percent number stuck. Suddenly gays had a voting bloc very nearly as large and together as blacks.

Corporate America had cozied up to gays with even more affection than the politicians. Gay men, that is. They not only shopped and consumed beyond their numbers, but they also helped shape the shopping patterns of others, women in particular. As to lesbians, Madison Avenue did not quite see enough fashion potential in wide-bottomed overalls and flannel shirts to get excited.

Still, it took AIDS to get big business on board the gay express. The disease "perversely legitimized the gay community as a group of consumers," culture critic Daniel Harris argues. He contends that by presenting gays as "an object of pity," corporate America and its media allies could now welcome gays "into the fold of conventional shoppers." To do so, though, they felt "compelled to reinvent the homosexual, reshaping him in the image of the happily wedded heterosexual." Harris resents this reimaging not only because it is false, but also because it is destroying a distinctly gay subculture or, as he smartly phrases it, "laying waste to the natural habitat of homosexuals."

In the 1970s that habitat had indeed been pretty wild. As Shilts observes, "Promiscuity was practically an article of faith among the new gays of Castro Street." Shilts would himself later die of AIDS. Beyond the human tragedy of it all, AIDS and HIV have turned gays from a net plus to the city's tax base to a net minus. As of 2006, it cost an estimated $18,600 a year in medical care for each HIV patient. Roughly 14,000 out of San Francisco's estimated 58,000 gay men live with HIV. Astonishingly, given twenty-five years' worth of warnings and 18,000 AIDS deaths in the city alone, nearly 1,000 new HIV cases are diagnosed each year in San Francisco, some 87 percent of these among gay men. Among those to have died from AIDS was one Sweet Jimmy Simpson, O.J.'s father.

Despite minimal changes in behavior, the oversexed disco gay of the 1970s somehow morphed into the "desexualized, Teflon homosexual" of the 1990s. Now, urbanists began to take gays seriously as well, none more influentially than Richard Florida. Even in Kansas City, development types read his *Rise of the Creative Class* with highlighter in hand.

According to Florida, cities that attract creative people will do better economically than those that don't. To rank cities he employs a "creativity index" with four equally weighted variables. Three of the four make perfect sense: the number of creative workers, the number of high-tech workers, and the "innovation factor" as measured by patents per capita. The fourth variable, "diversity," Florida measures by the "Gay Index," the percentage of gays in the population, which he describes as "a reasonable proxy for an area's openness to different kinds of people and ideas." By this index, San Francisco not only ranks number one among American cities in diversity, but it also ranks number one in overall creativity.

In researching this book, I discovered that Florida and I are homeboys. We grew up within blocks of each other in Newark. In our communications Florida tells me that the city's racial tension and overall decay had "a haunting effect" on him. Personally, I still have nightmares. This background accounts for much of our shared enthusiasm for cities that work. Where we disagree is on what "work" means.

Florida argues that cities do well to recruit those sundry scientists, engineers, academics, designers, architects, entertainers, actors, rock and rollers, jugglers, and, of course, the "thought leadership" that compose the "creative class."

Like contemporary cargo cultists, many of the development specialists that I know have convinced themselves that if they can only create a groovy, gay-friendly, rock and rolling, Frisbee-throwing environment in Topeka or St. Joe or Kansas City the high-tech cargo will follow. To be sure, they misread Florida, but not entirely.

There is an oddly unexplored flaw in Florida's thesis: He does not take into account the possibility that a city might "tip," that it just might attract one creative person too many. The tipping point is not hard to gauge. I call it the "Mime Index." When the first mime artist shows up on a city street, you know that the creative class has officially reached critical mass, and from then on bad things will begin to happen—the more mimes, the worse the things. Here are six of them.

1. The "thought leadership" becomes the "thought police." It is not just Christians that bug the good burghers of San Francisco. They have little tolerance for lots of people. When handsome young mayor Gavin Newsom squired *CSI: Miami* star Sofia Milos to a gala dinner, the thought police issued an Orange Alert. Did the mayor not know or care that that Milos was a—gasp!—Scientologist? "Mayor Deflects Chatter on Social Life," read the subhead of the *Chronicle* article. "He responds to talk about relationship with Scientologist." I'm not making this up.

In Kansas City, people would not care a lick if their mayor dated a Scientologist. They would care, however, if that mayor still were married to someone else as Newsom was. Newsom blew it all off. "Relax," he told reporters. "I'm a practicing Irish Catholic. I'm not a Scientologist, and I couldn't tell you two things about it." Only in San Francisco could a Catholic mayor publicly run around on his wife while still married, perform wedding ceremonies for gay couples, which Newsom also did, and dare to pass himself off as "practicing." And for the record there is no such theological beast as an "Irish Catholic."

To get Scientology's take on the rift, I called Heber Jentsch, the Hollywood-based president of the Church of Scientology, and asked him how his organization has managed to tie San Francisco's collective underwear in a knot. In nicely Socratic style, he asked me why I thought that was so. I suggested that Scientology's position on homosexuality might have something to do with it. "We don't have a position," he told me. "In San Francisco," I answered, "that's position enough." In fact, Scientology stands accused of trying to turn its gay members, including at least two Hollywood biggies, straight—a crime against nature in San Francisco very nearly as grave as turning Republican.

Indeed, the later revelation that Mayor Newsom cuckolded his best friend and campaign manager, Alex Tourk, troubled the citizenry less than did his dating of a Scientologist. In fact, 67 percent of those San Franciscans polled said the affair with Tourk's wife (a non-Scientologist!) either did not change or actually *improved* their image of Mayor Newsom.

2. *The creative class ceases to be procreative.* Although some might see this as blessing, the creative class has little interest in sustaining itself. Gays have devised a handy slur for those who dare to try or even look like they might: "breeder." Precious few deserve the insult. "I'm thirty-six years old," says the yuppie Brian in Maupin's *Further Tales*, "and I've never bred so much as a goldfish." He is hardly unique. San Francisco has only fourteen children under eighteen per hundred people, the lowest such figure in the nation for a major city. This kind of demographic hara-kiri would impress even a European—if there are any left by the time this book comes out.

The state's smaller "People's Republics"—Berkeley and Santa Monica come to mind—also register scarily low on sperm count, meaning sperm that count. The humble, mid-American Modesto produces more kids per hundred than Berkeley and Santa Monica combined.

3. *Faith in science goes blind.* In November 2004, at the prompting of its creative class, Californians voted to approve the $3 billion Stem Cell Research and Cures Initiative, better known as the CCEA, the Creative Class Employment Act. They did so in no small part because South Korean veterinarian Woo-Suk Hwang (real name) had them convinced that theirs was a good investment.

Eight months before the election the major media had trumpeted Hwang's stem cell breakthrough. The "debate is over," the *San Francisco Chronicle* insisted. Much depends on how you define "over." A year later, the *Chronicle* was quietly reporting, "Scientists said they had no way to predict how long it might take to complete the experiments [in generating stem cells] or what chance they have to succeed." You see, in the interim, Hwang had been exposed as a charlatan. It seems that he had fabricated his proofs. California, however, is still intent on finding creative ways to spend that $3 billion.

4. The working class disappears. Almost everywhere the creative class rules, it prices the working and lower middle classes out of town. In the not-so-creative Kansas City, a family of median income can afford to buy 87 percent of the homes in the market place. In 2006 San Francisco, a median-income family could afford to buy 7 percent of the homes. In San Diego, that figure is 5 percent.

In San Francisco, white ethnic neighborhoods have almost fully disappeared, and black neighborhoods are not far behind. Between 1970 and 2000, a time when the city was gaining population, San Francisco lost 38 percent of its black population. The historic black Fillmore district became the not-so-historic, yuppified Fillmore District. The blacks who have remained are largely concentrated in isolated *banlieus* on the fringe of the city like Hunter's Point and Bayview.

Florida acknowledges that creative cities "rapidly outpaced the average national increase" in housing prices. This he attributes to increased demand. Demand, however, is only part of the equation. The other is artificially restricted supply. When they come to power, the ecological hard cases that drive the agenda for the creative class vie with each other to restrict new development.

5. The population becomes Balkanized. San Francisco has devolved into a Yugoslavia with lawyers. Forty years ago, for instance, San Francisco had reasonably successful schools: 41 percent of its ninety-four thousand students were white and 26 percent were black. Today, after a generation of Mad Hatter social engineering, 9 percent of its fifty-seven thousand students are white and just 13 percent are black. What's impressive, even by urban school standards, is that the school district managed to lose 40 percent of its student body while the city's population was increasing by 8 percent.

Recently freed from a twenty-two-year federal court order that the judge decreed a "failure," the district is now free to screw things up on its own. Although 78 percent of the students are something other than black or white, the two groups for which the word "segregation" was coined, the school board has convinced itself that the schools have become "resegregated." The problem board members now face is how to "desegregate" the schools according to their not-so-very bright lights.

Proposition 209 presents something of a roadblock in that it prohibits public agencies from using race as an educational criterion. The parents present another one in that they typically want to choose a good school for their kids. Neither consideration deters the board. School board member Eric Mar argued that school choice—of a sort—might be a useful option. If the proposed plan forces parents to choose a private school, said Mar with royal indifference, "that's their choice." As to Proposition 209, Mar and the board could care less. Six of its seven members have come out publicly for reintroducing race into school assignments, and so has the school commissioner.

"California law takes the use of race off the table—it's just clear as can be," said an attorney representing a group of Chinese families. Nothing is ever clear on the yonder side of the Looking Glass. Besides, board members always figure they can find a sympathetic judge. Berkeley did in a similar case. And if push comes to shove, the whole mess ends up in the dependably injudicious Ninth U.S. Circuit Court of Appeals, right in

San Francisco, where good thoughts are being thunk anew on a daily basis.

6. Spontaneous diversity dies. Wherever the creative class prevails, the whole notion of diversity grows legalistic and oppressive. Citizens are no longer asked to tolerate their neighbors. They are compelled to "celebrate" them, often with consequences if they don't. As a result, the "Gay Index" no longer measures "openness" in any American city hipper than Branson, Missouri.

A more contemporary "openness" test might measure an area's receptivity to its outcasts, and no group has been cast further out than the Boy Scouts of America. Other than street mimes, the clearest sign of creative critical mass is the first anti-BSA pogrom. Recently, for example, the City of Berkeley nixed an understanding it had with a local Sea Scout chapter to provide free berthing at the city's marina. Never mind that the agreement dated back sixty years or that many in this racially diverse troop come from impoverished families.

When the Sea Scouts appealed, just about all the do-gooders in California rushed to the defense, not of the Sea Scouts, but of the City of Berkeley. This included the League of California Cities, the California Association of Counties, the Anti-Defamation League, the Lawyers' Committee for Civil Rights, and three foundations of the ACLU. True to form, the California Supreme Court ruled unanimously in the city's favor. As an Eagle Scout—okay, I only got twenty-one merit badges, but they were the right ones—I tend to take this personally.

As a long-term strategy, Florida would do his clients more justice if he retooled the index, just a little. The first three variables—creativity, high tech, innovation—still work, but on the fourth variable, diversity, the "Gay Index" should yield to the "Boy Scout Index."

Tolerance of the Boy Scouts suggests not only a genuine openness to "unpopular" ideas, like being "reverent" and "morally straight," but also an openness to children and the having of them. As development specialists will tell you, the young people most likely to live in an area are the ones who have grown up there. These smart kids will in turn have their own smart kids, a "procreative class" if you will, the ultimate in real sustainability and renewable resources, the gift that keeps on giving.

★ 35. San Fernando Valley ★

The reign of Christian terror at this magazine is now over. We're smut peddlers again. We're going back to our roots. We are porn again.
—Larry Flynt, *The People vs. Larry Flynt*

I thought they said "Paste," which struck me as a weird name for a restaurant even in West Hollywood, but it turned out to be "Taste" on Melrose. That night we had dinner, me and these three amiable guys in the "industry," none of whom I had ever met before. This meeting, however, proved serendipitous. It led me to a series of discoveries that would shed stunning new light on the last hours of Steven Nary's freedom and Juan Pifarre's life in the early morning hours of March 24, 1996.

Here's how it happened. In the course of the dinner, one of the guys asked me what *I* thought was the matter with California. Among other problems, I cited "fatherlessness."

"Hell, yeah," said the one guy, an agent. "You should check out the Valley." The Valley? I had no idea what he was referring to beyond the literal, much-maligned territory on the nether side of the Hollywood Hills, the San Fernando Valley.

"That's where all the porn is," added another guy, a screenwriter, sensing my confusion.

"You mean like strip clubs," I said naïvely.

"No, no," he said. "That's where porn comes from. That's where they make the films." He then explained how the producers feed on the fatherless girls who wash up on the streets of LA from wherever and how, after they have used them up, they spit them back out on the streets, often drugged and/or diseased. Without intending to, these Hollywood people were talking about the pornography industry the way other people talk about Hollywood.

Personally, I had always given the porn industry and its product wide berth. Under the no harm–no foul rule, I was libertarian enough not to begrudge others their tastes. My research would change my opinion. What these guys were telling me proved true. The porn industry has a number of unfortunate material consequences, among them the brutalization of young girls. For the more reckless of producers, the younger the girls, the better. "People were surprised that girls started in porn when they were underage," porn star Sharon Mitchell reveals in a fascinating oral history, *The Other Hollywood*, "but I wasn't surprised because I started underage, you know?"

To get the girls to perform on camera it sometimes helped to drug them, Quaaludes being the narcotic of choice, and not just for amateurs like Polanski. "That was what that prick Lenny used to do—get all them girls strung out," said one insider about producer Lenny Camp, imprisoned for exploiting underage girls. "That way they'd do what he told them." When it came to drugs, the performers, male and female both, turned Nancy Reagan on her head. There was little to which they didn't "just say yes."

John Holmes, the grandest of the male stars, lived out every pathology that the profession—and the state—had to offer. His father abandoned him when he was a tot. Subsequent stepfathers abused him. He left his own wife for a sixteen-year-old after the girl's family fell apart. An active bisexual, he pimped for both her and himself, both ways. He did enough coke to pay down Colombia's national debt. He invaded a dealer's house, the reprisal for which left four people dead. He survived the attack but not AIDS, which took him out at age forty-three, along with who knows how many of the men and women he had infected.

For all of Holmes's derangement, there was little about his

life that the people in this drug-soaked industry had not seen before. Still, if the porn industry victimized only the willing, like Holmes, one could justify its existence. Many have tried to, including the ACLU and the numerous Hollywood luminaries who have shown up at the industry's gala award shows and Free Speech Coalition Dinner Dances. To get me beyond this almost comic exercise in euphemism and self-deception, I found an unlikely guide in Ben Shapiro, an unusual young man from Burbank, porn's ground zero.

At twenty-one, during his first year at Harvard Law School, Ben Shapiro wrote the impressively insightful book *The Porn Generation,* about the corrosive effect of pornography, hard and soft, on his own peers. The oldest of four kids in an Orthodox Jewish family, Shapiro credits his parents and his faith for keeping him on the straight and narrow despite what he told me was the area's "massive intolerance for people who choose moral behavior."

On the softer side of the equation, as Shapiro explains, the relentless infusion of sexual imagery into everything from soda pop ads to hip-hop music serves to wear away at cultural restraints. In 1993, the effects of this trend became painfully manifest in the famously improvised town of Lakewood, just south of LA. In March of that year, sheriff's deputies arrested nine popular students from the town high school on charges ranging from rape to lewd conduct with girls as young as ten. The kids belonged to a clique that called itself the Spur Posse. Posse members kept a competitive point count on the number of girls they could successfully penetrate. When released from custody, the boys were greeted as heroes back at Lakewood High and rewarded for their derring-do with "a whirlwind of appearances" on national TV including *Dateline NBC* and *The Jenny Jones Show.*

"The kids' friends become their family," said a divorced mom whose sons were at the center of the scandal. "They watch TV and want more and more. They aren't content with just living."

The same month the kids in Lakewood were arrested, three young men on the East Coast were convicted of sexual assault for a comparable offense. The details are appalling. The three and their high-school buddies in suburban Glen Ridge, New Jersey, had grown bored with merely watching porn flicks. So they decided to make one of their own. For a "star" they lured in a trusting, mentally impaired girl and proceeded to sexually violate her with a broom handle and a baseball bat. As in Lakewood, the towns' parental class was slow to see that something had gone wrong. The media, which captured this story in both book form and TV movie, were even slower to understand *what* had gone wrong. In both cases, reporters traced the breakdown to the boys' participation in sports.

As Ben Shapiro points out, these cases are hardly unusual. A ten-year LAPD study found pornography to be a factor in 62 percent of child molestation cases. An FBI study reported that 81 percent of serial killers described hard-core porn as their "highest sexual interest." The explosion of Internet porn promises, if anything, even higher numbers in the future.

On the day before he was executed, the most infamous of serial killers, Ted Bundy, granted a final interview that deserves far more attention than it got. He invited Christian leader Dr. James Dobson to his cell to talk about one specific subject. "I take full responsibility for all the things that I've done," said Bundy carefully. "That's not the question here. The issue is how this kind of literature contributed and helped mold and shape the kinds of violent behavior." He was talking, of course, about pornography.

Bundy never knew his real father. He split before Bundy was born. Were Bundy more introspective he might have seen how vulnerable that abandonment had left him. But after his mother married Johnny Bundy, Ted grew up in a decent enough home, one that he chose not to fault. His descent into hard-core savagery began, in his own mind, with a chance discovery of soft-core porn outside the home when he was twelve or thirteen. "Once addicted," he observed, "you look for more potent, more explicit, more graphic kinds of material." The most dangerous of all, he insisted, is the kind "that involves violence and sexual violence." Bundy was speaking from some serious experience. He had murdered at least twenty-eight girls and women, the last a twelve-year old whose body he left stuffed in a dumpster.

In his many years in prison, Bundy had met any number of violent men. "Without exception," he said, "every one of them was deeply involved in pornography—deeply consumed by the addiction." As a final plea, he cut to the heart of what seems like a sincere appeal. "You are going to kill me," he told Dobson, "and that will protect society from me. But out there are many, many more people who are addicted to pornography, and you are doing nothing about that." Not exactly nothing. American society was about to usher in the golden age of porn. This would include Hollywood's own tribute to the industry, *The People vs. Larry Flynt,* which the IMDb describes as an "idealized film of the controversial pornography publisher and how he became a defender of free speech for all people." As it happens, this celebration of Flynt's "freedom" premiered the same year that Steven Nary lost his.

★ 36. San Diego ★

As it was, innocence was his blinder.
—Herman Melville, *Billy Budd*

Just nineteen when Ted Bundy died, Andrew DeSilva paid Bundy's final antipornography plea no heed. The San Diego native had developed an attraction to porn that was beginning to mirror Bundy's own. "Mirror" here suggests both reflection and reversal, as DeSilva was unapologetically gay. Half-Filipino and half-Sicilian, the handsome preppy captured the increasingly exotic look and lifestyle of the young Californian, which seemed somehow appropriate for a kid born the same year as Stonewall and the same month as the Manson murders.

By 1989, the year Bundy died, porn had become what culture critic Daniel Harris calls a "wholesale substitute" for sex in gay circles. Early in the decade, the VCR and AIDS had hit America just about simultaneously. The timing proved useful. The former stimulated a massive new demand for sexual videos, and the latter had made voyeurism—and onanism—a safer, if not entirely welcome or wholesome, community pastime. For instance, a character in Maupin's 1987 volume, *Significant Others,* invites Michael to a self-pleasuring, porn-watching (aka "JO") party as though "he might have been recruiting for a parish bake sale." According to Maureen Orth, a *Vanity Fair* reporter who has done the best research on this subject, gay videos had come to account for 30 percent or more of the entire porn video market. The wife of NBC's Tim Russert, Orth has taken a harder look at a subject than most reporters would dare to.

In the nether reaches of the San Diego gay underground, bootleg "candid" videos became all the rage. The videos featured performers who had no idea they were being recorded. Some of

these performers had no idea they were being raped. The producers would slip their subjects, typically young boys, a date rape
drug like Ketamine, better known as Special K, sexually abuse
them, and record the abuse on video. When performing under
the drug's influence, the boys were said to be in the "K Hole."

While still in San Diego, DeSilva found a mentor in a character named Vance Coukoulis, a notorious party thrower and
producer of candid videos. Court documents allege that Coukoulis would befriend young men under some pretext or another,
ply them with drug-laced booze, and then have sex with them
on camera. According to the documents, "Young boys appear to
be unconscious or drugged to the extent that they cannot resist
the sexual advances made upon them." Even those in Coukoulis's circle were reluctant to take a drink from him. "People
walked away from there doing things they really did not want to
do," one of Coukoulis's associates told Orth.

A born hustler, DeSilva shuttled back and forth between
San Diego and the Bay Area throughout the early 1990s, selling
anything he could, including a wide variety of drugs, and living off various sugar daddies. His "dark fantasies," writes Orth,
"were fueled by crystal meth, cocaine, and pornography." His
porn tastes now moved more and more deeply into sadomas-
ochism, but at the time and place, that was hardly unusual. San
Francisco has neighborhoods and festivals dedicated to the same.
Its highly public Folsom Street Fair boasts of a whirlwind of
people "in their most outrageous leather/rubber/fetish attire
enjoying the worlds largest and best loved Leather fair"—not, of
course, that there's anything wrong with that.

In early 1997, DeSilva met a young fellow named Tim
Schwager at a gay dance club in San Francisco and took him
back to the hotel where he was staying. "I think I was drugged
that night, or I had too much to drink," Schwager told Orth. He
recalled having "memory flashbacks of trying to fight [DeSilva]
off during the night." This was a story that Orth had heard from

other DeSilva acquaintances as well. When Schwager woke up the next morning he had three hickeys and no clothes on. "After that night," he said of DeSilva, "I knew he had a rough side to him."

Schwager's comments stopped me cold. I read them in Orth's book late in my research, but I knew I had read comments almost exactly like these before. I thought I knew where. I went tearing through my correspondence file with Steven Nary, and Eureka! I found just what I was looking for. Before I share what Nary wrote to me from Pleasant Valley State Prison on May 15, 2006, allow me to backtrack a little to Saturday, March 23, 1996.

That was the evening the eighteen-year-old apprentice airman ended up in North Beach drunk and alone at the Palladium, a co-ed dance club that catered to the under-twenty-one crowd. There, he was approached by Juan Pifarre, a fifty-three-year-old Latino activist from Potrero Hill. Pifarre had started the evening at a friend's house in the Castro where he and his friends had a few drinks. Pifarre left his friends about 10:00 PM. Sometime that evening he also did at least a few lines of cocaine, as residue would be found in his blood days later. He then drove to the most unlikely of places for a middle-aged gay man, the Palladium.

Pifarre had likely been there before. His one-time attorney and neighbor, Ralph Johansen, would testify that he once defended Pifarre on an assault charge stemming from an incident at an unnamed club whose description perfectly matched the Palladium. Apparently, Pifarre had grabbed the crotch of a nineteen-year-old male and asked for oral sex. This led to a fight in which both were charged with battery.

Johansen had lived downstairs from Pifarre in the Castro for thirteen years until 1993. Many a night he saw Pifarre come home with what appeared to be young military types. Often he heard "lots of noise, lots of screaming," and at least once he heard

a full-blown fight that culminated in a fist going through a window. Johansen characterized Pifarre as being "cold and angry"
all of the time and often drunk. Pifarre's behavior apparently did
not change a whole heck of a lot when he moved to Potrero
Hill. There, according to trial testimony, the downstairs neighbor gave "sort of a smirk" when the police asked whether she
had ever heard altercations upstairs before. In the early morning
hours of March 24 the sounds of violence had frightened her to
tears, but tellingly, neither she nor her husband had thought to
call the police.

That March night at the Palladium in 1996, Pifarre was
on the prowl. He saw the drunken young sailor and sized him
up quickly. As to the girls Pifarre originally sat down with, they
put Nary at ease, and the ploy worked. Nary suspected nothing.
When Pifarre offered him a ride back across the Bay Bridge to
the Alameda Naval Station, Nary accepted.

On the way back to the base, Nary would testify, Pifarre
told him that he had been to a party earlier. There he had had
too much to drink and done too much cocaine, both likely true.
He wasn't sure that he could make it across the bridge and back,
likely false. "His wife was out of town," he told Nary. He suggested that Nary "could stay at his house. He could call some
girls." Pifarre, in fact, did have a wife, however sham a marriage
that was, and Nary had seen him with girls. A naïve eighteen-
year-old, he had no reason to be overly suspicious, and he consented.

Along the way, Pifarre pulled the car over in a commercial area, promised to come right back, and exited. When he
did come back, the interaction began to change. "He started
touching my leg," Nary testified, "and asking for a blow job."
Nary scooted away from him and pushed his hand off. He was
shocked. Pifarre persisted, and Nary continued to resist. Pifarre
then flashed some twenties he had gotten at the ATM where
he had stopped. Exasperated and still inebriated, Nary finally

accepted the forty dollars, as he claimed, just to shut Pifarre up. Nary volunteered the information about accepting the money to the police. The prosecutors would hang him with it.

When they got to the house, the first thing that Pifarre did was to offer Nary some more alcohol. Nary tells me that he declined the booze and asked for water. Pifarre went with him to show him where the glasses were. "I don't remember if I filled the glass up or if he did," says Nary. After drinking the water, all that Nary wanted to do was go to sleep, and he told Pifarre this. But now Pifarre started hounding him for oral sex. "I told him I just wanted to go to sleep," Nary testified, but Pifarre would not let up. "The next thing I remember," Nary testified, "was laying on the bed and him putting a condom on me and giving me a blow job." Prosecutor John Farrell ridiculed Nary on this point:

"You don't know how your clothes got off."

"No."

"You don't know how your shirt got off."

"No."

"And you don't know how your penis got erect, right? Is that right?"

"I guess, I mean. It just happened. I was there and he was putting a condom on me and giving me a blow job."

The scene got quickly more unsettling. Pifarre persisted, now demanding anal sex. What follows is the critical excerpt from Nary's letter of May 15:

I have struggled with trying to understand why I let it all just happen. When I rolled over and pulled up my pants he continued to ask me if he could give me anal sex. I said no and that I just want to go to sleep. After some time, he started pulling my shorts down to force anal sex on me. He succeeded in pulling my pants down enough for him to try to continue. I felt stuck. I could not speak. I could not move, and I could not do anything. He just kept trying and trying over and over. In fact it brings me to tears as I write this because I have avoided this image for so long.

The reader does well to recall that Tim Schwager had had "memory flashbacks of trying to fight [DeSilva] off during the night," and when he came to, he had no clothes on and no memory of how they came off. And then too there was the testimony of Samantha Geimer. "I was going, 'No come on, stop it,' but I was afraid." Paralyzed by drugs and fear, she watched helplessly as Roman Polanski anally raped her.

Had Nary's public defender, Bruce Hotchkiss, introduced the idea of a drugging—and there was also ample opportunity at the Palladium for Pifarre to have done so—Nary's behavior would have made perfect sense. At the time, the use of date-rape drugs was widespread in both gay and straight society. As it happens, Patrick Arnold, the fellow who supplied BALCO with its steroids, was also dealing the date-rape drug GHB. Hotchkiss may not have known how prevalent the drugs were in gay society. Given their sensitivity on gay issues, especially in the Bay Area, the media have completely avoided the topic.

Still, Pifarre and DeSilva inhabited the same city at the same time, used many of the same drugs, and ran in overlapping circles. There is no evidence that they knew each other, but they shared certain pathologies—excuse me, I'm being judgmental—lifestyle choices. One has to wonder where Pifarre got the confidence to go to a straight club, hustle a straight kid, and expect to succeed. Some part of it may have been his skill at exploiting the loneliness and isolation of boys like Nary, especially if they were drunk. Part of it too may have been his willingness, perhaps even his eagerness, to take on rough trade. But given Nary's behavior, the best explanation is that Pifarre drugged him.

Ironically, however, Nary is not looking for excuses. In his conversion to Catholicism he feels the need to accept responsibility for everything he has done, including the oral sex and the death of Pifarre. Besides, he knows that if he goes into his first parole hearing a few years hence playing innocent victim, "This system will never let me out." In fact, though, Nary responded to Pifarre's assault the way any rape victim would, at least one who had a fighting chance of success and who could summon the will and courage that Nary did. Hotchkiss asked:

"What did you do at that point?"

"I then tried to push him away?"

"Were you able to push him off?"

"No."

"What was he saying, if anything?"

"He continued to tell me he wanted to give—screw me from behind."

"What did you do at that point?"

"I then grabbed a cup that was by the bed that had previously had water in it and hit him in the head with it."

As Nary testified honestly, he had never been in a fight before in his life, never even lost his temper, but when he somehow got his mind back that night, and his will, he fought off Pifarre like a man possessed. Pifarre had picked the wrong kid to rape. Nary does not really remember the sequence of events, never did. At his attorney's request, he tried to fill in the blanks as best he could, but the prosecutor walked all over him, made him sound evasive as well as violent, mocking Nary with every question.

"Well, you hit him with the mug again and again at the door, right?"

"I don't remember hitting him with the mug again and again."

"But you might have, right?"

"It's a possibility, yes?"

"So, it's a possibility you hit him with the mug, but you just don't remember that detail?"

"After the first hit it went very quickly, so it wasn't a matter of remembering anything."

Although the prosecutor would portray Pifarre as small and pudgy, he outweighed Nary and was not without power of his own. His friend Raymond Sloane testified to this at the trial. "Mr. Pifarre had a bravado, had a charisma, and I think it, you know, expanded as he was drinking." When Hotchkiss asked if Pifarre could become belligerent when he drank, Sloane answered simply, "He could."

After the blow by the bedside, the fight shifted into the bathroom, where Nary contends Pifarre tried to gouge his eyes out, and where Nary countered by grabbing a towel rack and striking back. It was likely here that Nary broke his hand, a fact that was used against Nary at trial. There were also choke marks on Pifarre's neck, which may well have caused his death, but the exact cause was never quite settled.

When Nary had finally subdued the relentless Pifarre, he grabbed his clothes as best he could, fled into the early morning darkness, and eventually made his way back to the base. Four days later, after talking to the chaplain, Nary called the police and turned himself in, not knowing that Pifarre was dead. Fearful of upsetting the Clinton administration in an election year and the host city on a gay issue, the Navy shamefully ignored its own regulations in its haste to rid itself of this now troublesome sailor.

The judge set bail at $1 million. The figure shocked Nary's public defender because, as the *San Francisco Chronicle* would report, "The suspect called police voluntarily and asked to be picked up." Besides, Nary had "defensive wounds," and the bail for first-time defendants in a passion crime almost never exceeded $250,000. No matter. Nary was about to learn lesson one in his unwilled study of San Francisco tectonics: Don't expect justice when you oppose two powerful cultural plates. Expect, in fact, to be crushed. While awaiting trial in the San Francisco City Jail, Nary was denied exercise and sunlight for the next three years.

Nary's working-class parents could not offer much help.

The whole "nightmare" overwhelmed them. "We were told the worst he could get was involuntary manslaughter," confided Edith Nary, just thirty-five at the time of the arrest. Steven did not want his parents to share his humiliation in any case and asked them not to come to the trial. After seventeen uneasy years in California, the Narys returned home to Arkansas with their younger daughter before the trial began.

As to Andrew DeSilva, Orth reports, "The drugs and pornography he fed on kept his cruel and domineering sexual fantasies at a fever pitch." That pitch was about to get more feverish still. In April 1997, a year after the death of Pifarre, DeSilva told acquaintances in San Diego that he was moving to San Francisco for good. First, though, he had to visit some friends in Minneapolis. He neglected to tell anyone that the ticket he bought was one-way.

DeSilva's Minneapolis friends were not eager to see him. His behavior had grown progressively more anxious and eccentric. He was also broke and desperate. No one knows what caused DeSilva to turn on buddy and would-be beau Jeff Trail. Trail may have owed him money, and DeSilva may have wanted him to retail his steroids, another of the drugs that DeSilva peddled. As in the Pifarre death, neighbors reported hearing yelling and scuffling but called no one. What they heard was DeSilva bludgeoning Trail in the head and face with a claw hammer as many as thirty times. He then coerced former beau David Madson into rolling the body into a carpet. The two stayed with the body for two days in the apartment and did nothing else with it. Five days later, DeSilva and Madson drove to a lake about an hour out of town and there DeSilva shot Madson through the eye at close range, killing him instantly. Now, the manhunt was on in earnest. For the first time, old friends were learning that Andrew, in true California fashion, had given himself the name "DeSilva." His real name was Cunanan.

On May 4, 1997, two events of note took place. In Chicago, Cunanan seized seventy-two-year-old developer Lee Miglin in the garage of his Gold Coast home, bound him, wrapped his head in duct tape, and severed his throat with a bow saw. In San Francisco, on May 4, members of the United Satanic Apache Front seized Steven Johnson Leyba, bound him, stripped him, carved a Satanic pentagram on his back, and had a woman member of the group urinate on his open wound. In Chicago, after the Miglin killing, authorities stepped up their pursuit of Cunanan. In San Francisco, after the Leyba outrage, authorities stood and applauded.

You see, Leyba and his performance troupe were the featured attraction at a birthday bash for gay activist Jack Davis. In attendance were the city's political elite, including Mayor Willie Brown, Sheriff Mike Hennessy, City Attorney Louise Renne, several members of the Board of Supervisors, including its president, and District Attorney Terrence Hallinan, who was overseeing the impending trial of Steven Nary. Davis, a prominent political consultant, had successfully orchestrated the election of two consecutive San Francisco mayors and had been hired by the NFL 49ers to help steer passage of a $100 million bond deal for a new stadium.

Although further descent may not seem possible, the evening headed downhill after the ritual bleeding of the "Reverend" Leyba, an ordained minister in Anton LaVey's Church of Satan. None of the major newspapers would print what happened next: A woman, dressed as Pocahontas and using a Jack Daniel's bottle as a dildo, actually sodomized Leyba with the bottle in full view of the audience. Leyba, who claims to be one-quarter Apache, more than enough for victim status in San Francisco, described the ritual in question as "a literal metaphor for how alcohol was forced on my people."

The *San Francisco Chronicle* reporters who covered the event did so under the assumption that they were supposed to be amused. They did not know any better. The paper's initial reporting reflects as much. "San Francisco 49ers campaign manager Jack Davis' birthday parties are legendary for their abandon," read the lighthearted lead, "but none compared to the wild, Caligulan scene that went down at his politically packed, 50th-year bash Saturday night." Although the reporters conceded that some people were "disgusted" by the "bizarre" proceedings, they gave the last word to Davis himself. "Most people said it was the best party they'd ever been to," he enthused. "And it wasn't anything compared to the after-party at my house." The tone would change within days, especially when the 49ers brass and the saner heads in San Francisco weighed in with their outrage and the national media started clucking.

Cunanan was shedding no glory on his state or his orientation either. As the world knows, he made his way south and east, killing an inconvenient security guard in New Jersey en route. Once in Miami, he shot and killed the famed designer Gianni Versace before eventually turning the gun on himself.

In San Francisco meanwhile, the Nary case slugged through the preliminaries with precious little attention being paid beyond the city. Lacking an external counterbalance, the postmodern local powers, led by the district attorney, could define the "narrative" as they saw fit. In their rewriting, Nary was a brutal, calculating killer, not unlike Aaron McKinney and Russell Henderson, the two "homophobic" desperadoes who killed helpless gay Wyoming University student Matthew Shepard in a fit of "gay panic."

Although Hollywood would turn out at least three TV movies about the "crucifixion" of Shepard, two of which premiered in the week before Easter 2002, the homophobic story line did not match the Wyoming reality. As the truth began to leak out of Laramie, that line grew more and more suspect. Best evidence now suggests that McKinney, the actual killer, had previously expressed no homophobic sentiments. One good reason why is that he was an active bisexual himself. Apparently, he and

Shepard, who had a known drug problem, had done meth together a number of times. On the night in question, McKinney
went on a meth-fueled rampage. He pistol-whipped the vulnerable Shepard for drug money, drove into town to rob Shepard's
apartment, and then pistol-whipped a stranger who got in his
way, fracturing his skull in the process.

Jacob Marsden of the *Caspar Star Tribune* would later tell
ABC's *20/20*, "I remember one of my fellow reporters saying
to me, 'This kid's gonna be the new poster child for gay rights.
Matt Shepard, gay bashed, symbol of the oppression of the gay
community.'" How right he was. Matthew Shepard died just
four weeks before the 1998 midterm elections. For the next four
weeks, much to their own surprise, the killers were presented to
America as poster children for the religious right and one more
reason not to vote Republican.

Of course, McKinney and Henderson were not products
of Christian culture, but of its antithesis: a crude, soulless, fatherless, sexually libertine, drug-addled pop culture. Those who
controlled the narrative, however, could shape it as they saw fit.
In the weeks before the 2006 midterms, that same machinery
would be used to smear Republicans as pedophile-friendly in
the Mark Foley imbroglio.

When the defense tried to redefine the narrative in the Nary
case, the local powers turned the very attempt against them. As
one gay legal source observed, "Community activists expressed
outrage at the defense tactics of trying to depict Pifarre, a well-
known community activist and journalist, as a dangerous sexual
predator." District Attorney Terrence Hallinan, feeling the heat
from both the gay and the Hispanic communities, threw Nary
into the fire. On a more personal level, the newly elected Hallinan had enjoyed Pifarre's public support in his campaign for
district attorney. For reasons only he can explain, his office rejected the defense's request for a change of venue.

In late-century San Francisco, as Nary was about to learn,

the truth mattered no more than it had in early-century Selma or Scottsboro. Pifarre was, in fact, a sexual predator with a history of violence. He had secured his permanent residency through a fraudulent marriage. He was shortchanging the City of San Jose on his working hours and on health benefits for his "wife." He regularly used illegal drugs, including cocaine. He was drunk often and was a mean drunk. He had been arrested at least once for indecent exposure and on another occasion for battery stemming from a sexual molestation. He had a history of seducing young men, almost assuredly under false pretenses, and did not stop to ask for "proof." He likely drugged them, and he had no compunction about raping them. He lived the ethos that rocket scientist Jack Parsons merely conceived: "Do what thou wilt shall be the whole of the Law." And in San Francisco, he had juice enough to get away with it all.

Still, if Nary had been a female sailor under identical circumstances, this case would never have come to trial, not even in San Francisco. The feminist plate would have pushed harder on that sailor's behalf than the Hispanic plate would have pushed against it. Indeed, there was more public sympathy for a woman whose breasts had been fondled by an assistant DA at the Jack Davis party than there was for Nary.

The prosecutors had hoped to stage the trial during Gay Pride week in June but settled for March 1999, conveniently just a week before the start of Russell Henderson's trial in Laramie. For Nary, the time was as inauspicious as the place. On one occasion during the trial, members of the audience stood up and faced the jury wearing large bright orange lapel tags saying "Recuerda [Remember] Juan," "Stop Homophobia," and "Stop Immigrant Bashing." Judge Kevin Ryan ignored the demonstration. Later, these demonstrators lobbied the jurors as they went to and came from lunch.

John Farrell, the prosecutor, hammered the "homophobia" theme throughout the trial. Incredibly, he attacked Nary for his honest admission of feeling "disgusted" after coerced oral sex. In his summation, Farrell argued that the only kind of person "who feels bad about what they did"—meaning oral sex with another man—is the kind of "person who is homophobic."

"Where is that rage coming from?" he asked the jury of Nary's self-defense. "Where is the motive for all that: That word 'faggot' written on the board." Farrell insinuated that the military's presumed antigay ethos had reinforced Nary's native bigotry, although there was no evidence at all that Nary ever used the word "faggot" or anything like it. Farrell also invented a flourishing gay club scene just blocks from Cathedral City High to suggest that Nary may well have gay-bashed before.

Nary never had a chance. After a generation of propaganda, locals had convinced themselves that only a bigoted young man would find sex with another man something other than perfectly natural. By coming back with a guilty verdict, each juror could claim his or her rightful place in this town's zone of decency—sensitive to immigrants and gays and hostile to a homophobic military. The temptation proved irresistible.

Without intending to, the daily journal *Gay Today* showed just how the tectonic deck was stacked against "hustler" and "crazed assailant" Steven Nary and his "racist" handful of supporters like Peter Verzola. "The 2nd-degree jury verdict for Nary is really a heartening victory," read its editorial, "especially during this week when the bogus concept of 'Gay Panic' is being tested again in Laramie, at the most visible anti-gay murder trial since Dan White got away with the murder of Harvey Milk by admitting to being a Twinkie junkie."

Under the California Penal Code, an individual convicted of second degree murder "subjectively knows, based on everything, that the conduct that he or she is about to engage in has a high probability of death to another human being." As I write, Steven Nary is serving the eleventh year of a sixteen-year-to-life sentence.

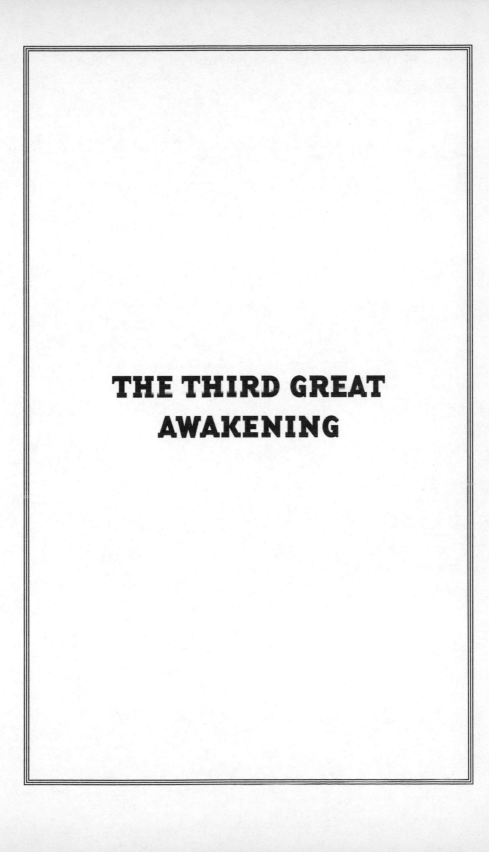

THE THIRD GREAT
AWAKENING

★ 37. Santa Paula ★

There are thousands upon thousands who are searching for, and at the same time rebelling against, authority and solidity in their lives. They, as I was, are looking for something that will hold still and be true. They are looking for a real family.
—Susan Atkins, *Child of Satan, Child of God*

Midwest Flight 87 soared through the chill rain of a Kansas City night and put me down three-plus hours later on the tarmac of LAX. From LAX I shuttled past the airport's appropriately manic light pylons to the Emerald Aisle at the National Car Rental. There were no cars. I went downstairs and informed the lady at the desk. "Carlos," she boomed to the unseen Carlos, "there are no cars in the Emerald Aisle." "There will be," the unseen Carlos boomed back.

Welcome to LA.

Carlos was as good as his word. Fifteen minutes later, I was heading north on the 405, which I took to the 101 north— "Ventura Highway in the sunshine"—and that to the 126 east, a route that Father Junipero Serra likely traversed in journeying between Mission San Buenaventura and Mission San Fernando. An hour and a few minutes after leaving the Emerald Aisle, just before midnight, I exited the 126 in the humble but still functional downtown of Santa Paula, population thirty thousand and change. From Santa Paula I took the Ojai Road north out of town. So sinewy and remote was the road that I drove high beams all the way and passed no one. A guide met me at the gate of my destination six miles from town and led me down an unlit switchback no wider than the car to my lodgings. It was midnight now, and I fell right to sleep.

The next morning I awoke on the set of *Ramona,* or so it seemed. They call the place the Doheny Hacienda after the family that built it seventy some years ago, a near-perfect, open-aired, U-shaped replica of an Alta California abode right down to the chapel, which happened to be next to my room. I almost expected to hear Señora Moreno welcome the morning with a hymn, but the only sounds I heard were the local birds—species unknown—a serenading brook, and the soft rustling of the Santa Anas through the trees. And this, just seventy-five minutes from LAX.

I had come here looking for an answer. I had convinced myself that the state has too much entrepreneurial zeal and hybrid vigor to be undone by its problems, however serious. Fate, or perhaps Providence, had drawn me to Santa Paula. In May 2006, I had received a copy of a magazine called *The American Enterprise.* "You have been selected to receive this FREE IS-SUE," declared a label affixed to the cover, "plus your choice of a riveting new book, also FREE." I never bothered with the book, but an article by Chris Weinkopf caught my eye. "America has a growing string of countercultural towns where religion, traditional culture, and family life are taken very seriously," read the article's subhead. "Come visit one of them." I do not think Weinkopf, the editorial page editor of the *Los Angeles Daily News,* expected anyone to take his invite literally, but I did.

At the heart of Santa Paula and other such countercultural towns—Catholic or Protestant or Jewish—there is almost inevitably an institution that serves as magnet, usually a church or college. For Santa Paula, it's Thomas Aquinas College. Some of those who live in Santa Paula are faculty members. Others are alumni. Others are friends of faculty or just folks who have heard about the environment, some of those not Catholic.

One alumna with whom I spoke came back to Santa Paula with her two children from Washington, D.C., after her husband died. She was looking for a welcoming place to call home. This she found. Her parents and her sister and brother-in-law soon followed, with her sister tending to their father full-time before he died. Strong extended families take care of their elders as well as their children, another material advantage to the larger society.

I wondered if others might find their way to Santa Paula as well, particularly abandoned souls like Steven Nary. I shared his story at lunch one day, and an older priest in our company smiled in astonishment. Father Cornelius Buckley had instructed Nary in the faith at the San Francisco City Jail. He renewed their correspondence immediately. "I must say his letter brought tears of joy," Nary wrote me soon afterward, "and I wondered what God could be doing bringing us all together." Father Buckley was equally pleased to receive Steven's letter in return. "Steven was always an extraordinary humble man," he told me by email, "and I was so happy to see that the spiritual potential in him that was so apparent has been realized."

What moved Buckley was Steven's knowing acceptance of his fate. "I do not see my trial and punishment as an injustice any more. After all I did take the life of another human being," Steven wrote in his return letter to Buckley. "God is clearly showing me a path through friends and family to use my life's experience as a way to inform others and to live a faith-based life."

Thomas Aquinas president Tom Dillon had graciously invited me to stay at his residence, the Doheny Hacienda. I was in good company. Mother Teresa had stayed there before me. I took a walk that first early morning and surfaced on the meadow up above. In front of me lay the lovely, clustered Mission-style buildings that compose the Thomas Aquinas campus. Surrounding the meadow on three sides were mountains of the Los Padres National Forest. A month earlier, I had to postpone the trip because a fire on the far side of those mountains had forced the evacuation of the campus. The setting is not quite paradise, merely close. In fact, it was just down the road a few miles on the way to Ojai that Frank Capra filmed the money shot in *Lost Horizon*: the moment when his refugees see, for the first time, the valley of Shangri-La.

I saw no students out and about and understood why only when I passed the chapel, which was full. This was Sunday morning, but it is close to full on weekdays as well. No one has to go to mass—not all the students are Catholic, for that matter. It's just that very nearly everyone does. The students all followed the mass in Latin. That seemed to make more sense in contemporary California than the unwitting apartheid that results from separate masses in English and Spanish, which many churches now offer.

Over the next few days, I would speak to any number of these students and sit in on perhaps ten classes. The college, which was founded in 1971, features a great books curriculum and aggressive seminar-style interaction. None of the classes I attended had more than fifteen students.

"Miss Rack, have you yet had any of that Book Thirteen glory?" asked the class "tutor" with a smile. Miss Rack responded to his invitation. She promptly went to the board and with chalk in hand explained how Euclid arrived at a particular geometric proof. It was impressive. Every class was. The students spoke concisely and to the point, and those not speaking listened intently. I saw none of the empty grandstanding that passes for student participation in too many college classrooms.

I was particularly struck by how confidently the girls held their own in the debates that characterize all classes, including math and science. I asked a student where the confidence comes from. "The boys respect us," she told me. "They even open doors for us. They make us feel confident." That same student told me that she hoped to go to Harvard Law School after college, then get married and have children. "How many?" I asked. "Oh, a dozen or so," she answered.

The girls wear dresses or skirts to class. The boys wear shirts, neatly tucked, with collars. No jeans. This is code. So are separate dorms and the ban on intergender visitation. Few object. Most prefer it. They knew what they were getting into. I asked a few kids how much drug use there was on campus. They looked at me as if I had asked how much voodoo there was on campus. Although Catholics don't object to drinking, there is close to none on campus either.

One student told me that she was reluctant to come for fear that the college was "an Amish-style sackcloth and ashes kind of place," but one visit assured her otherwise. After his stay at the campus, British social critic Christopher Derrick wrote a book around the experience. "What struck me first," he observes in the well-titled *Escape from Scepticism*, "was the exceptional happiness of the students." President Dillon told me that just about everyone notices this. I did.

Although a tad smarter than average, these kids are otherwise not that exceptional. Few among them come from wealthy homes or fancy prep schools, and many come from large, struggling families. The kind of life they lead—or at least try to—is materially accessible to most of their peers. Many of different faiths already live this way, such as, say, Ben Shapiro, author of *Porn Generation*. Restricting the argument to the here and now, if 90 percent of young California exercised a comparable "controlling power upon will and appetite," the state would change in some intriguing ways.

Tattoo parlors would go out of business. Piercing enterprises would have to survive on ears, and girls' ears at that. Doctors would find something better to do with their time than breast implants and nose jobs, let alone abortions. AIDS and STD clinics could shift their attention to unavoidable diseases. ER staffers could focus on the victims of accidents and illnesses; shootings, stabbings, and ODs would consume them no more. The police and rescue people could do the same. Drug cartels would take their business elsewhere. Like Alcatraz, prisons could become museums, and the prison unions would no longer run the state. Pimps and pornographers would just about close up shop—"It's hard out there" for them anyhow. So would divorce lawyers and most personal-injury lawyers as well. The Crips could shift from larceny and other louche behavior to lawn care and cut the need for illegal immigration along with the grass. The LA school district could sell its fences for scrap iron. The state payouts for welfare, housing, food stamps, and Medicaid would shrivel. Taxes would fall, and still there would be additional revenue for infrastructure, schools, universities, and, yes, even new green technologies.

The remaining 10 percent of the population could choose to behave or misbehave as they would. It is just that they would have to do far less injustice to themselves and to society to get attention. A half-century ago, about the worst thing the then-provocative Beats imposed on California was bad literature. "That's not writing," Truman Capote said accurately of Jack Kerouac's *On the Road*. "That's typing."

For those who remember the California of fifty years ago, the Thomas Aquinas scenario may not appear all that novel. The difference, however, is that the college, in becoming a fully postracial community, has moved beyond the fifties, moved beyond the nineties, for that matter. Here, a student's race or ethnicity scores him or her absolutely no points for or against. A few years back, the credentialing authorities attempted to impose race consciousness on the curriculum under the guise of "multiculturalism." The college stared them down and ultimately prevailed. As President Dillon explained, "The fact that they're African is not why we teach Augustine and Ptolemy." The "second language" at Thomas Aquinas is Latin.

On the bookshelf of my room at the Hacienda, I found a copy of the Bible, and sitting next to it, a copy of Tocqueville's *Democracy in America*. For an institution as distinct as a Thomas

Aquinas to work within the state, this placement suggests a necessary understanding, namely an adherence to the larger principles of the nation. That adherence is the great stabilizer, the one that assures that friction among and between cultural plates, though inevitable, is manageable.

As attractive as the Thomas Aquinas model might seem, the state's Blue establishment does not exactly embrace it. There is one fundamental reason why. A Red plate thrust, Santa Paula style, would surely check the progress of the "Do as thou wilt" revolution and perhaps even reverse it. A Thomas Aquinas grad, after all, drafted Proposition 85, the ultimately unsuccessful 2006 initiative that would have mandated parental notification on abortion.

From their redoubts in places like Santa Barbara and Santa Monica and San Francisco, the good thought thinkers will continue to resist a Red revival until their personal fortunes are at risk. In the meantime, they will hover nervously behind their iron gates and, like the characters who people their films, repeat as mantra, "It's not supposed to be like this."

The families in Santa Paula, by contrast, have a clear-eyed sense of how things are supposed to be. I met with several of them, including Chris Weinkopf's, and asked whether their vision of the good life was likely to spread on its own. In general, they were more optimistic for the long haul than the short. They see their strength in their children, both the quantity and the quality thereof. Unlike some of their Protestant peers, however, they are not aggressively evangelistic. They prefer to "bear witness" quietly.

Those secularists who fret about a potential theocracy in a state like California or even a city like Santa Paula do so with an impressive disregard for history or reality. The Catholic Church has nothing close to a monopoly. The Mormons, for instance, have missionaries in Santa Paula actively proselytizing among the city's 70 percent Hispanic population. There are also, of course, effective and influential evangelical churches in Santa Paula and throughout the state.

The state's Hispanic population, legal and otherwise, will likely determine the state's future, and everyone suspects it. The unions are recruiting hard. The merchandisers are selling hard. The multiculturalists are dividing hard. The Aztec wannabes are radicalizing hard. Christians are evangelizing, but not as hard as they might. Nonetheless, they have an advantage—the state does as well—in that these new arrivals come from a Western Christian tradition. The seamless, timeless California that Santa Paula represents is very much the summation of that tradition, the California that Junipero Serra envisioned two hundred years ago but with a little butt-kicking American enterprise thrown in.

To save itself, California will need to spread the spirit of Santa Paula. The state government cannot do this, but it can at least stay out of the way. The leadership will have to come from within the ranks of the Hispanic Christian community. People like auxiliary bishop Gabino Zavala and union leader Dolores Huerta are not likely candidates. By preaching socialism, separatism, and materialism, they are leading their troops not to a City on the Hill but to a city like Compton—or something quite like it.

One senses among the Hispanics of California a hunger for something more, a hunger for stability and meaning. They will not find these in the false gods that have diverted their more jaded Anglo peers or in the Aztec concoctions that distract their own confused children or in the unending victim trip that has paralyzed the black community. Where they will find them is where Susan Atkins found them and where Steven Nary found them—in the very same Christian God their ancestors have been worshipping for generations. The Second Great Awakening saved the Scotch-Irish of Appalachia and points west from nihilism and lawlessness. A Third Great Awakening could do the same for California. And the place to start, right now, is the prisons. The mud-dancers at Burning Man, the hot-tubbers at Esalen, the naked runners on Hayes Street, even the leather folk on Folsom have a stake in seeing this happen. Real revolutions have little tolerance for liberals and even less for libertines.

This revived California, the California of Santa Paula, is the one our Hispanic friends ought to come home to, the home we all can come to if we have to, the one California "that will hold still and be true."

★ Notes ★

Prologue

On Saturday evening: Unless specified otherwise, all factual descriptions of the events of March 23, 1996, come from the *Reporter's Transcript of Proceedings, The People of the State of California vs. Steven Nary*, Court No. 1639231.

As naturalist John McPhee: John McPhee, *Assembling California* (New York: Farrar, Straus and Giroux, 1993), p. 108.

"A big one": McPhee, p. 253.

California-based social theorist: Shelby Steele, *A Dream Deferred: The Second Betrayal of Freedom in Black America* (New York: HarperCollins, 1998), p. 163.

THE BLUE PLATE COMES UNGLUED

1. Beverly Hills

By 1920: Scott Bottles, *Los Angeles and the Automobile: The Making of the Modern City* (Berkeley: University of California Press, 1987), p. 93.

By 1940: Bottles, p. 188.

In 1923: Kevin Starr, *The Dream Endures: California Enters the 1940s* (New York: Oxford University Press, 1997), p. 5.

Westbrook Pegler called: Starr, p. 197.

"Growing up here": Thomas Frank, *What's The Matter With Kansas?: How Conservatives Won the Heart of America* (New York: Metropolitan Books, 2004), p. 47.

"Deep in the subconscious": Julia Phillips, *You'll Never Eat Lunch in This Town Again* (New York: New American Library, 2002), p. 314.

Bret Easton Ellis: Bret Easton Ellis, *Less Than Zero* (New York: Vintage, 1998), p. 189.

In the 2005–6 school year: Sandy Banks, "A Northridge Junior High Tells L.A. Unified: Don't Fence Us In," *Los Angeles Times,* June 8, 2006.

the state prison population: As of December 31, 2005, "California Prisoners & Parolees 2005," California Department of Corrections and Rehabilitation.

In his dazzling book: Mike Davis, *City of Quartz: Excavating the Future in Los Angeles* (New York: Vintage, 1992), p. 239.

"Watts Rebellion": Davis, p. 67.

"the social polarizations": Davis, p. 223.

Julia Phillips takes: Phillips, p. 488.

The notorious Crip: Sanyika Shakur, *Monster: The Autobiography of an L.A. Gang Member* (New York: Grove Press, 1993), p. 275.

"utter despair": Shakur, p. 252.

"It is so warm": Wendy Leigh, *Arnold: An Unauthorized Biography* (Chicago: Congdon & Weed, 1990), p. 91.

2. Alta California

Spanish explorer Pedro Font: Pedro Font, "The Colorado Yumans in 1775," in *The California Indians: A Source Book,* edited by R. F. Heizer and M.A. Whipple (Berkeley: University of California Press, 1971), p. 253.

"As with all of nature's children": Carl Meyer, "The Yurok of Trinidad Bay, 1851," in Heizer and Whipple, p. 267.

Indeed, before the first Spanish: James J. Rawls, *Indians of California: The Changing Image* (Norman: University of Oklahoma Press, 1986), p. 6.

"disorderly and beastlike": Font in Heizer and Whipple, p. 249.

"They are certainly a race": Rawls, p. 28.

"The native in his primitive condition": Rawls, p. 34.

"wild beauties": Rawls, p. 64.

James Ohio Pattie: Rawls, p. 57.

Ten years later: Richard Henry Dana, *Two Years Before The Mast* (New York: Penguin, 1986), p. 236.

"The [Catholic] Faith": Msgr. Francis J. Weber, *The Life and Times of Fray Junipero Serra* (San Luis Obispo: EZ Nature Books, 1988), p. 23.

"You marry an Indian": Helen Hunt Jackson, *Ramona* (New York: Avon Books, 1970), p. 126.

"One cannot help thinking": Rawls, p. 34.

"About Serra's worth": Josiah Royce, *California: A Study of American Character* (Berkeley: Heyday Books, 2002), p. 14.

"During the height": Jackson, p. 24.

"The old monastic order": Rawls, p. 39.

The frijol: Dana, p. 59.

The Hawaiians: Dana, p. 205.

"The Californians": Dana, p. 125.

"Among the Spaniards": Dana, p. 123.

"a curse had fallen": Dana, p. 128.

He describes the Yankees: Dana, p. 131.

"In the hands": Dana, p. 237.

"The final decade": Kevin Starr, *Americans and the California Dream, 1850–1915* (New York: Oxford University Press, 1973). p. 7.

"In politics, as in morals": Royce, p. 28.

This little history: El Plan Espiritual de Aztlán was adopted by the First National Chicano Liberation Youth Conference, a March 1969 convention.

"California in a nutshell": Starr, p. 7.

Anthropologist James Rawls: Rawls, p. 81.

"civilized warfare": Royce, p. 25.

"We exhibited": Royce, p. 4.

Its boundaries: Jackson, p. 15.

"These Americans will destroy": Jackson, p. 178.

Even the normally sober: Starr, p. 415.

San Francisco naval commander: Rawls, p. 84.

In San Francisco: Colonel William Thompson, *Reminiscences of a Pioneer*, 1912, available online at books-about-California.com.

He acknowledges: Royce, p. 217.

3. Lakewood

To know how future governor: Ethan Rarick, *California Rising: The Life and Times of Pat Brown* (Berkeley: University of California Press, 2005), pp. 8–9.

Sixth-generation Californian: Joan Didion, *Where I Was From* (New York: Alfred A. Knopf, 2003), pp. 16–17.

From the end of World War II: Curt Gentry, *The Last Days of the Late, Great State of California* (New York: G.P. Putnam's Sons, 1968), p. 29.

"Buyers needed only": D. J. Waldie, *Holy Land: A Suburban Memoir* (New York: St. Martin's Press, 1996), p. 49.

In 1953: Waldie, p. 102.

A century earlier: Rawls, p. 148.

Expectations were lofty: Rarick, p. 210.

The national magazines: Peter Schrag, *Paradise Lost: California's Experience, America's Future* (Berkeley: University of California Press, 2004), p. 27.

"Most important of all": Schrag, p. 28.

4. North Beach

In her autobiography: Susan Atkins, *Child of Satan, Child of God* (New York: Bantam Books, 1978), photo section.

"This is a whole different time": Atkins, p. 30.

"moral chaos": Atkins, p. 31.

That trade traces: Gentry, p. 101.

Hard to believe: Gentry, p. 104.

"There wasn't a place": Steven Nary, correspondence with the author. This correspondence began May 15, 2006, and has continued to the present.

Unless otherwise specified, all personal observations by Nary come from this correspondence.

In early 1967: Atkins, p. 60.

"a black flower of sin": Quoted in Starr, *Americans and the California Dream* p. 264.

"witches' sabbath": Atkins, p. 62.

"Everything is a racket": Blanche Barton, *The Secret Life of a Satanist: The Authorized Biography of Anton LaVey* (Portland, Ore.: Feral House, 1992), p. 26.

"Man is the only god": Barton, p. 60.

In fact, he designed: Barton, p. 88.

"You have to take Satan": Barton, p. 205.

Not one to shy: John Carter, *Sex and Rockets: The Occult World of Jack Parsons* (Los Angeles: Feral House, 2004), p. 4.

"Without his contribution": Carter, p. 195.

There, Parsons discovered Crowley: Carter, p. 33.

In 1913, the young Duranty: S. J. Taylor, *Stalin's Apologist* (New York: Oxford University Press, 1990), pp. 36–37.

"Russians may be hungry": Quoted in Taylor, p. 185.

Jayson Blair: Jayson Blair, *Burning Down My Masters' House* (Beverly Hills: New Millennium Press), p. 85.

There is no god but man: Carter, p. 180.

"Some still say": Robert Anton Wilson, Foreword, in Carter, p. xii.

Wilson, in fact: Carter, p. xviii.

There is little to doubt: Carter, p. 102.

Later, Hubbard's people: Carter, p. 119.

As she is cleaning out: Joan Didion, *The White Album* (New York: Pocket Books, 1980), p. 47.

When challenged: Ellis, p. 189.

At one point: Carter, p. 87.

Among the charred ruins: Carter, p.183.

"Father/Yes son": "The End," The Doors, 1967.

"Christian piety": Carter, p. xii.

5. El Monte

"God is everywhere": Atkins, p. 98.

"I felt he might be Christ": Atkins, p. 85.

"All your roots": Atkins, p. 83.

"Charlie had instantly": Atkins, p. 76.

In the way of background: Timothy White, *The Nearest Far Away Place: Brian Wilson, the Beach Boys, and the Southern California Experience* (New York: Henry Holt and Company, 1996), p. 49.

"*Dennis's only ambition*": White, p. 97.

"*I'm lonesome*": White, p. 339.

"*I'm the devil*": Atkins, p. 127.

"*kill a priest*": Atkins, p. 134.

"*They were a clean-cut*": Karlene Faith, *The Long Prison Journey of Leslie Van Houten: Life Beyond the Cult* (Boston: Northeastern University Press, 2001), p. 27.

"*Manson's followers*": Faith, p. 48.

After all, America: Faith, p. 29.

"*The Tate-LaBianca snuffs*": James Ellroy, *My Dark Places* (New York: Vintage Books, 1996), p. 169.

"*I took it hard*": Ellroy, p. 105.

"*The 50s divorce boom*": Ellroy, pp. 24–25.

"*I saw more*": Ellroy, p. 169.

"*stigmatized little kids*": Ellroy, p. 105.

Not that Californians: Royce, p. 318.

"*He wanted to do something*": Michael Reagan, *Twice Adopted* (Nashville: Broadman & Holman, 2004), p. 42.

Marin County divorce authority: Judith Wallerstein, *The Unexpected Legacy of Divorce: The 25 Year Landmark Study* (New York: Hyperion, 2000), p. xxviii.

In 1970, the first full year: California's historical divorce statistics can be accessed at www.christianparty.net/divorcecalifornia.htm.

Only Oklahoma had no-fault: Judy Parejko, *Stolen Vows: The Illusion of No-Fault Divorce and the Rise of the American Divorce Industry,* available online at http://www.stolenvows.com/chapter3.htm.

These divorce reforms: Wallerstein, p. xiii.

"*Divorce is a life-transforming*": Wallerstein, p. xxxiii.

In general, adolescence: Wallerstein, p. 299.

Even as adults: Wallerstein, p. 300.

In July 1999: As reported in Wallerstein, p. xxvii.

He remembers his own: Ellroy, p. 106.

"*Oh, my dear Katie*": Chris Columbus, director, *Mrs. Doubtfire*, 1993.

One shared trait: Wallerstein, p. 301.

Susan Atkins and the others: Atkins, p. 108.

6. Pleasantville

"*I didn't want to be*": Interview, *Dateline NBC*, October 15, 2004.

"*The family grows best*": Royce, p. 319.

"*Man existing alone*": Nicholas Ray, director, *Rebel Without a Cause*, 1955.

When sixteen-year-old Natalie: Suzanne Finstad, *Natasha: The Biography of Natalie Wood* (New York: Harmony Books, 2001), p. 139.

"a shadow figure": Finstad, p. 144.

These included an affair: Finstad p. 143.

a brutal rape: Finstad, p. 148.

a marriage to movie star: Finstad, p. 235.

That Wagner walked away: Finstad, pp. 385–86.

In writing about Gold Rush: Royce, p. 313.

"The film addresses the limits": Harry's Reviews, *Ain't It Cool News*, October 2, 1998.

A typical review: Anonymous, www.epinions.com/mvie_mu-1124997/display_~full_specs.

7. South Central

The unbloodied thirteen-year-olds: Lawrence Kasdan, director, *Grand Canyon*, 1991.

In 1969, the same year: Randall Sullivan, *Labyrinth* (New York: Grove Press, 2002), p. 47.

In 1953, the year: All statistics from the California Crime Index, Office of the Attorney General—California Department of Justice. For a quicker summary, check www.disastercenter.com/crime/cacrime.htm.

"was killing all white people": This quotation comes from Williams's trial transcript (2189, 2193) as cited in Charles Montaldo, "The Crimes of Stanley 'Tookie' Williams," *About: Crime/Punishment*, July 2, 2006.

"The statistics freeze the blood": Prison statistics come from the "Population Reports" of the California Department of Corrections and Rehabilitation.

In Tookie's case: Press release, ACLU of Northern California, November 7, 2002.

"My mom's house": Shakur, p. 122.

"An oppressed nation": Shakur, p. 351.

"playing God": Shakur, p. 226.

"And there has not": Shakur, p. 332.

"Absentee fatherhood was despicable": Shakur, p. 372.

"You guys have turned": Shakur, p. 332.

"My homeboys became": Shakur, p. 25.

"If you died": Shakur, p. 103.

"We had done so many": Shakur, p. 195.

Williams remembers: Stanley "Tookie" Williams, *Blue Rage, Black Redemption: A Memoir* (Pleasant Hill, Calif.: Damamli Publishing, 2004), pp. 5–7.

In this powerful: Williams, p. 9.

"a colony of poverty": Williams, p. 9.

he sees himself: Williams, p. 13.

"The Crips became my family": Williams, p. 96.

In his well-observed book: Diego Vigil, *Barrio Gangs, Street Life and Identity in Southern California* (Austin: University of Texas Press, 2003), pp. 65–81.

In time, he hooked up: David Thibodeau and Leon Whiteson, *A Place Called Waco: A Survivor's Story* (New York: Public Affairs, 1999), p. 27.

In fact, more than half: Thibodeau and Whiteson list the Waco victims by name and race, pp. 355–57.

It would take seven years: Thibodeau and Whiteson, pp. 316–17.

The gang, says Vigil: Vigil, p. 81.

"We frankly haven't gotten gang": Patrick McGreevy, "Study: Effort to Rid L.A. of Gangs Is Failing," *Los Angeles Times,* August 3, 2006.

THE UPHEAVAL OF THE BEIGE

8. Sacramento

The reforms of the 1960s: Janice Shaw Crouse, "Leaving on a Jet Plane: Illegitimacy Trends and the Nation's Children," Beverly LaHaye Institute, January 16, 2004.

By 1990 only Alaska: George J. Borjas, "Immigration & welfare," *National Review,* June 16, 1997.

Although the percentage: Heather McDonald, "Hispanic Family Values?" *City Journal,* November 15, 2006.

The impact of this breakdown: State of California Budgets for the Fiscal year July 1, 1959, to June 30, 1960; July 1, 1968, to June 30, 1969; and July 1, 1977, to June 30, 1978.

To understand how: "Gross State Product, 1963–2004," California Department of Finance.

Jobs were plentiful: Paul W. Rhode, "The Evolution of California Manufacturing," Public Policy Institute of California, 2001.

In 1910, however, citizens: Schrag, pp. 189–90.

Among the most righteously wrathful: Howard Jarvis, *I'm Mad As Hell* (New York: Times Books, 1979), pp. 206–209.

"Finally Churchill said": Jarvis, p. 269.

"I advised Nixon": Jarvis, p. 273.

In still another: Jarvis, p. 267.

His crusade began: Jarvis, p. 5.

"the chief spokesman": as quoted in Jarvis, p. 95.

As Peter Schrag concedes: Schrag, p. 133.

They believed that property owners: Jarvis, p. 32.

In a generation: Jarvis, p. 110.

Not surprisingly: Jarvis, p. 30.

Of the 148 initiatives: Jarvis, p. 29.

By the end of 1977: Jarvis, p. 8.
He predicted that Prop 13: Jarvis, p. 56.
As Schrag acknowledges: Schrag, p. 145.
The media treated: Jarvis, pp. 92–95.
Howard Jarvis and friends: Schrag, p. 151.
Indeed, only twenty thousand: Jarvis, p. 9.
In the ten years: Stephen Moore, "Proposition 13: Then, Now and Forever,"
    CATO Institute, July 30, 1998.
"The Tax Revolt": these and following articles are cited in Moore, July 30,
    1998.
And, in book form: Schrag, p. xix.
Twenty years after: cited in Moore, July 30, 1998.

9. Malibu

The worst place: Los Angeles Times online, July 18, 2006.
The scariest road: Los Angeles Times online, July 19, 2006.
The average August high: All weather statistics come from The Weather Chan-
    nel, weather.com.
The housing opportunity index: This index is published by the National As-
    sociation of Home Builders in association with Wells Fargo, accessible at
    www.nahb.org.
Stockton resident: Jim Christie, "State's middle class is relocating inland," *San
    Diego Union-Tribune,* September 17, 2006.
In fact, when Ted Costa: Joe Mathews, *The People's Machine: Arnold Schwarzenegger
    and the Rise of Blockbuster Democracy* (New York: Public Affairs, 2006), p. 115.
Costa had even less standing: Ted Costa, interview with author, November 13,
    2006.
Still working on his college degree: Mathews, p. 107.
"He had deliberately mischaracterized": Melanie Morgan, interview with author,
    November 12, 2006.
If there was a defining moment: Mathews, pp. 126–28.
A month later: Mathews, p. 140.

THE FALL OF THE SKY BLUES

10. Big Sur

Although not radically inclined: Starr, *The Dream Endures,* p. 341.
Ever since the Franciscans: Starr, p. 197.
Like Hazel Motes: Flannery O'Connor, *3 by Flannery O'Connor* (New York:
    Signet Books), p. 60.

"There is only one truth": O'Connor, p. 90.

The story might profitably: Walter Truett Anderson, *The Upstart Spring, Esalen and the Human Potential Movement: The First Twenty Years* (Lincoln, Neb.: Authors Guild, 2004), pp. 34–42.

They named their creation: Anderson, p. 48.

In that the tribe: Anderson, p. 18.

As a philosophy: The manifesto can be found at www.americanhumanist.org.

In 1939: The Humanist Society can be accessed at http://www.humanist-society.org.

"Esalen was remarkably cozy": Anderson, p. 183.

"astonishing impact": Carl R. Rogers, *A Way of Being: The Founder of the Human Potential Movement Looks Back on a Distinguished Career* (Boston: Houghton Mifflin Company, 1995), p. 49.

To self-realize: Rogers, p. 58.

"The Good Person": A. H. Maslow, *The Farther Reaches of Human Nature* (Penguin: New York, 1993), p. 18.

"I do my thing": Anderson, p. 90.

His creation: Anderson, p. 95.

"the human potentiality": Anderson, p. 64.

Bhagwan Shree Rajneesh: Anderson, p. 234.

At the end of the 1970s: Anderson, p. 304.

11. Marin County

Before fleeing to St. Louis: Steven Pressman, *Outrageous Betrayal: The Dark Journey of Werner Erhard from est to Exile* (New York: St. Martin's Press, 1993), pp. 3–8.

In March 1971: Gerald Derloshon and James Potter, *The Success Merchants: A Guide to Major Influences and People in the Human Potential Movement* (Englewood Cliffs, N.J.: Prentice-Hall, 1982), p. 131.

To get the dope: Interview with author, May 19, 2006.

"Don't give me your": Pressman, p. 405.

He was "the Source": Don Lattin, "Ex-Employees Describe Abuse in Suit Against est's Erhard," *San Francisco Chronicle,* April 3, 1990.

"I am who sent him": Pressman, p. 147.

"he stirred up Hollywood": Pressman, p. 267.

"You have no rights": Pressman, p. 149.

"Writing for a penny": Russell Miller, *Bare-Faced Messiah, The True Story of L. Ron Hubbard* (New York: Henry Holt and Company, 1987), p. 148.

"In Scientology no one is asked": Church of Scientology Official Site, www.scientology.org.

"It is despicable and utterly": L. Ron Hubbard, *Professional Auditor Bulletin,* #31, July 23, 1954.

"We found that as soon": Alcoholics Anonymous, *Big Book,* Chapter 4, available online at www.recovery.org/aa/bigbook.

"You can use vitamins": "Cruise Slams Shields' Drug Use," Hollywood.com, May 25, 2005.

"His comments are dangerous": "Shields Attacks Cruise for Criticizing Drug Use," Hollywood.com, May 30, 2005.

"He beats his wife": Quoted in Pressman, p. 256.

12. Hollywood

"terrific human being": Dr. William Coulson, interview with Dr. William Marra, "The Story of a Repentant Psychologist," *Latin Mass,* January–February issue, 1994.

Back in 1965: Carol Lynn Mithers, *Therapy Gone Mad: The True Story of Hundreds of Patients and a Generation Betrayed* (New York: Addison-Wesley, 1994), pp. 17–18.

Lennon would enthuse: Cited in Mithers, p. 41.

"cruel hoax": Mithers, p. 72.

These budding therapists: Mithers, p. 70.

"In this world, all that mattered": Carol Lynn Mithers, "When Therapists Drive Their Patients Crazy," *California,* August 1988.

"Your whole mythology": Mithers, *Therapy Gone Mad,* p. 192.

"I refuse to give in": Mithers, *Therapy Gone Mad,* p. 384

shorthand for "repressed": Mithers, *Therapy Gone Mad,* p. 78.

"Forget the old ways": Mithers, *Therapy Gone Mad,* p. 202.

"Center values were beginning": Mithers, *Therapy Gone Mad,* p. 180.

A moment of real possibility: Mithers, *Therapy Gone Mad,* p. 404.

"poverty, war, racism": Mithers, *Therapy Gone Mad,* p. 405.

"The children that seemed to matter": Mithers, *Therapy Gone Mad,* p. 124.

"Every man and every woman": Carter, p. 160.

"The new alchemical dream": Tom Wolfe, "The Me Decade and the Third Great Awakening," *Mauve Gloves & Madmen, Clutter & Vine* (New York: Random House, 1976), p. 83.

Remember, Julia Phillips: Phillips, p. 380.

Werner Erhard's mercenary: Pressman, p. 47.

At the time: Mithers, *Therapy Gone Mad,* p. 179.

A prayer composed: Mithers, *Therapy Gone Mad,* p. 90.

The media didn't quite get: Mithers, *Therapy Gone Mad,* p. 179.

"They got caught up in something": Mithers, *California,* August 1988.

13. Nob Hill

The only child: David M. Robertson, *A Passionate Pilgrim: A Biography of James A. Pike* (New York: Alfred A. Knopf, 2004), pp. 8–25.

In his first posting: Robertson, p. 59.

In July 1953: Robertson, pp. 80–81.

A late 1960 article: Robertson, p. 111.

When certain Georgia bishops: Robertson, p. 113.

Yet this was a truism: Robertson, p. 145.

Joan Didion, who: Didion, *White Album*, p. 57.

He first spoke at Esalen: Roberston, p. 117.

The timing was inauspicious: Robertson, pp. 159–80.

For all of his personal foibles: Robertson, p. 176.

As unfashionably late: Robertson, pp. 195–96.

"one great effect": Robertson, p. 199.

"Our Christian/Lutheran feminist prayers": herchurch.org.

What motivated Pike: Robertson, p. 214.

"where the trolley": Robertson, p. 206.

"The majority of my colleagues": For a more complete account, see Jack Cashill, "Religious Studies Professor Slurs Christians, Jews," *WorldNetDaily*, December 1, 2005.

In the southern end of the state: "Robert Schuller Biography," Academy of Achievement, www.achievement.org.

The message he developed: CrystalCathedral.org.

In that same year: Jeffrey Sheler, "Preacher With A Purpose," *U.S. News & World Report*, October 31, 2005.

Warren had a specific goal: "Purpose Driven Project," *Red Mountain*, Fall 2005.

14. La Jolla

Dr. William Coulson tells: Dr. William Coulson, interview with Dr. William Marra, "The Story of a Repentant Psychologist," *Latin Mass* magazine, January–February issue, 1994. Unless specified otherwise, this full account comes from the Coulson interview.

More than a few times: Armistead Maupin, *Significant Others* (New York: HarperPerennial, 1994), pp. 234–36.

"I felt my life was over": Steven Nary, correspondence with the author.

In his regretful look: Michael S. Rose, *Goodbye Good Men: How Liberals Brought Corruption into the Catholic Church* (Washington: Regnery Publishing, 2002), p. 27.

The Boston diocese: Christina Hoff Summers and Sally Satel, M.D., *One Nation Under Therapy: How the Helping Culture Is Eroding Self-Reliance* (New York: St. Martin's Press, 2005), p. 81.

15. Ukiah

In a mass grave: Denice Stephenson, ed., *Dear People, Remembering Jonestown: Selections from the Peoples Temple Collection at the California Historical Society* (Berkeley: Heyday Books, 2005), p. 160.

"More people have been slaughtered": Harvey Milk quotes, en.thinkexist .com.

As all the world was learning: cited in *Dear People,* p. 5.

"I decided how": Jim Jones, "Jim's Commentary about Himself," 1977-1978, cited in *Dear People,* p. 77.

"I believed I was unfairly forsaken": Deborah Layton, *Seductive Poison: A Jonestown Survivor's Story of Life and Death in the Peoples Temple* (New York: Anchor Books, 1998), p. 20.

"We are not really a church": Layton, p. 85.

Layton remembers him: Layton, p. 53.

"Free at last, free at last": Layton, p. 99.

At Jones's request: Layton, p. 55.

"I had come to believe": Layton, p. 99.

"We called him Dad": Armistead Maupin, *Further Tales of the City* (New York: HarperPerennial, 1994), p. 112.

"He fucked everything": Maupin, *Further Tales,* p. 148.

"You could start with the governor": Maupin, *Further Tales,* p. 139.

"I figured if these people": From Deposition, *Peoples Temple* v. *Attorney General of California* in *Dear People,* p. 152.

That same year: Dear People, p. 69.

"In my later years": Jim Jones, "Jim's Commentary about Himself," 1977–78, as cited in *Dear People,* p. 78.

"#4, Any Socialism teacher": "Instructions from JJ," March 17, 1978, as cited in *Dear People,* p. 83.

He denounced Ryan: Jim Jones, "Reading and Commentary in the News Today," November 9–10, 1978, cited in *Dear People,* p. 108.

proclamation #75: "Follow-up Notes from Peoples Rally," August 8, 1978, as cited in *Dear People,* p. 87.

Only the San Francisco Examiner: cited in *Dear People,* p. 6.

Twenty-five years after the fact: Tim Reiterman, "Hell's 25-Year Echo: The Jonestown Mass Suicide," *Los Angeles Times,* November 19, 2003.

16. Manhattan Beach

That year, Peggy: Paul and Shirley Eberle, *The Abuse of Innocence: The McMartin Preschool Trial* (Amherst, N.Y.: Prometheus Books, 2003), pp. 16–17.

The provocateur in this case: Eberle and Eberle, p. 28.

The forces that crushed: Dorothy Rabinowitz, *No Crueler Tyrannies: Accusation, False Witness, and Other Terrors of Our Times* (New York: A Wall Street Journal Book, 2004), p. 25.
the stylish Kee McFarlane: Eberle and Eberle, p. 26.
Detective Hoag had: Eberle and Eberle, pp. 19–20.
Using the McMartin database: Eberle and Eberle, p. 19.
"Peggy put her vagina": Eberle and Eberle, p. 331.
"all the stuff that usually goes on": Eberle and Eberle, p. 137.
The station promoted: Eberle and Eberle, p. 21.
"It's an uneven struggle": Eberle and Eberle, p. 94.
One survey showed: Eberle and Eberle, p. 34.

17. Chinatown

Days before the Oscars: Patrick Goldstein, "Judge 'The Pianist,' not Roman Polanski," *Los Angeles Times*, March 12, 2003.
"I should be sent to prison": Roman Polanski, *Roman by Polanski* (New York: Ballantine Books, 1985), p. 379.
The description that follows: The People of the State of California v. *Roman Polanski*, Reporter's Transcript of Grand Jury Proceedings, March 24, 1977, posted at www.thesmokinggun.com.
"I could sense a certain erotic tension": Polanski, p. 368.
"traditional moral code": David McClintick, *Indecent Exposure: A True Story of Hollywood and Wall Street* (New York: HarperBusiness Essentials, 2002), p. 5.
"There's nothing wrong": McClintick, p. 42.
When exposed: McClintick, p. 55.
A public opinion survey: Michael Medved, *Hollywood vs. America: Popular Culture and the War on Traditional Values* (New York: HarperPerrenial, 1993), p. 71.
Hollywood filled the spiritual void: Phillips, p. 130.
"I like to think of myself": as cited in McClintick, p. 169.
True to form: McClintick, p. 139.
With more therapists per capita: McClintick, p. 241.
"I have learned a great deal": McClintick, p. 231.
"I understand the motivation": McClintick, p. 511.
Says Dominick Dunne: Dominick Dunne, *Another City, Not My Own* (New York: Crown Publishers, 1997), p. 67.
one Justice Department spokesman: Mark Fainaru-Wada and Lance Williams, *Game of Shadows: Barry Bonds, Balco, and the Steroids Scandal That Rocked Professional Sports* (New York: Gotham Books, 2006), p. 211
Barry started honing: Jeff Pearlman, *Love Me, Hate Me: Barry Bonds and the Making of an Antihero* (New York: HarperCollins, 2006), p. 34.

By the time major: Pearlman, p. 48.

In Pittsburgh, his: Fainaru-Wada and Williams, p. 29.

Born in Fresno: Fainaru-Wada and Williams, pp. 5–7.

Always a charmer: Fainaru-Wada and Williams, pp. 8–9.

In the midst of all this: Fainaru-Wada and Williams, p. 23.

Before that unfortunate turn: Fainaru-Wada and Williams, pp. 10–11.

Conte and Bonds hooked up: Pearlman, p. 234

Bonds's stats bewildered: Pearlman, p. 231.

The man is a saint: Pearlman, p. 295.

In a random ballpark survey: Pearlman, p. 333.

The email Williams and Fainaru-Wada: Fainaru-Wada and Williams, p. 241.

"San Francisco led the league": Pearlman, p. 214.

A twelve-year-old fan: Demian Bulwa and Cicero A. Estrella, "Bonds finds plenty of support at the ballpark Giants faithful are fed up—opposing fans not so forgiving," SFGate.com, July 21, 2006.

Bonds proved just as obstinate: Fainaru-Wada and Williams, p. 268.

18. Black Rock

I realized that I had seriously: Larry Harvey, interview with author, May 22, 2006. Unless specified otherwise, all references to Harvey derive from this interview.

"We're putting the force of law": Bob Pool, "Smoking Ban Moves Outdoors," *Los Angeles Times,* March 18, 2006.

"Inclusive is illusive for burners": Vanessa Martin, "Burning Man at 20, "Inclusive is illusive for burners," SFGate.com, September 3, 2005.

"have simulated sex": "Yahoo Education Pamphlet," Burning Man, 2000.

Burning Man summarizes its prohibitions: www.burningman.com/prepara tion.

THE WEARING OF THE GREEN

19. San Mateo

The revival's first major camp meetings: Susan Zakin, *Coyotes and Town Dogs: Earth First! And The Environmental Movement* (New York: Penguin Books, 1993), p. 35.

It is not possible here: Ted Kesik, "Perspectives on Sustainability," *Architectural Science Forum,* January 2002.

"The world, we are told": Chris Highland, ed., *Meditations of John Muir: Nature's Temple* (Berkeley: Wilderness Press, 2002), p. 55.

"All things are hitched": Zakin, p. 263.

"humans occupy a special place": Christopher Manes, *Green Rage: Radical Environmentalism and the Unmaking of a Civilization* (Boston: Back Bay Books. 1990), p. 145.

Deep ecologists: Manes, p. 247.

"The women got tubal ligations": Zakin, p. 352.

Earth First's Dave Foreman: Zakin, pp. 399–400.

"The battle to feed": Paul Ehrlich, *The Population Bomb* (New York: Ballantine Books, 1968), p. 36.

Ehrlich then lays out three: Ehrlich, *The Population Bomb*, pp. 77–80.

"We see ourselves": Manes, p. 164.

"The place seemed holy": Highland, p. 15.

"Praise God from whom": Highland, p. 81.

20. Altamont

"Everybody, just cool it": Albert and David Maysles, directors, *Gimme Shelter,* 1970.

"Never in my long lifetime": K. C. Clarke and Jeffrey J. Hemphill, "The Santa Barbara Oil Spill, A Retrospective," *Yearbook of the Association of Pacific Coast Geographers,* Darrick Danta, ed., (Honolulu: University of Hawaii Press), vol. 64, pp. 157–62.

To please the free market people: Jerry Taylor and Peter Van Doren, "California's Electricity Crisis: What's Going On, Who's to Blame, What's to Do," CATO Institute, July 3, 2001.

At the depth of the state's power crisis: Jill Darling Richardson, "Poll Analysis: Californians Conserve Electricity, Oppose Easing Environmental Regulations," *Los Angeles Times,* February 18, 2001.

In his good-looking film: Alex Gibney, director, *Enron: The Smartest Guys in the Room,* 2005.

Gibney gropes to explain: Alex Gibney interview with Ivana Redwine, *About: Home Video/DVD,* January 13, 2006.

The crime is an ongoing one: James M. Taylor, "New Studies Show Greater-Than-Expected Harm to Humans, Wildlife," *Environment News,* March 1, 2004.

21. Eel River Valley

In 1997, to ward off the chainsaws: "Julia Butterfly Hill," Ecology Hall of Fame, www.ecotopia.org.

Although raised Catholic: Gar Smith, "An Interview with Julia Butterfly Hill," *The Edge,* May 26, 2005.

She was then preparing: Associated Press, "L.A. Tree-Sitter Hill Comes Down to Earth," June 10, 2006.

Paul established some: Paul Bassis, interview with author, May 8, 2006.

In Werner Herzog's documentary: Werner Herzog, director, *Grizzly Man,* 2005.
An already classic episode: South Park, "Smug Alert!" Episode number 141, first
   aired March 29, 2006.

22. Mount Washington
Vigilant as they are: Ron Russell, "Return of the Swami," *Los Angeles Times,*
   July 1, 1999.
"They started looking": Tomas Osinski, interview with author, April 19, 2006.
It's a whole lot easier to bump: Barry Witt, *San Jose Mercury News,* ran an ex-
   tended series on this issue in 2002–3.

23. East of Indio
I met Gene: Initial author interview with subject, April 20, 2006; subsequent
   interview, August 6, 2006.
In fact, as late as 1973: Davis, *City of Quartz,* p. 181.
To test Gene's contention: Published by the National Association of Home
   Builders in association with Wells Fargo, accessible at www.nahb.org.
"If they gathered": Author interview with Paul Bassis.
Niskala practices: Judith Lewis, "Astroturf Wars," *Los Angeles Weekly,* April 5, 2006.
The Sierra Club and five other: Sierra Club press release, April 21, 2005.
"How many gay bars": The People of the State of California v. Steven Nary, Court
   No. 1639231.
I talked to Gloria Hernandez: Gloria Hernandez and Mark Morrison, inter-
   view with author, April 21, 2006.
When I met Funair: Artie Funair, interview with author, April 21, 2006.

24. Whittier
Michael and Deborah Grumbine: Michael and Deborah Grumbine and family,
   interview with author, April 23, 2006.
In his recent book: Mark Steyn, *America Alone: The End of the World As We Know
   It* (Washington, D.C.: Regnery Publishing, 2006), p. 3.

THE BENNETON COLORS DISUNITE

25. Gold Mountain
Last school year: Although the University of California keeps racial and ethnic
   statistics system-wide, accessing them is more difficult than one might
   suspect. I found no single easily accessible source.

Soon the Chinese: Iris Chang, *The Chinese in America: A Narrative History* (New York: Penguin Books, 2003), p. 17.

In the early days of the Gold Rush: Chang, p. 30.

"China boys will yet": Chang, p. 51.

Among them was Yung Win: Chang, p. 110.

Over the years: Chang, p. 127.

In 1978, a young Ph.D.: Wen Ho Lee with Helen Zia, *My Country Versus Me: The First-Hand Account by the Los Alamos Scientist Who Was Falsely Accused of Being a Spy* (New York: Hyperion, 2001), pp. 96–107.

"I do know," Trulock elaborates: Notra Trulock, *Code Name Kindred Spirit: Inside The Chinese Nuclear Espionage Scandal* (San Francisco: Encounter Books, 2003), p. 6.

"worst case since the Rosenbergs": "Helen Zia: From Minority to Majority, Invisible to Envisioning," profile, www.speakoutnow.org.

In his book, Lee claims: Lee, p. 26.

"I didn't know that the FBI": Lee, p. 24.

Says Lee unconvincingly: Lee, p. 28.

By the late 1990s: Trulock, p. 73.

In 1996, a Chinese military officer: Stephanie Lieggi, "Going Beyond the Stir: The Strategic Realities of China's No-First-Use Policy," *Nuclear Threat Initiative Issue Brief,* December 2005.

"With what I now understood": Lee, p. 65.

"Asian American / Arrest me too": Lee, photo section.

"They were all excused": Lee, p. 93.

"Nobody even whispered": Lee, p. 119.

26. Maywood

"The size of the pro-immigrant march": Ernesto Cienfuegos, "Aztlan Arising: 700,000+ March in Los Angeles," *La Voz de Aztlan,* March 26, 2006.

The Mexica movement headlined: http://www.mexica-movement.org/gran marcha.htm.

"Why should we punish people": Name withheld, interview with author, April 18, 2006.

the charming book: City of Maywood and Edward W. Ahrens, *Maywood: Images of America* (San Francisco: Arcadia Publishing, 2005).

A deft politician: Ed Ahrens, interviews with author, April 20, 2006; July 27, 2006.

"I'm afraid we're testing": Hector Becerra, "Welcome to Maywood, Where Roads Open Up for Immigrants," *Los Angeles Times,* March 21, 2006.

"Buy your Aztlan postage stamps": www.aztlan.net, August 26, 2006.

"The garbage covered the U.S. team": Bill Plaschke, "U.S.-Based Players Should Not Be Pelted with Debris by U.S.-Based Fans," *Los Angeles Times*, February 17, 1998.

"growing despair and uncertainty": Victor Davis Hanson, *Mexifornia: A State of Becoming* (San Francisco: Encounter Books, 2003), p. 5.

When I caught up with him: Victor Davis Hanson, interview with author, September 23, 2006.

27. Army Street

"Most of the Spanish names": Joshua Brandt, "Proposition O," *Golden Gater Online*, November 9, 1995.

"its corruption and misappropriation": Hanson, p. 77.

Said activist Eva Royale: Joshua Brandt, "Old Fashioned Street Fight," *Golden Gater Online*, October 31, 1995.

"San Franciscans to Save Army Street": Brandt, October 31, 1995.

According to probate records: This information is contained in a letter sent by Martin Rios on behalf of the Pifarre estate to Superior Court Judge Isabella Grant. The purpose of the letter was to prevent the activist in question, Sharon Martinas, "acting out of selfish greed and paranoia," from securing any part of the estate. Probate case #267324.

In February 1987: Berry Barnacle, "SJ Official Cited on Two Sex Charges," *San Jose Mercury News*, February 20, 1987.

According to San Francisco supervisor: Thaai Walker, "Latino Publisher Found Slain in S.F.," *San Francisco Chronicle*, March 28, 1996.

According to a spokesperson: Walker.

"the opposition of an easily caricatured": Hanson, p. 98.

Speaking for many: Brandt, October 31, 1995.

"It would be a terrible embarrassment": Brandt, November 9, 1995.

"Latino Publisher": Walker, March 28, 1996.

28. Downtown LA

"California's leading union organization": Joe Mathews, "In a Shift, Union Group Backs Abortion Rights," *Los Angeles Times,* August 7, 2006.

29. Glendale

"Maybe [the DA] wants": Jaxon Van Derbeken, "All Stops Pulled Out in Mauling Trial, Knoller-Noel Case Should Go to Jury Today," *San Francisco Chronicle*, March 19, 2002.

"If radical environmentalists were": As quoted in Zakin, pp. 350–51.

Eco-novelist Edward Abbey: Zakin, pp. 184–85.

The fact that immigration raises: Paul and Anne Ehrlich, *The Population Explosion* (London: Hutchinson, 1990), pp. 63–64.

"I'm for gay marriage": Larry David, "Meanwhile: Cowboys Are My Weakness," *New York Times,* January 10, 2006.

"Trash—excuse me—Crash": Annie Proulx, "Blood on the Red Carpet," The *Guardian,* March 11, 2006.

"For those that don't know": Ronald Chatman, "My Side of the Racial Divide," Streetgangs.com, July 1, 2005.

The ratio of Hispanics: The school was 31 percent Hispanic, 20 percent black. Simone Sebastian, "San Leandro Police Patrol High School After Fights," *San Francisco Chronicle,* April 28, 2006.

"There are big fights": Elliot McGregor, "Blacks v. Mexicans: Round 6," *Youth Outlook,* May 11, 2006.

A Hispanic principal in Oakland: Jorge Lopez, interview with the author, October 6, 2006

"It is often volatile to mix": Chatman, July 1, 2005.

Literary wunderkind Ben Shapiro: Ben Shapiro, *Porn Generation: How Social Liberalism Is Corrupting Our Future* (Washington: Regnery Publishing, 2005), p. 73.

Bakari Kitwana, author: Bakari Kitwana, *Hip-Hop Generation: Young Blacks and the Crisis in African-American Culture* (New York: Basic Civitas Books, 2002), p. 202.

This urge to succeed: Carlos Mencia: Not for the Easily Offended, 2005.

30. Oakland

I met with Lance Izumi: Lance Izumi and Xiaochin Claire Yan, interview with author, May 23, 2006.

Chavis has a story to tell: Ben Chavis, interview with author, May 23, 2006.

Aguilar claims to be teaching: Marcos Aguilar, interview with Maribel Santiago, in *Teaching to Change LA,* Issue 2, 2004.

Under the leadership: "Comparing California," Ed-Data, Education Data Partnership, November 2005.

Only Mississippi sends: How California Ranks: A National Perspective, Educational Opportunity High School Report, 2006.

When Jorge Lopez took over: Jorge Lopez, interview with author, May 23, 2006, and subsequent phone interviews.

THE RAINBOW LOSES ITS LUSTER

31. Potrero Hill

Of all those acts: Dunne, p. 277.

"Resourceful gays staked out": Randy Shilts, *The Mayor of Castro Street: The Life and Times of Harvey Milk* (New York: St. Martin's Press, 1982), p. 49.

There was, to be sure, trouble: Timothy Roche, Brian Bennett, Anne Berryman, Hilary Hylton, Siobhan Morrissey, and Amany Radwan, "The Making of John Walker Lindh," *Time,* October 7, 2002. Unless specified otherwise, the Lindh story comes from this six-thousand-plus-word article. Frank Lindh turned down my request for an interview.

"lifelong learners": Tamiscal High School, "Mission Statement," tamiscal. org.

They are required: Grade Seven, History-Social Science Content Standards, California State Board of Education, www.cde.ca.gov.

Students in Byron: Bob Egelko, "Appeal on School's Lesson in Muslim Culture Is Rejected," *San Francisco Chronicle,* October 3, 2006.

Melanie Morgan: Melanie Morgan, interview with author, May 22, 2006.

In 2002, a union spokesman: David Limbaugh, *Persecution: How Liberals Are Waging War Against Christianity* (Washington, D.C.: Regnery Publishing, 2003), p. 72.

"Berkeley may have": Joe Garofoli, "Peace Efforts Credible at Santa Cruz Campus, Pentagon Notes 'Counter-Recruiting' Strategy," *San Francisco Chronicle,* March 15, 2006.

There, his supporters: Philip Sherwell, "The new Malcolm X?" Telegraph. co.uk, April 9, 2006.

The New York Times' *Frank Rich:* Frank Rich, "Ding, Dong, the Cultural Witch Hunt Is Dead," *New York Times,* February 24, 2002.

The public debate started: P. J. Corkery, "Central Gossip Agency," *San Francisco Examiner,* December 18, 2001,

In high ABETTO dudgeon: Cited in Michelangelo Signorile, "Did Homophobia Corrupt John Walker?" *New York Press,* January 4, 2002.

Michelangelo Signorile, a gay columnist: Signorile.

According to sympathetic biographer: Mark Kukis, "*My Heart Became Attached*": The Strange Odyssey of John Walker Lindh (Washington, D.C.: Brassey's, 2003), p. 10.

He rejects the notion: Kukis, p. xiv.

In one of the very few analyses: David Gutmann, "In the Absence of Fathers," *First Things,* February 1995.

Tookie Williams, among others: Williams, p. 4.

Boys with no dad: Gutmann, February 1995.

Says Dunne, speaking for many: Dunne, p. 313.
"The rage of white citizenry": Dunne, p. 318.

32. The Castro

In New York, at the time: Dudley Clendinen and Adam Nagourney, *Out for Good: The Struggle to Build a Gay Rights Movement in America* (New York: Simon & Schuster, 1999), pp. 22–23.
By 1969, the city had emerged: Clendinen and Nagourney, p. 172
On recalling his move: Armistead Maupin, *Tales of the City* (New York: Harper-Perennial, 1994), p. 109.
"Boosterism has largely displaced": Daniel Harris, *The Rise and Fall of Gay Culture* (New York: Ballantine Books, 1999), p, 2.
The result, he laments: Harris, p. 22.
In 1971 the city's gay community: Randy Shilts, *And the Band Played On: Politics, People, and the AIDS Epidemic* (New York: Penguin Books, 1988), p. 15.
By decade's end: Armistead Maupin, *More Tales of the City* (New York: Harper-Perennial, 1994), p. 120.
"The truth was": Clendinen and Nagourney, p. 364.
"Lesbianism had simply": Maupin, *More Tales,* p. 125.
"Are you off men completely": Armistead Maupin, *Babycakes* (New York: Harper-Perennial, 1994), p. 292.
Something of a "spoiled child": Shilts, *Mayor,* p. 134
Looking for big cosmic hugs: Clendinen and Nagourney, p. 160.
Provocateurs hounded the shrinks: Clendinen and Nagourney, pp. 199–204.

33. Roseville

In his own odd way: Peter Verzola, interview with author, May 17, 2006.
The seeds of this: Clendinen and Nagourney, pp. 293–95.
"Homosexuals should avoid": Clendinen and Nagourney, p. 311.
In San Francisco, gays coped: Clendinen and Nagourney, p. 312.
A few weeks after the vote: Shilts, *Mayor,* p. 164.
"I never needed saving": Maupin, *More Tales,* p. 221.
In May 2006, for instance: Greg Lucas, "Senate OKs Bill on Gays in Textbooks," *San Francisco Chronicle,* May 12, 2006.
In March 2006: Joe Garofoli, "Evangelical Teens Rally in S.F.," *San Francisco Chronicle,* March 25, 2006."
"It is an insult to all San Franciscans": Rachel Gordon, "Supervisors Slam Vatican on Adoptions Resolution," *San Francisco Chronicle,* March 22, 2006.
When he was alive, even his friends: Shilts, *Mayor,* p. 286.
They just lined up: Shilts, *Mayor,* p. 317.

When asked what the verdicts: Shilts, *Mayor,* p. 235.
How about thousands: Shilts, *Mayor,* p. 328.

34. The Creative City

Just ten days after Orange Tuesday: Shilts, *Mayor,* p. 161.
Just five years later: Clendinen and Nagourney, pp. 472–74.
Mondale would not even: Shilts, *Band,* p. 495.
"For Democrats AIDS": Shilts, *Band,* p. 474.
What boosted the cause immensely: The most comprehensive and objective source on Kinsey is James H. Jones, *Alfred C. Kinsey: A Public/Private Life* (New York, W.W. Norton & Co., 1997).
Still, it took AIDS: Harris, p. 109.
"compelled to reinvent": Harris, p. 84.
"laying waste": Harris, p. 83.
"Promiscuity was practically an article": Shilts, *Mayor,* p. 88.
As of 2006: "Who Should Be Providing HIV Care? A Roundtable Discussion," *AIDS Clinical Care,* February 15, 2006.
Roughly 14,000: Adam Tanner, "New Statistics Suggest San Francisco Has the Highest Percentage of Gay Men," Reuters, April 7, 2006.
"desexualized, Teflon homosexual": Harris, p. 236.
According to Florida: Richard Florida. "The Rise of the Creative Class: Why Cities Without Gays and Rock Bands Are Losing the Economic Development Race," *Washington Monthly,* May 2002.
"Mayor Deflects Chatter": Rachel Gordon, "Mayor Deflects Chatter on Social Life," *San Francisco Chronicle,* March 3, 2006.
I called Heber Jentsch: Heber Jentsch, interview with author, April 13, 2006.
Indeed, the later revelation: "Does San Francisco Care About Its Mayor's Morals?" *World Journal,* Translated by Eugenia Chien, Posted: Feb 16, 2007.
"I'm thirty-six years old": Maupin, *Further Tales,* p. 167.
The "debate is over": David Ewing Duncan, "Bush No Match for Science in Debate Over Stem Cells," *San Francisco Chronicle,* May 29, 2005.
A year later: Carl T. Hall, "UCSF Resumes Human Embryo Stem Cell Work," *San Francisco Chronicle,* May 6, 2006.
In the not-so-creative: The housing opportunity index, www.nahb.org.
Between 1970 and 2000: San Francisco Planning Department, Census Data Analysis.
Florida acknowledges: Richard Florida, "Where the Brains Are," *Atlantic Monthly,* October 2006.
Forty years ago: Leslie Fulbright and Heather Knight, "With More Choice Has Come Resegregation," *San Francisco Chronicle,* May 29, 2006.

Recently, for example: Bob Egelko, "Sea Scouts Lose Suit Over Rent," *San Francisco Chronicle*, March 10, 2006.

35. San Fernando Valley

"People were surprised": Legs McNeil and Jennifer Osborne, *The Other Hollywood, the Uncensored Oral History of the Porn Film Industry* (New York: ReganBooks, 2005), p. 155.

"That was what that prick": McNeil and Osborne, p. 158.

John Holmes: McNeil and Osborne, pp. 316–21.

Many have tried to: McNeil and Osborne, pp. 574–575.

At twenty-one, during his first year: Ben Shapiro, interview with author, September 17, 2006.

In 1993, the effects: David Ferrell and Somini Sengupta, "A Stain Spreads in Suburbia," *Los Angeles Times*, April 6, 1993.

"The kids' friends": Janet Wiscombe, "An American Tragedy: One Spur Posse Mother Struggles to Understand," *Los Angeles Times*, March 22, 1996.

The details are appalling: The best source on this story is Bernard Lefkowitz, *Our Guys: The Glen Ridge Rape and the Secret Life of the Perfect Suburb* (Berkeley: University of California Press, 1997).

A ten-year LAPD study: As cited in Shapiro, p. 162.

On the day before: "Fatal Addiction: Ted Bundy's Final Interview," available online at www.pureintimacy.org.

36. San Diego

The San Diego native: The biography of Andrew Cunanan, aka DeSilva, is best told in Maureen Orth, *Vulgar Favors: Andrew Cunanan, Gianni Versace, and the Largest Failed Manhunt in U.S. History* (New York, Delacorte Press, 1999).

"wholesale substitute": Harris, p. 131.

Maupin's 1987 volume: Maupin, *Significant Others,* p. 31.

According to Maureen Orth: Orth, p. 115.

In the nether reaches: Orth, pp. 107–8.

According to the documents: Orth, p. 112.

Its highly public Folsom Street Fair: Folsomstreetfair.com.

"I think I was drugged": Orth, p. 173.

Pifarre had likely been there before: Reporter's Transcript of Proceedings, The People of the State of California vs. Steven Nary, Court No. 1639231.

As it happens, Patrick Arnold: Fainaru-Wada and Williams, p. 50.

"The suspect called police voluntarily": Glenn Martin, "Sailor's Lawyer Fails in Bid For Lower Bail," *San Francisco Chronicle*, April 16, 1996.

Nary's working-class parents: Edith Nary, interview with author, April 10, 2006.

"The drugs and pornography": Orth, p. 179.

In April 1997: Orth, p. 177.

No one knows: Orth, pp. 187–217.

In Chicago, Cunanan seized: Orth, pp. 230–40.

In San Francisco, on May 4: Phillip Matier and Andrew Ross, "Davis' Big Birthday Bash Turns Heads (And Some Stomachs)," *San Francisco Chronicle,* May 5, 1997.

Although further descent: For a complete description of events, see the Danielle Willis website, www.neitherday.com/danielle_willis. Willis, the sodomizer in question, "was kicked out of Barnard in 1986 and has since worked as a nanny, poodle groomer, stripper and dominatrix."

The tone would change within days: Mary Curtius and Maria L. La Ganga, "Party Proves Even San Francisco Can Blush," *Los Angeles Times,* May 8, 1997.

Best evidence now suggests: Stephen Jimenez, Glenn Silber and Elizabeth Vargas, "A Murder in Laramie: The Mystery and the Myth," *20/20,* May 29, 2004.

"Community activists expressed": "Litigation Notes," Lesbian/Gay Law Notes, December 1999.

On a more personal level: Along with Nancy Pelosi, Tom Lantos, and other prominent Bay Area residents, Pifarre lent his name to a *San Francisco Chronicle* ad for Terence Hallinan before the December 12, 1995, election.

Indeed, there was more public sympathy: Phillip Matier and Andrew Ross, "2nd Sex Scandal Hits DA's Office," *San Francisco Chronicle,* May 30, 1997.

On one occasion: Peter Verzola, author interview.

"The 2nd-degree jury verdict": Jeffrey Montgomery, "Pace Quickens in Aaron McKinney's Trial for Murder," *Gay Today,* October 28, 1999.